Busy Woman's

SLOW COOKER
COOKBOOK

By Sharon and Gene McFall
with Linda Burgett

First Printing 2005

Copyright © 2005
Sharon McFall
Creative Ideas Publishing
Edmond, Oklahoma

ISBN: 1-930170-16-5

Additional copies may be ordered for $18.95, plus $3.50 shipping.

Creative Ideas Publishing
PMB 115
7916 N.W. 23rd St.
Bethany, OK 73008-5135
800-673-0768

www.busywomanscookbook.com

Design by Barbara Jezek
Production by Kate Withrow

Printed in China

You may substitute light or fat-free ingredients in any recipe calling for milk, cream, butter or cheese to create a delicious low calorie dish.

Most recipes in this cookbook can be cooked longer than indicated without changing the recipe.

Acknowledgements

We want to express our heartfelt appreciation for the approximately 400,000 cooks who have bought BUSY WOMAN'S COOK-BOOK, making it far more successful than we ever dreamed. They gave us the courage and inspiration to do this follow-up volume.

We are very grateful for the family harmony that enables a husband and wife in Oklahoma and a daughter in New Mexico to work together-utilizing the best talents of each person-to bring this book to fruition.

We are especially thankful for the compliments we have received about BUSY WOMAN'S COOKBOOK from people all over the country. Our favorite is, "I use this cookbook all the time." We hope the same is said about this book.

Table of Contents

Beverages, Dips, & Appetizers   9

Soups, Stews, & Chili   37

Vegetables, Pasta, Casseroles, & Rice   75

Beef, Pork, Poultry, & Seafood   157

Desserts & Fondues   227

Adaptations, Substitutions, Herbs & Spices   245

Index   252

Foreword

How do you have a home cooked meal ready at dinner time when you have to be at work or school all day? How can you have delicious dishes ready to eat after shopping, an afternoon at the movies, or after church?

Turn to your trusted slow cooker or Crock Pot . A few minutes of preparation, turn it on, then come home and enjoy. Fix it, do what you have to do, or want to do, then enjoy good homemade food.

In 2000 we published *Busy Woman's Cookbook*, a compilation of over 500 recipes with only three or four ingredients each, Its tremendous success has led us to follow these guidelines in all of our cookbooks.

1. Practically nobody today wants to spend all day in the kitchen.

2. They don't want to have to buy a large number of ingredients to make one dish.

3. They don't want a lot of ingredients of which they have never heard. They want things that are found in a normal cupboard.

The slow cooker has had a great upsurge in popularity recently. We decided to write a cookbook for the slow cooker, and each recipe would have only a very few ingredients. Of course, the true test of any recipe is, "Does it taste good?" The recipes in *Busy Woman's Slow Cooker Cookbook* have been carefully chosen for ease of preparation and for great taste.

Another extremely popular feature of *Busy Woman's Cookbook* was the stories about women and their accomplishments. We decided to follow the same format in this book. We hope you find the stories interesting and informative. In the back of this book is a list of women honored in *Busy Woman's Cookbook*. You may want to read further about these talented or famous women. We have not been able to name all deserving women-even in two volumes-so any omissions are due to lack of space.

We are sure you will enjoy the ease of using *Busy Woman's Slow Cooker Cookbook*, eating the great food, and reading the interesting bits about women of note.

About the Authors

Busy Woman's Slow Cooker Cookbook is the fifth cookbook co-authored by husband and wife team, Sharon and Gene McFall. It is a companion book to their national best-seller, *Busy Woman's Cookbook*. Daughter Linda Burgett has collaborated with them on this book.

SHARON MCFALL is a native of Des Moines, Iowa, and has worked extensively in publicity and promotion and in the retail management field. She gained her knowledge of cooking and food as the mother of four children with diverse tastes, and as an executive with a dinner theatre. She and Gene have also owned and operated a restaurant and concessions in tourist areas.

GENE MCFALL is a former teacher and basketball coach from Kentucky. Since 1982 he has performed as an actor in his nationally acclaimed one-man show, "Witty World of Will Rogers," appearing in 45 states and around the world.

LINDA BURGETT lives in New Mexico with her husband Stan and son Tyler. Her love of different cultures and cuisine makes traveling around the United States and around the world as Executive Producer of Passion Play Ministries a true pleasure. She enjoys entertaining and collecting recipes at the many functions she attends. She is the author of the highly successful *Mild To Wild Mexican Cookbook*.

Bever-
ages,
Dips &
Appetizers

Infamous Women

1. AXIS SALLY, 1900-1988, (Mildred Elizabeth Gillars) was an American English teacher from Ohio who made Nazi propaganda broadcasts from Tunisia after the Allies landed in North Africa in World War II. She shockingly sometimes broadcast information that was supposed to be secret. The Allies laughed at her heavy propaganda, but enjoyed the jazz music she played, and they gave her the nickname, Axis Sally. She was convicted of treason in 1949 and served twelve years in a U.S. prison. After her release, she finished her college education and again taught school in Ohio.

2. During World War II the Japanese broadcast radio programs featuring English speaking women announcers and American music. They were meant to make U.S. personnel homesick and discouraged, but they had little effect on morale. U.S. troops nicknamed them TOKYO ROSE. The name became associated with Iva Toguri d'Aquino, a U.S. citizen of Japanese ancestry who was stranded in Tokyo when World War II began. In 1949 she was the seventh person convicted of treason in the history of the United States, served 6 years in prison and paid a $100,000 dollar fine. Many believe she was wrongly convicted. In 1977 President Gerald Ford granted her a full and unconditional pardon.

3. MATI HARI (Gertrude Margarethe Macleod) was executed on October 14, 1917, for betraying Allied military secrets to the German Secret Service in World War I.

4. ETHEL ROSENBURG was electrocuted in 1952 (along with her husband, Julius) for obtaining classified atomic secrets and turning them over to the Soviet Union. She may have been a victim of an over-reaching government due to Cold War tension, communist witch-hunting by McCarthy, and the Great Red Scare—Russia had just detonated and atomic bomb. A case was built against her to get her husband to talk. The very weak evidence against her came from dubious testimony that she was present when conversations about espionage took place and typed notes on classified information. After 26 months on death row, she was the first woman executed by the U.S. government since Mary Surratt.

WIDE AWAKE COFFEE

3 cups half and half

¾ cup maple syrup

3 cups strong coffee

In slow cooker, combine all ingredients. Cover. Cook on high 1 or 1½ hours. Makes 6 servings.

MOCHA COFFEE

1 cup instant cocoa mix

½ cup instant coffee crystals

8 cups hot water

Whipped topping

In slow cooker, combine all ingredients. Mix well. Cook on high 1 or 1½ hours. Mix, reduce heat to low. Cover. Cook until hot. Serve with whipped topping. Makes 8 servings.

MOCHA CAPPUCCINO

6 cups hot strong coffee

¾ cup half-and-half

6 tablespoons chocolate syrup

7 teaspoons sugar

In slow cooker, combine all ingredients. Cook on high 1 or 1½ hours. Makes 6 servings.

*The American people and the press showed a great warmth for First Lady **BARBARA BUSH**, wife of President George H. Bush. She attributed this to her image of "everybody's grandmother." People are comfortable with her white hair, relaxed manner and her keen wit. She says people like her because they know "I'm fair and I like children and I adore my husband." During her tenure as First Lady, she adopted the promotion of literacy as her special cause.*

HOT IRISH MOCHA

6 cups hot strong brewed coffee

4 (1.25 ounce) envelopes Irish cream instant cocoa mix

2 cups half and half

In slow cooker, combine all ingredients. Mix well. Cook on high 1 to 1½ hours or until very hot. Note: great for a brunch. Makes 8 servings.

HOT PARTY PUNCH

1 quart cranberry juice

1 cup orange juice

1½ cups sugar

¼ cup lemon juice

2 quarts hot water

¼ cup red hot candies

In slow cooker, combine all ingredients. Mix until sugar has dissolved. Cover. Cook on high 1½ to 2 hours. Makes 12 to 15 servings.

HOT JUICE WARM-UPS

1 cup pineapple juice

1½ cups cranberry juice

1½ cups hot water

3 cups orange juice

1½ teaspoons lemon juice

In slow cooker, combine all ingredients. Cover. Cook on low 1 to 1½ hours. Makes 6 servings.

NANCY DAVIS *appeared in 11 movies from 1949 to 1956. In her last movie, "Hellcats of the Navy," she played opposite her husband, Ronald Reagan. She gave up acting for the permanent role of wife and mother. As First Lady she gave support to the Foster Grandparent Program and concentrated on the fight against drug and alcohol abuse among young people. She was very devoted to the care of her husband in his last years battle with Alzheimers.*

HOT CIDER PUNCH

2 quarts apple cider

1 cup orange juice

1 cup pineapple juice

4 cinnamon sticks

In slow cooker, combine all ingredients. Cover. Cook on low 2 to 4 hours before serving.

SPICY HOT CIDER

8 cups apple cider

1 cup red cinnamon candies

In slow cooker, combine all ingredients. Mix well. Cover. Cook on high 1½ hours or until candies are melted. Makes 8 servings.

CARAMEL APPLE CIDER

1 gallon apple cider

6 cinnamon sticks

1 (10 ounce) jar caramel ice cream topping

1 (14 ounce) can whipped topping

In slow cooker, combine cider and cinnamon sticks. Cover. Cook on low 2 to 4 hours. Pour into mugs. Top each with 1 teaspoon caramel topping and whipped cream. Drizzle additional caramel topping over whipped cream. Makes 15 servings.

*The first woman to undergo astronaut tests was **JERRIE COBB** of Oklahoma City, OK, who passed a series of 75 examinations conducted in February, 1960, at the Lovelace Foundation in Albuquerque, NM. The tests were the same as those given to male astronauts. In August, 1960, she underwent additional examinations. Many feel that she should have been the first United States female astronaut, but the timing was not right.*

HOT CRAN-APPLE CIDER

6 cups apple cider

2 cups cranberry juice

1 (4 inch) cinnamon stick

In slow cooker, combine all ingredients. Mix well. Cook on high 1½ to 2 hours. Makes 8 servings.

SIPPIN APPLE CIDER

1 gallon apple cider

2 cups sugar

3 cups orange juice

½ cup lemon juice

In slow cooker, combine apple cider and sugar. Mix well. Cook on high 1½ hours. Add orange juice and lemon juice. Mix well. Cover. Cook an additional 1 hour. Makes 15 to 18 servings.

CHILL OUT APPLE JUICE

8 cups apple juice

1 (10 ounce) package sweet frozen sliced strawberries

½ teaspoon whole cloves

In slow cooker, combine all ingredients. Mix well. Cover. Cook on low 2½ to 3 hours. Makes 8 servings.

VIRGINIA DARE was the first child born of English parents in America. She was born at Roanoke Island, NC, to Ananias and Eleanor Dare on August 18, 1587. On August 27, her grandfather, John White, governor of the colony, sailed for England for more supplies. When he returned four years later, there was no sign of the 150 colonists and the fort was in ruins. Their fate remains a mystery to this day—with much speculation when blue-eyed Indians were later discovered further inland.

MAD ABOUT MUSHROOMS

1 (1 ounce) package beefy mushroom soup mix

¼ cup sour cream

¼ cup half and half

2 pounds button mushrooms

In slow cooker, combine soup mix, sour cream, and half and half. Add mushrooms. Mix well. Cover. Cook on low 2 to 3 hours.

ARTICHOKE DIP

2 cups frozen spinach, cooked, drained, chopped

1 (14 ounce) can artichoke hearts, drained, chopped

½ cup mayonnaise

½ cup Alfredo sauce

¾ teaspoon garlic salt

1 cup shredded Swiss cheese

In slow cooker, combine all ingredients. Mix well. Cover. Cook on low 2 to 3 hours. Serve with tortilla chips, vegetables or bread.

*On March 16, 1697, during an attack on Haverhill, MA, Indians killed her one-week old baby and captured **HANNAH DUSTIN**. The Indians also murdered or captured 39 other persons and destroyed six houses. On April 29 at the Indian camp Hannah killed ten Indians with a tomahawk and escaped. She scalped the Indians as proof of her deed. The Great and General Court of Massachusetts honored her by awarding her 25 pounds out of the public treasury.*

EASY ARTICHOKE DIP

1 (14 ounce) can artichoke hearts, drained, chopped

1 (8 ounce) container sour cream

1 (1 ounce) package onion soup mix

1 cup shredded mozzarella cheese

1 cup mayonnaise

In slow cooker, combine all ingredients. Cover. Cook on low 2 to 3 hours.

SEASIDE CLAM DIP

2 pints clams

2 (8 ounce) packages cream cheese

1 cup sour cream

⅓ cup creamy horseradish

In slow cooker, combine all ingredients. Mix well. Cover. Cook on low 2 to 3 hours. Serve with chips. Makes 8 to 10 servings.

DON'T BE A CRAB DIP

1 pound Velveeta® cheese, cubed

1 stick butter or margarine, cubed

2 (6 ounce) cans crab meat

In slow cooker, combine all ingredients. Cover. Cook on low 2 to 3 hours.

PHYLLIS DILLER, a comedienne known for her wild hair, zany laugh and self-deprecating monologues (usually about her imaginary husband, Fang) did not start in show business until age 36. She has appeared in supper clubs, movies, TV, has recorded comedy albums and has performed with over 100 symphony orchestras as a piano soloist. She was honored by the American Academy of Cosmetic Surgery for publicly acknowledging her plastic surgery, "bringing it out of the closet."

CHEESY CRAB DIP

1 pound Velveeta® cheese, cubed

2 cups cream cheese

2 (6 ounce) cans crab meat, drained

In slow cooker, combine all ingredients. Mix well. Cover. Cook on low 1½ to 2 hours. Serve with crackers.

CHEESE & SHRIMP DIP

2 (8 ounce) packages cream cheese

2 (10¾ ounce) cans cheddar cheese soup

2 (4½ ounce) cans shrimp, drained

¼ cup diced green onion

In slow cooker, add cream cheese. Cover. Cook on low until cheese melts. Add remaining ingredients. Mix well. Cover. Cook on low 1½ to 2 hours. Makes 8 to 12 servings.

PARTY TIME SHRIMP DIP

1 (10¾ ounce) can cream of shrimp soup

1 (8 ounce) package cream cheese, softened

¼ cup finely chopped green bell pepper

2 tablespoons finely chopped onion

In slow cooker, combine all ingredients. Mix well. Cover. Cook on low 2 to 3 hours. Stir after 1 hour of cooking. Makes 2½ cups.2¹/₃

ELIZABETH I, (1533–1600) Queen of England's peaceful and prosperous 45 year reign was one of the most outstanding periods in English history. She was extremely popular-a cult figure to the populace-and showed great regard for her subjects' economic welfare. It was a Golden Age of Literature with authors such as William Shakespeare, Francis Bacon, Christopher Marlow and Sir Walter Raleigh flourishing.

TACO DIP

2 cups shredded cheddar cheese

2 (16 ounce) cans refried beans

1 (2¼ ounce) can chopped black olives

1 (1 ounce) package taco seasoning mix

In slow cooker, combine all ingredients. Mix well. Cover. Cook on low 3 to 4 hours. Serve with tortilla chips.

TACO CHEESE DIP

2 pounds Velveeta® cheese, cubed

2 (10 ounce) cans diced tomatoes with green chiles

2 teaspoons taco seasoning

In slow cooker, combine all ingredients. Cover. Cook on low 2½ to 3 hours. Stir after 1 hour and before serving. Serve with tortilla chips. Makes 6 to 8 servings.

CON QUESO DIP

1 (14.5 ounce) can chopped tomatoes

1 (4 ounce) can green chiles

½ cup diced onions

2 cups shredded Monterey Jack cheese

In slow cooker, combine all ingredients. Mix well. Cover. Cook on low 2 to 3 hours or high 1½ hours. Serve with tortilla chips. Makes 6 to 8 servings.

Who made the first United States flag? Every school child knows that it was **BETSY ROSS** *who made the first Stars and Stripes in June, 1776, at the request of a committee composed of George Washington, Robert Morris, and her uncle George Ross. Unfortunately, historians have been unable to find a historical record of such a meeting or committee. But until further evidence is found, let's go ahead and give her the honor.*

CHILE CON QUESO DIP

2 (15 ounce) cans chili without beans

⅓ cup diced onion

1 (16 ounce) jar hot picante sauce

1 (8 ounce) package shredded cheddar
cheese

In slow, cooker, combine all ingredients. Cover.
Cook on low 2½ to 3 hours. Serve with chips.
Makes 6 to 10 servings.

SALSA MEXI DIP

2 (16 ounce) cans refried beans

2 cups shredded cheddar cheese

1 cup salsa

1 cup chopped green chile pepper

In slow cooker, combine all ingredients. Mix
well. Cover. Cook on low 2 to 3 hours. Serve
with tortilla chips. Makes 2 cups.

NACHO PARTY SNACK DIP

2 (16 ounce) packages shredded cheddar
cheese

½ cup chopped green chiles

⅓ cup diced onion

½ teaspoon chili powder

1 cup diced tomatoes

Coat inside slow cooker with cooking spray. In
slow cooker, combine all ingredients. Mix well.
Cover. Cook on high 1½ hours. Mix well.
Cover. Cook on low until hot and cheese has
melted.

DINAH SHORE *was the first major vocalist to break away from the big-band format and begin a solo career. She remained popular from the 1940s through the 1980s. She pioneered the prime time variety show. On her 1950s television show she had the whole country singing, "See the USA in your Chevrolet." She had polio at 18 months and was left with a shortened leg, always covered by long pants or long skirts. When she kissed Nat King Cole on her TV show, 26 stations dropped the show.*

GAME TIME CHEESE DIP

2 pounds ground beef, browned, drained

½ cup diced onion

1 (16 ounce) jar cheese spread

1 (8 ounce) jar salsa

In slow cooker, combine all ingredients. Mix well. Cover. Cook on low 3 to 4 hours. Serve with tortilla chips. Makes 8 to 10 servings.

TIPSY CHEESE DIP

2 (8 ounce) packages Mexican cheese

1 cup thick and chunky salsa

½ cup beer

In slow cooker, combine all ingredients. Mix well. Cover. Cook on low 2 to 3 hours. Serve with tortilla chips. Makes 2½ cups.

SIZZLIN BEEF DIP

1½ pounds lean ground beef, browned, drained

1 (15 ounce) can no bean chili

1 (8 ounce) package hot Velveeta® Mexican cheese, cubed

½ cup green chiles

In slow cooker, combine all ingredients. Mix well. Cover. Cook on low 2½ to 3 hours. Makes 6 to 8 servings.

PEPPERONI DIP

2 (16 ounce) jars pizza sauce

2 (10 ounce) packages pepperoni slices, diced

½ cup grated Parmesan cheese

1 cup shredded mozzarella cheese

In slow cooker, combine all ingredients. Mix well. Cover. Cook on low 2 to 3 hours. Serve with crackers or bread sticks. Makes 10 to 15 servings.

ITALIAN PIZZA DIP

1 pound Italian sausage, browned, drained

⅓ cup chopped onion

⅔ cup sliced pepperoni, chopped

2 (16 ounce) jars pizza sauce

1 cup shredded mozzarella cheese

In slow cooker, combine all ingredients. Mix well. Cover. Cook on low 3 to 4 hours. Serve with bread sticks or crackers. Makes 6 to 8 servings.

PIZZA DIP

1 pound ground beef

2 (14 ounce) jars pizza sauce

1 (16 ounce) package shredded mozzarella cheese

In slow cooker, combine all ingredients. Mix well. Cover. Cook on low 3 to 4 hours. Serve with bread sticks or crackers. Makes 10 to 12 servings.

ANNE FRANK (1929–1945) was a German-Jewish girl whose family fled to the Netherlands in 1933. In 1942 during the Nazi occupation the family hid in a secret annex behind her father's Amsterdam office Anne wrote her diary as a series of letters to an imaginary friend. In it the 13 year old school girl expressed her feelings and thoughts while in hiding from the Nazis. Two years later the family was betrayed and arrested. Anne died in a Nazi concentration camp in March, 1945. Her diary was published in 1947 and was later made into a play and movie called "The Diary of Anne Frank."

HAM & CHEESE DIP

1 (8 ounce) package cream cheese, softened

1 cup sour cream

2 (2½ ounce) packages ham, diced

2 green onions, diced

In slow cooker, combine all ingredients. Cover. Cook on low 2 to 3 hours. Serve with bagel chips, tortilla chips, or crackers.

HAM & VEGGIE DIP

2 (4 ounce) packages vegetable cream cheese, softened

1 cup sour cream

1 teaspoon garlic powder

2 (2½ ounce) packages ham, diced

2 green onions, diced

In small bowl, combine cream cheese, sour cream, and garlic powder. Mix until smooth. Add ham and onion. Mix well. Cover. Cook on low 2 to 3 hours. Serve with bagel chips, mini bagels, or crackers

ONION DIP

3 (8 ounce) packages cream cheese, softened

2 cups grated Parmesan cheese

1 onion, finely chopped

½ cup mayonnaise

In slow cooker, combine all ingredients. Mix well. Cover. Cook on low 2 to 3 hours. Serve with crackers or chips.

Over a period of ten years **MARGARET MITCHELL** *wrote her only novel, "Gone With the Wind." Published in 1936 it became one of the most popular novels of its time. It sold more than twenty million copies in 27 languages, and won the Pulitzer Prize for fiction. In 1939 it was made into one of the most popular movies of all time. People were shocked when Clark Gable's Rhett Butler said, "Frankly my dear, I don't give a damn."*

C'MON OVER CHEESE DIP

3 (15½ ounce) cans chili

½ cup diced onion

2 (8 ounce) packages cream cheese

2½ cups shredded cheddar cheese

In slow cooker, combine all ingredients. Mix well. Cover. Cook on low 3 to 4 hours. Serve with tortilla chips. Makes 10 to 12 servings.

EASY PARTY CHEESE DIP

2 (16 ounce) packages Velveeta® cheddar cheese, cubed

2 cups salsa

½ cup diced onion

2 cups sour cream

In slow cooker, combine all ingredients. Mix well. Cover. Cook on low 2½ to 3 hours. Makes 12 to 15 servings.

For over 45 years a Catholic nun, **MOTHER TERESA** *(1910–1997), ministered to the destitute, diseased and dying of Calcutta and other parts of the world with a selfless devotion that caused her to become known as the "saint of the gutters." She founded a religious order that operates 2,500 orphanages, clinics and hospices in more than 120 countries. She received the Nobel Peace Prize in 1979, and has received the U.S. Presidential Medal of Freedom, the first Pope John XXIII Peace Prize and many other awards. In 2003 Pope John Paul II beatified her—the first step toward being declared a saint.*

BROCCOLI CHEESE DIP

2 (10 ounce) packages frozen chopped broccoli, thawed

2 (10¾ ounce) cans cream of mushroom soup

¼ cup sour cream

½ pound Mexican style Velveeta ® cheese, cube

½ pound Velveeta® cheese, cubed

1½ teaspoons garlic salt

In slow cooker, combine all ingredients. Mix well. Cover. Cook on low 2 to 3 hours.

BROCCOLI DIP

3 (10 ounce) packages frozen chopped broccoli, thawed

½ cup sliced mushrooms

2 (10¾ ounce) cans cream of chicken soup

2 (3 ounce) packages cream cheese with chives and garlic

In slow cooker, combine all ingredients. Mix well. Cover. Cook on low 2 to 3 hours. Stir after 1 hour. Serve with crackers, chips or corn tortillas

When Clara Ann Fowler began singing on the radio in Tulsa, OK, she was asked to change her name at the request of the sponsor, the Page Milk Co. She was the third singer to perform on the radio program under the same name. She became so popular that when she left the show, the sponsor agreed to let her keep the name, **PATTI PAGE**. *She went on to become a major recording artist. Her big hit was "Tennessee Waltz."*

PUMPKIN BUTTER SPREAD

1 (15 ounce) can pumpkin

1 cup apple, peeled, grated

½ cup packed brown sugar

¾ teaspoon pumpkin pie spice

1 cup apple juice

In slow cooker, combine all ingredients. Mix well. Cover. Cook on high 1½ hours. Reduce heat to low. Cook 5 to 6 hours. Makes 3 cups.

REUBEN SPREAD

½ pound chopped cooked corned beef

1 (16 ounce) can sauerkraut, rinsed, drained

¾ cup Thousand Island salad dressing

2 cups shredded Swiss cheese

1 (3 ounce) package cream cheese, cubed

In slow cooker, combine all ingredients. Mix well. Cover. Cook on low for 2 to 3 hours. Serve with cocktail rye bread slices.

SARAH BERNHARDT (1844–1923), a French actress, was the first theatrical superstar, an actress of such magnitude that she became a cultural icon. She was celebrated for her graceful movements and the bell-like clarity and rich tones of her voice. She performed only in French, but toured the U.S. and Canada nine times between 1890 and 1918. She was as notorious for her love affairs, her unpredictable behavior and outrageous eccentricities as she was for the intensity and passion of her acting.

CHICKEN CHEESE SPREAD

2 (12.5 ounce) cans white chicken, drained

2 (8 ounce) packages cream cheese, softened

1½ cups mayonnaise

½ cup diced green onion

½ cup diced red bell pepper

In slow cooker, combine all ingredients. Mix well. Cover. Cook on low 2 to 3 hours. Serve with crackers. Makes 8 to 10 servings.

CRAB CHEESE SPREAD

2 cups flaked crab

2 (8 ounce) packages cream cheese, softened

1½ cups mayonnaise

½ cup chopped green onion

1 cup shredded Swiss cheese

In slow cooker, combine all ingredients. Mix well. Cover. Cook on low 2 to 3 hours. Serve with crackers. Makes 8 to 10 servings.

KATHLEEN MARY KENYON (1906–1978), *an English archeologist, excavated the Old Testament site of Jericho and showed that it was one of the earliest continuous settlements in the world—dating to c. 11,000 B.C. She was named Honorary Director of the British School of Archeology in Jerusalem. In 1973 Queen Elizabeth II named her DBE (Dame of the Order of the British Empire) , the female version of knighthood.*

HAVING A PARTY CHEESE BALL

2 (8 ounce) packages cream cheese

4 cups grated cheddar cheese

4 tablespoons diced onions

4 tablespoons apple juice

1 cup chopped pecans

In slow cooker, add cream cheese. Cover. Cook on low until cheese melts. Mix in cheddar cheese, onions and apple juice until smooth. Cover. Cook on low 1 hour. Pour mixture into medium bowl. Chill slightly. Form into ball. Roll in pecans. Serve with assorted crackers. Makes 12 to 15 servings.

NACHOS

1 pound ground beef, browned, drained

1 (19 ounce) can black beans, rinsed, drained

1 (1 ounce) package onion soup mix

1 cup salsa

1 (8½ ounce) package tortilla chips

1 cup shredded cheddar cheese

In slow cooker, combine beef, beans, soup mix, and salsa. Mix well. Cover. Cook on low 3 to 4 hours. Arrange tortilla chips on platter. Spread beef mixture over chips. Sprinkle with cheese.

DOROTHEA DIX *was appalled by the horrible treatment of the mentally ill who were lodged in jails and prisons in the mid 1800s. In her campaign for humane treatment of the mentally ill, she personally founded 32 hospitals for the insane in the U.S. and was the inspiring force for 123 additional facilities. During the Civil War she served without pay as the Union's Superintendent of Female Nurses. She recruited only plain looking women over 30 and enforced a dress code of modest black or brown skirts and no hoops or jewelry.*

NUTS ABOUT WALNUTS

4 cups walnuts

$\frac{1}{2}$ cup butter, melted

$2\frac{1}{2}$ tablespoons sugar

1 teaspoon allspice

1 teaspoon cinnamon

In slow cooker, add walnuts. Pour butter over nuts. Mix well. Cover. Cook on low 2 hours. Remover cover. Cook 30 minutes. Sprinkle nuts with sugar and spices. Mix well. Pour on cookie sheet to cool. Makes 6 to 8 servings.

JALAPEÑO COCKTAIL WIENERS

1 (10.5 ounce) jar Jalapeno jelly

1 (10 ounce) jar chili sauce

2 (16 ounce) packages smoked cocktail wieners

In slow cooker, combine jelly and chili sauce. Mix well. Add wieners. Mix well. Cover. Cook on low 3 to 4 hours.

"One dark night, when people were in bed, Mrs. O'Leary lit a lantern in her shed, The cow kicked it over, winked its eye and said, There'll be a hot time in the old town tonight." Legend has it that while **MRS. CATHERINE O'LEARY** *was milking, her cow started the Great Chicago Fire of 1871. The Board of Police and Fire Commission held an inquiry and could not ascertain the fire's cause. The O'Leary home survived the conflagration.*

SWEET AND SOUR COCKTAIL WIENERS

2 cups ketchup

¾ cup orange juice

¾ cup packed brown sugar

2 tablespoons mustard

1 tablespoon minced onion

1 pound cocktail wieners

In slow cooker, combine all ingredients except cocktail wieners. Mix well, add cocktail wieners. Mix well. Cover. Cook on low 3 to 4 hours.

GOTTA HAVE HOT DOG ROLL UPS

2 (16 ounce) packages hot dogs, cut in half

1 pound bacon, cut in half

2 tablespoons brown sugar

Wrap each hot dog piece with bacon, stick toothpick through bacon and hot dog to hold. Place in bottom of slow cooker. Sprinkle with brown sugar. Cover. Cook on low 3 to 4 hours.

WILMA RUDOLPH (1940–1999), an American athlete, was the first woman runner to win three gold medals in track and field at one Olympic Games. In the 1960 Games at Rome she won the 100 meters, 200 meters, and the 400 meter relay. At the age of four, she had double pneumonia and scarlet fever, followed by polio. She was unable to walk properly until she was 11 years old. At age 16 she competed in the 1956 Olympics and won the bronze medal in the 400 meter relay.

MAE WEST (1892–1980) became famous for the humorous bawdy sexuality of her stage and film performances. Her racy wisecracks won her world fame. The success of her 1933 films, "She Done Him Wrong," and "I'm No Angel" resulted in the Motion Picture Production Code to regulate the content of movies. To avoid the censors, she spoke in double meanings. As a tribute to her ample female endowments, American airmen and sailors in World War II named their life vests "Mae Wests."

LITTLE SMOKIES LINKS

2 cups barbeque sauce

½ cup ketchup

½ cup packed brown sugar

2 tablespoons diced onion

2 (16 ounce) packages little smokies

In slow cooker, combine all ingredients. Mix well. Cover. Cook on low 3 to 4 hours. Makes 10 servings.

BUDGET PARTY LINKS

2 (16 ounce) packages hot dogs, sliced 1-inch thick

2 cups barbecue sauce

¼ cup packaged brown sugar

1 teaspoon dry mustard

2 tablespoons maple syrup

In slow cooker, combine all ingredients. Mix well. Cover. Cook on low 3 to 4 hours. Makes 10 to 15 servings.

BBQ COCKTAIL WIENERS

36 cocktail wieners

2½ cups barbeque sauce

1 teaspoon dry mustard

¼ cup packed brown sugar

In slow cooker, combine all ingredients. Cover. Cook on low 3 to 4 hours or high 1½ to 2 hours. Makes 6 to 8 servings.

PARTY COCKTAIL WIENERS

2 pounds package cocktail wieners

1 cup ketchup

1 cup barbecue sauce

1 cup brown sugar

½ teaspoon Worcestershire sauce

In slow cooker, combine all ingredients. Cover. Cook on high 1½ hours. Remove lid and cook on low an additional 60 minutes. Makes 8 to 10 servings.

BARBECUE CHICKEN WINGS

2 ½ pounds chicken wings, separated at joints, tips discarded

1 cup barbecue sauce

2 tablespoons maple syrup

1 teaspoon sugar

1 teaspoon Worcestershire sauce

In slow cooker, place chicken wings. In small bowl, combine barbecue sauce, maple syrup, sugar and Worcestershire sauce. Pour mixture over wings. Cover. Cook on low 6 to 8 hours. Makes 6 to 8 servings.

Actress **BETTY GRABEL** became America's favorite pin-up girl. Her famous bathing suit photo became the most popular pin-up for American GI's in World War II. In fact, the term "Betty" became war-era slang for a good looking woman. At one time she was the highest paid entertainer in the U.S., $300,000 salary in 1947. Betty was best known for her "Million Dollar Legs," insured for that amount by 20th Century Fox with Lloyds of London.

SPICY HONEY WINGS

1 (1.5 ounce) envelope dry onion soup mix

½ cup honey

1 tablespoon spicy brown mustard

18 chicken wings, separated at joints, tips discarded

In slow cooker, place chicken wings. In small bowl, combine onion soup mix, honey and mustard. Mix well. Pour mixture over wings. Mix well. Cover. Cook on low 6 to 8 hours. Makes 36.

SMOKE 'N HOT WINGS

2½ pounds chicken wings, separated at joints, tips discarded

2 cups chili sauce

½ cup hot pepper sauce

In slow cooker, place chicken wings. In small bowl, combine remaining ingredients. Mix well. Pour mixture over wings. Cover. Cook on low 6 to 8 hours or high 3 to 4 hours. Makes 8 to 10 servings.

THEDA BARA was one of the most successful and glamorous stars of the 1910's, and is the most mysterious and inaccessible today. Of her more than 40 films, only three and a half remain. She is responsible for the word "vamp" being placed in the dictionary and in everyday use. She became an instant overnight star in her first movie role, The Vampire, in "A Fool Like This" in 1915. Dangling earrings, kohled eyes, languorous glances and the line, "Kiss me, my fool," were Theda's projected public personna.

SO GOOD CHICKEN WINGS

½ cup soy sauce

½ cup packed dark brown sugar

12 large chicken wings, separated at joints, tips discarded

In small bowl, combine soy sauce and brown sugar. Mix well. Let set 10 minutes. Coat each wing with mixture, place in slow cooker. Cover. Cook on low 6 to 8 hours or high 3 to 4 hours. Makes 12 servings.

SAUCY SWEET CHICKEN WINGS

12 chicken wings, separated at joints, tips discarded

3 cups barbeque sauce

¼ cup maple syrup

¼ cup ketchup

1 tablespoon sugar

In slow cooker, place chicken wings. In medium bowl, combine remaining ingredients. Mix well. Pour mixture over wings. Cover. Cook on low 6 to 8 hours or high 3 to 4 hours. Makes 12 servings.

MARGARET MEAD (*1901–1978*) *was the foremost anthropologist of our day. After expeditions to Samoa and New Guinea, her best selling books, "Growing Up In Samoa" and "Sex and Temperament in Three Primitive Societies" made anthropology a fascinating subject to the public at large. In her works she argued that personality characteristics, especially as they differ between male and female, are shaped by cultural conditioning instead of heredity.*

JUST WING IT

3 pounds chicken wings, discard tips

1 cup honey

2 cups barbecue sauce

Cut each wing into 2 parts. In slow cooker, combine all ingredients. Mix well. Cover. Cook on low 6 to 8 hours.

BEEF BURGER BITES

1 pound ground beef, cooked and drained

2 tablespoons ketchup

2 teaspoons instant minced onion

1 teaspoon mustard

2 cups cubed American cheese

24 miniature sandwich buns

Spray slow cooker with vegetable spray. In slow cooker, combine beef, ketchup, onion, and mustard. Mix well. Top with cheese. Cover. Cook on low 3 to 4 hours. Serve on miniature buns. Makes 24 appetizers.

PARTY TIME MEATBALLS

2 (18 ounce) packages frozen cooked meatballs

1 (12 ounce) jar savory beef gravy

1 (1 ounce) package dry onion soup mix

In slow cooker, place meatballs. In medium bowl, combine gravy and onion soup mix. Mix well. Add mixture to meatballs. Cover. Cook on low 6 to 8 hours. Makes 72 meatballs.

Women have reigned in the Netherlands (Holland) since 1890. **QUEEN WILHELMINIA** *inherited the throne at age 10. She helped her country remain neutral in World War I. When the Nazis overran the Netherlands in 1940 she escaped to England. She became the symbol of resistance for her countrymen, bringing hope to her occupied nation through regular radio broadcasts. She returned home in 1945 and abdicated three years later in favor of her daughter.*

BARBECUED MEATBALLS

1 (36 ounce) package frozen meatballs

3 cups barbeque sauce

⅓ cup packed brown sugar

¼ cup ketchup

In slow cooker, combine all ingredients. Mix well. Cover. Cook on low 6 to 8 hours. Makes 72 meatballs.

PRETZEL TWIST NIBBLERS

1 (14 ounce) package pretzel nuggets

3 cups tiny twist shape pretzels

⅓ cup vegetable oil

1 (1 ounce) envelope ranch dressing mix

In slow cooker, add pretzels. In small bowl, combine oil and ranch dressing. Pour mixture over pretzels. Mix well. Cook on low 3 hours. Remove lid. Stir. Cook 30 additional minutes. Pour on cookie sheet to cool. Makes 6 to 8 servings.

ROSEMARY GOLDIE holds a special place in Catholic church history. On January 10, 1967, Pope Paul VI named the Sydney, Australia, native as Undersecretary in the Council of the Laity. She was the first woman to be appointed to so high a rank in the Vatican. She also became the first full time woman teacher in a pontifical University in Rome, although she had no formal training in theology.

SWISS CHEESE FONDUE

1 (16 ounce) package shredded Swiss cheese

1 cup apple juice

1 (10¾ ounce) can cheddar cheese soup

¼ teaspoon garlic salt

In slow cooker, combine all ingredients. Mix well. Cover. Cook on low 2 to 3 hours. Stir after 1 hour of cooking. Serve with vegetables, bread chunks, and fruit. Makes 4 cups.

CHEDDAR CHEESE FONDUE

1 (16 ounce) package cheddar cheese cubes

½ cup apple cider

½ teaspoon hot pepper sauce

In slow cooker, spray with non-stick cooking spray. Add ingredients; mix well. Cover. Cook on low 2 to 3 hours. Serve with French bread cubes, tortilla chips, or fresh vegetables.

PEGGY FLEMING was the only American to win a gold medal in the 1968 Tenth Winter Olympic Games in Grenoble, France, when she won the figure skating championship. ABC televised these games live and in color for the first time. She captivated American audiences. She starred in five TV specials, one of which won two Emmys. In 1980 she was the first figure skater to perform at the White House.

Soups
Stews,
& Chili

Infamous Women

5. MARY E. SURRATT was convicted by a military commission of conspiracy in the assassination of President Abraham Lincoln at Ford's Theatre in Washington, D.C., on April 14, 1865. Her home had supposedly been a meeting place for the Southern sympathizers. She became the first woman hanged by the United States Government when she and three male conspirators went to the gallows on July 7, 1865. Her guilt is still a subject of much controversy.

6. "LIZZIE BORDEN took an axe and gave her father forty whacks. Then when she was done, she gave her mother forty-one." One of the most notable murders in history took place in the small town of Fall River, Massachusetts, in 1892, and gave birth to the above verse. Lizzie was acquitted and lived out her life in Fall River. You can see the home where the murders (never solved) took place, Lizzie's later home, and the cemetery where the participants in the drama are buried.

7. BONNIE PARKER was the female half of a notorious Depression Era crime duo with Clyde Barrow. They robbed stores, filling stations and small banks in a murderous crime spree in Texas, Oklahoma, New Mexico and Missouri. They became almost folk heroes and the object of a massive manhunt. On May 23, 1934, they were killed in an ambush at Blue Lake, Louisiana. The 4' 11", 90 pound pretty Bonnie helped make the criminal duo unique. Faye Dunaway portrayed her (opposite Warren Beatty) in the extremely popular movie, "Bonnie and Clyde."

8. KATE "MA" BARKER was a plump matronly mother extremely devoted to her four criminal sons. She traveled with them around the Midwest, condoned their criminal lifestyle, made sure they ate well, and would have done anything to protect them. FBI chief, J. Edgar Hoover, called her "one of the most vicious, dangerous, and resourceful criminal brains " of his era. However, there was never any evidence she committed or planned any of the criminal activities committed by her sons. Historians believe the legend of Ma Barker was launched by Hoover after she and her son Freddie were killed by FBI agents in a bloody four-hour gun battle in Lake Weir, Florida. Was she a "veritable beast of prey" or just a simple-minded mother devoted to her four no-good sons?

CREAMY BROCCOLI SOUP

1 small onion, chopped

1 tablespoon butter

1 (20 ounce) package frozen broccoli

2 (10¾ ounce) cans cream of celery soup

1 (10¾ ounce) can cream of mushroom soup

1 cup grated American cheese

2 soup cans milk

In medium skillet, sauté onion in butter over medium heat. Place in slow cooker. Add broccoli, celery soup, mushroom soup, cheese, and milk. Cover. Cook on low 3 to 4 hours. Makes 6 to 8 servings.

BROCCOLI CHEESE SOUP

1 (8 ounce) package Velveeta® cheese

2 (10¾ ounce) cans cream of celery soup

1 pint half and half

1 (10 ounce) package frozen chopped broccoli

In slow cooker, combine all ingredients. Cover. Cook on low 2 to 3 hours. Makes 4 to 6 servings.

GERTRUDE STEIN (1874–1946) was a novelist with a unique writing style-her language the equivalent of cubism in art. She used little punctuation and simple words and repeated basic words, as in her statement, "Rose is a rose is a rose is a rose." She felt such repetition of words helped communicate the feelings they expressed, and she placed more importance on the feelings of the characters than on telling a story. Her best known book is "The Autobiography of Alice B. Toklas" (1933).

CHEESY BROCCOLI SOUP

1 (16 ounce) package chopped frozen broccoli, thawed

1 (8 ounce) jar Cheese Whiz®

1 (10¾ ounce) can cream of celery soup

1 (16 ounce) carton half and half

In slow cooker, combine all ingredients. Mix well. Cover. Cook on low 2 to 3 hours. Makes 6 servings.

BROCCOLI CHEDDAR CHEESE SOUP

1 (8 ounce) package shredded cheddar cheese

1 pint half and half

1 (10 ounce) package frozen broccoli

In slow cooker, combine all ingredients. Cover. Cook on low 2 to 3 hours. Makes 6 to 8 servings.

CHEDDAR CHEESE SOUP

2 (10¾ ounce) cans cheddar cheese soup

1½ cans water

½ cup chopped tomatoes

¼ cup chopped green chiles

In slow cooker, combine all ingredients. Mix well. Cover and cook on low 2 to 3 hours. Makes 4 servings.

DR. ALETTA JACOBS *was a pioneering physician and feminist, with a 20ᵗʰ century vision, who lived most of her life during the Victorian era. She was the first woman to attend university and receive a medical degree in the Netherlands. She established what is considered the first birth control clinic in the world in Amsterdam in 1881. She worked for deregulation of prostitution, improved working conditions for women, and women's suffrage in Holland.*

BROCCOLI CHEESE SOUP

2 (16 ounce) packages chopped broccoli

2 (10¾ ounce) cans cheddar cheese soup

2 (12 ounce) cans evaporated milk

¼ cup finely chopped onion

½ teaspoon salt

In slow cooker, combine all ingredients. Cover. Cook on low 4 to 6 hours. Makes 8 servings.

CHEDDAR CHEESE SOUP

2 (10 ounce) cans cream of mushroom soup

1 pound cheddar cheese, cubed

1 cup evaporated milk

1 teaspoon Worcestershire sauce

¼ teaspoon paprika

In slow cooker, combine all ingredients. Mix well. Cover. Cook on low 3 to 4 hours. Makes 4 servings.

VEGETABLE SOUP

4 cups vegetable broth

3 cups water

2 (8 ounce) cans tomato sauce

2 cups dried pasta

2½ cups frozen vegetables, thawed

Salt and pepper

In slow cooker, combine all ingredients. Mix well. Cover. Cook on low 8 to 9 hours or high 3 to 4 hours. Makes 4 to 6 servings.

WALLIS WARFIELD was married and residing in London when she met Edward, Prince of Wales, who became King Edward VIII. They became friends and gradually fell in love. Wallis filed for divorce with the intention of marrying Edward, but as a woman twice divorced she was socially and politically unacceptable as a prospective British Queen. Edward abdicated his throne and they were married On June 3, 1937, in France. In a radio broadcast he said, "I have found it impossible to carry the heavy burden of responsibility and to discharge my duties as king, as I wish to do, without the help of the woman I love."

MORE THAN CHICKEN SOUP

2 (10¾ ounce) cans cream of chicken soup

1 cup broccoli florets, thawed

1 cup cooked chicken cubes

1¾ cups milk

In slow cooker, combine all ingredients. Mix well. Cover. Cook on low 2 to 3 hours. Makes 4 servings.

GET A GRIP ONION SOUP

3 large onions, sliced

3 tablespoons butter or margarine, melted

3 tablespoons all-purpose flour

1 tablespoon Worcestershire sauce

1 teaspoon sugar

4 (14 ounce) cans beef broth

In slow cooker, combine onions and butter. Cover. Cook on high 40 minutes. In small bowl, combine flour, Worcestershire sauce and sugar. Add mixture and broth to onions. Stir well. Cover. Cook on low heat 7 to 9 hours. Makes 8 servings.

MARGARET CHASE SMITH (1899–1995) was the first woman to be elected to both houses of the U.S. Congress. When her husband, a Maine Republican Congressman, died in 1940, she replaced him and served four full two-year terms. In 1948 she was elected to the U.S. Senate and was reelected three times. In 1964, Smith campaigned for the Republican presidential nomination, the first woman to ever do so for a major party.

ON THE GO ONION SOUP

3 pounds onions, sliced

½ cup butter

2 (14 ounce) cans beef broth

1 can water

In large skillet, sauté onions in butter until lightly golden brown. Pour onions into slow cooker. Add remaining ingredients. Cover. Cook on low 8 to 10 hours. If desired, top each serving with grated mozzarella cheese. Makes 4 to 6 servings.

EASY FIX 'N BEEF SOUP

1 pound ground beef, browned, drained

2 cups beef broth

2 cups tomato juice

1 (16 ounce) package frozen mixed vegetables

1 teaspoon salt

In slow cooker, combine all ingredients. Mix well. Cover. Cook on low 4 to 6 hours. Makes 4 servings.

MADELINE ALBRIGHT *was nominated by President Bill Clinton to become our 64th Secretary of State, was unanimously confirmed, and sworn in on January, 28, 1997. She became the first female Secretary of State and the highest ranking woman ever in U.S. government.*

LITTLE BITE BEEF SOUP

2 pounds stewing beef, cut in ½-inch chunks

2 (15 ounce) can black beans, drained

2 cups frozen corn

2 cups chopped onions

2 (16 ounce) jars chunky salsa

4 cups water

2 teaspoons ground cumin

1 teaspoon red pepper

In slow cooker, combine all ingredients. Mix well. Cover. Cook on low 8 to 10 hours. Makes 10 to 12 servings.

CHILL OUT BEEF SOUP

1 (2.5 ounce) jar mushrooms, drained

¼ green bell pepper, diced

1 tablespoon butter or margarine

1 (10¾ ounce) can beef soup

2 (10¾ ounce) cans beef noodle soup

1½ soup cans water

In slow cooker, combine all ingredients. Cover. Cook on low 3 to 4 hours. Makes 4 to 6 servings.

DOROTHY DANDRIDGE *was the first black performer to receive an Academy Award nomination, for her performance in 1954's "Carmen Jones." She won a Golden Globe Award for her appearance with Sidney Portier in "Porgy and Bess," but was offered virtually no film roles and returned to night clubs. At age 41 she died of an overdose of antidepressants.*

VEGGIE BEEF SOUP

½ pound extra lean ground beef, browned, drained

1 (14 ounce) can ready to serve beef broth

1 (14.5 ounce) can stewed tomatoes, chopped, undrained

1 cup frozen mixed vegetables

1 (8 ounce) can tomato sauce

⅓ cup uncooked quick cooking barley

In slow cooker, combine all ingredients. Cover. Cook on low 4 to 6 hours. Makes 4 to 5 servings.

GROUND BEEF SOUP

1 pound lean ground beef, browned, drained

2½ cups tomato juice

1½ cups beef broth

3 cups frozen mixed vegetables

In slow cooker, combine all ingredients. Cover. Cook on low 4 to 6 hours. Makes 4 to 6 servings.

BETTY CROCKER *was created in 1921 after a promotion for Gold Medal Flour caused customers to flood the company with questions about baking. The fictitious kitchen expert was created to answer inquiries in a personal way. Betty hosted a radio show and became a star-voted the second most famous woman in America in 1945. A TV show, over 200 cookbooks since 1950 and a line of food products including cake mixes have carried the Betty Crocker name.*

NO FUSS VEGGIE BEEF SOUP

1 pound ground beef, browned, drained

2 cups tomato juice

2 cups beef broth

1 (16 ounce) package frozen mixed vegetables

In slow cooker, combine all ingredients. Cover. Cook on low 3 to 4 hours. Makes 4 to 5 servings.

BUTTER BEAN SOUP

1 pound butter beans

6 cups water

1 teaspoon salt

½ cup butter

1 cup cubed ham

In slow cooker, add beans and water. Cover. Cook on low 8 to 10 hours. Add salt, butter and ham. Cover. Cook and additional 1 hour. Makes 6 servings.

MAMA MIA'S MEATBALL SOUP

1 (16 ounce) package precooked meatballs

2 (10¾ ounce) cans garlic mushroom soup

2 soup cans water

In slow cooker, combine all ingredients. Cover. Cook on low 4 to 5 hours. Makes 4 to 6 servings.

JANE GOODALL revolutionized field research on animals in nature. She won their trust through daily contact with them, and observed them at close range. In her studies of chimpanzees in Tanganyika she discovered that they were adept at making and using tools. Her research suggests that hunting, tool use, and "warfare" are not unique to human beings.

MEATBALL SOUP

1 (16 ounce) package frozen precooked
   meatballs

2 (14 ounce) cans beef broth

2 (14 ounce) cans diced Italian seasoned
   tomatoes, undrained

1 cup water

1 (16 ounce) package frozen mixed
   vegetables

In slow cooker, combine meatballs, broth, tomatoes, and water. Cover. Cook on low 6 to 8 hours. Add vegetables. Cover. Cook an additional 1 hour. Makes 6 servings.

TERRIFIC TOMATO SOUP

1 cup chopped onion

2 cloves garlic, minced

1 tablespoon olive oil

9 medium tomatoes, chopped

In large saucepan, sauté onion and garlic in olive oil over medium heat until golden brown. Pour into slow cooker. Stir in tomatoes. Cover. Cook on low 6 to 8 hours. Makes 4 to 6 servings.

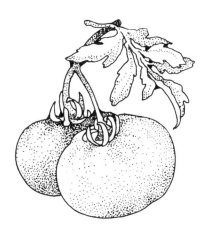

MARIE CALLAS (1923–1977), *a legendary soprano, was the dominant performer in opera for 20 years. She looked on opera as theatre as well as voice and put it all together. She is almost as well known for her 9 year affair with Aristotle Onassis, which ended with his marriage to Jackie Kennedy.*

CREAMY TOMATO SOUP

1 (28 ounce) can diced tomatoes, undrained

1 (26 ounce) jar tomato pasta sauce

2 (14 ounce) cans chicken broth

1 cup sour cream

½ cup milk

In slow cooker, combine tomatoes, pasta sauce, and chicken broth. Cover. Cook on low 4 to 6 hours. Add sour cream and milk. Mix well. Cover. Cook an additional 15 minutes. Makes 8 servings.

CURRY TOMATO SOUP

1 (46 ounce) can tomato juice

¼ cup sugar

¼ cup butter or margarine

1 teaspoon curry powder

¼ teaspoon onion powder

¼ cup flour

In slow cooker, combine all ingredients, except flour. Cover. Cook on low 3 to 4 hours. In small bowl, place 2 cups tomato soup mixture. Add flour slowly. Mix well. Add flour mixture to slow cooker. Mix well. Cover. Cook an additional 20 to 30 minutes. Makes 6 servings.

CHILI SOUP

1 pound Italian sausage

1 onion, chopped

1 (14½ ounce) can diced tomatoes, undrained

2 cups vegetable tomato juice

1 (15½ ounce) can Mexican style chili beans

1 teaspoon chili powder

In large skillet, brown sausage and onion over medium high heat, drain. In slow cooker, combine all ingredients. Mix well. Cover. Cook on low 5 to 6 hours. Makes 6 to 8 servings.

TURKEY & VEGETABLE SOUP

2 pounds turkey, cooked, drained

2 (14 ounce) cans beef broth

1 (28 ounce) can chopped tomatoes, undrained

1 (16 ounce) package mixed frozen vegetables

½ cup uncooked barley

1 teaspoon salt

½ teaspoon pepper

In slow cooker, combine all ingredients. Mix well. Cover. Cook on high 4 to 6 hours. Makes 6 to 8 servings.

JUDY GARLAND was only 17 when she starred as Dorothy in "The Wizard of Oz," in which she sang her signature song, "Just Over the Rainbow." She went on to win Grammy Awards for her records, Emmy Award nominations for TV, an Oscar nomination and a special Tony Award. Addiction to pills caused her many problems in later life.

ITALIAN POTATO SOUP

5 medium potatoes, sliced thin

½ cup diced onion

1¼ pounds Italian sausage, form bite size pieces

2½ teaspoons salt

1½ teaspoons pepper

6 cups water

¼ cup butter

2 cups milk

In slow cooker, layer ½ of potatoes, onion, sausage, salt, and pepper. Repeat layering. Add water and butter. Cover. Cook on low 10 hours. Add milk. Mix well and serve. Makes 6 to 8 servings.

ALMOST LIKE MOM'S POTATO SOUP

1 (5 ounce) package scalloped potato mix

4 cups chicken broth

1 onion, chopped

2 cups half and half

⅓ cup flour

In slow cooker, combine scalloped potato mix, broth, and onion. Cover. Cook on low 4 to 6 hours. In medium bowl, combine half and half and flour. Mix until smooth. Pour flour mixture into slow cooker slowly, stirring constantly. Cover. Cook an additional 1 hour, stirring occasionally. Makes 5 servings.

JEAN NIDETCH *weighed 214 pounds and was addicted to cookies. She began a diet plan that worked, and met with others with food problems in a support group. This was the beginning of Weight Watchers International, the most successful weight loss organization in the world. It currently has more than one million members.*

THICK POTATO SOUP

2 pounds potatoes, cut into 1 inch cubes

2 (10¾ ounce) cans cream of mushroom
  soup

1 cup sliced green onions

⅛ teaspoon red pepper

1½ cups shredded cheddar cheese

1 cup sour cream

1 cup milk

In slow cooker, combine potatoes, soup, green
onions, and red pepper. Mix well. Cover. Cook
on low 8 to 10 hours or high 4 hours. Add
cheese, sour cream and milk. Mix until cheese
melts. Cover. Cook 15 minutes. Makes 6 servings.

BEEF POTATO SOUP

1 pound ground beef, browned, drained

4 cups cubed potatoes

1 cup chopped onion

3 (8 ounce) cans tomato sauce

1½ teaspoons salt

Water

In slow cooker, combine beef, potatoes, onions,
tomato sauce, and salt. Add water to cover ingredients. Mix well. Cover. Cook on low 8 to 10
hours. Makes 6 to 8 servings.

CLARA BOW
*(1905–1965) was
the first sex symbol
in the movies. She
portrayed the plights
of working girls for
Flapper audiences
in the 1920s. The
saucy and pert
actress became
known as 'The "It"
Girl' when she
starred in the 1927
movie "It" which
made her a star.
"It" was just good
old sex appeal. She
retired in 1933 and
lived out her life in
quiet seclusion.*

POTATO AND CARROT SOUP

4 medium red potatoes, cubed

2 carrots, diced

1 onion, chopped

1 stalk celery, chopped

2 (14 ounce) cans chicken broth with garlic

2 strips bacon, cooked, crumbled

1 cup instant mashed potato flakes

1 cup milk

In slow cooker, combine potatoes, carrots, onion, celery, broth, and bacon. Mix well. Cover. Cook on low 8 to 10 hours. Add potato flakes and milk. Mix well. Makes 4 servings.

CHEESY POTATO SOUP

4 medium potatoes, cooked, cubed

1 small onion, chopped

1 (10¾ ounce) can cheddar cheese soup

1 (10¾ ounce) can cream of celery soup

2 cups milk

1 teaspoon salt

In slow cooker, combine all ingredients. Cover. Cook on low heat 2½ to 3 hours. Makes 4 to 6 servings.

PATSY CLINE was one of the first "crossover" female singers in Nashville. Her first break came on the Arthur Godfrey Talent Show, and was furthered by appearances on the Jimmy Dean Show. "Walking After Midnight" became her first Top 20 pop hit, quickly followed by several others. In 1973 she was the first female solo artist to become a member of the Country Music Hall of Fame. She died in a plane crash in 1963 at the height of her career.

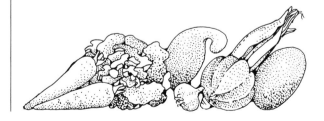

MINESTRONE SOUP

2 (14 ounce) cans chicken broth

1 (14 ounce) can crushed tomatoes

1 (14½ ounce) can kidney beans

1½ cups frozen mixed vegetables

3 teaspoons Italian seasoning

In slow cooker, combine all ingredients. Cover. Cook on low 3 to 4 hours. Makes 4 to 5 servings.

SANTA FE SOUP

1 cup dried red kidney beans, sorted, rinsed

1¼ pounds beef stew meat. Cut into bite size pieces

1 (15.25 ounce) can whole kernel corn, drained

1 (14.5 ounce) can diced tomatoes, undrained

1 (1.25 ounce) package taco seasoning mix

1 (4.5 ounce) can chopped green chiles

1½ cups water

1 onion, chopped

In large bowl, place beans. Cover with 3 cups water for 8 hours or overnight. Drain beans. In slow cooker, combine all ingredients. Mix well. Cover. Cook on low 8 to10 hours. Makes 6 servings.

MARIA TALLCHIEF, a half Osage Indian from Fairfax, OK, became the first American trained ballerina of international importance. She danced with the New York City Ballet from 1947–1965. She established her reputation when she danced in her husband, director George Balanchine's version of "The Firebird" in 1949. She founded the Chicago City Ballet and was its artistic director from 1980–1987.

TORTELLINI SOUP

1 (28 ounce) can diced tomatoes, undrained

1 (15.5 ounce) can great northern beans, drained, rinsed

2 (14½ ounce) cans chicken broth

2 medium zucchinis, halved, cut into 1-inch slices

1 onion, finely chopped

1 (8 ounce) package uncooked cheese filled tortellini

In slow cooker, combine all ingredients except tortellini. Mix well. Cover. Cook on low 6 to 8 hours. Add tortellini. Cover. Cook on high an additional 20 minutes. Makes 8 servings.

BELL PEPPER SOUP

1½ pounds lean ground beef, browned, drained

3 green bell peppers, chopped

1 onion, chopped

1 (28 ounce) can crushed tomatoes, undrained

2 (14½ ounce) cans beef broth

2 (10¾ ounce) cans tomato soup

1 cup instant rice, uncooked

1 cup water

In slow cooker, combine all ingredients. Mix well. Cover. Cook on low 6 to 8 hours. Makes 8 servings.

QUEEN ISABELL I, THE CATHOLIC, of Spain, (1457–1504), according to stories used her jewels to finance the three-ship expedition of Christopher Columbus on his voyage to the New World. Whether this is true or not, she was Columbus' supporter on his trip to America. She also was the protectoress of the American aborigines against ill usage by colonists and adventurers.

LAZY LASAGNA SOUP

1 pound ground beef, browned, drained

1 (14½ ounce) can diced tomatoes, undrained

1 (7¾ ounce) package lasagna dinner mix

1 (7 ounce) can whole kernel corn, undrained

5 cups water

1 small zucchini, chopped

½ cup chopped onion

2 tablespoons grated Parmesan cheese

In slow cooker, combine all ingredients. Cover. Cook on low 6 to 8 hours. Makes 8 to 10 servings.

CORN CHOWDER

4 medium potatoes, peeled, diced

2 (14½ ounce) cans diced tomatoes, undrained

2 (15 ¼ ounce) cans whole kernel corn, undrained

4 strips bacon, cooked, chopped

1 onion, chopped

In slow cooker, combine all ingredients. Cover. Cook on low 8 to 10 hours. Makes 8 to 9 servings.

*At 6 feet tall and 180 pounds, **CARRIE NATION** was an imposing figure, especially when she was yielding a hatchet. In 1899 she joined the Women's Christian Temperance Union, and felt divinely ordained to forcefully promote temperance. She set about destroying saloons with rocks, hammers and hatchets. She was arrested 30 times for destroying "watering holes" in the early 1900s.*

ON THE ROAD CLAM CHOWDER

2 (10¾ ounce) cans clam chowder soup

1 cup corn

2½ cups chopped cooked shrimp

1¾ cups milk

In slow cooker, combine all ingredients. Cover. Cook on low heat 2½ to 3 hours, stirring often. Makes 4 servings.

BAYSIDE CLAM CHOWDER

3 (10¾ ounce) cans cream of potato soup

2 (10¾ ounce) cans clam chowder soup

½ cup butter

1 small onion, diced

1 pint half and half

2 (6½ ounce) cans clams, chopped

In slow cooker, combine all ingredients. Cover. Cook on low 3 to 4 hours. Makes 4 to 6 servings.

SHANNON MILLER of Edmond, OK, one of the most talented gymnasts in history, won five Olympic medals at the 1992 Olympic Games. She was just 15 years old. In 1996 she led the U.S. Women's gymnastics team to its first Olympic gold medal, and won the first American gold medal on the balance beam. She is the only American to win two consecutive World Championship all-around titles.

CHICKEN & WILD RICE SOUP

½ pound skinless, boneless chicken thighs, cut into bite size pieces

3 (14½ ounce) cans chicken broth

2 carrots, thinly sliced

⅔ cup uncooked wild rice

½ cup chopped onion

1½ cups frozen broccoli florets, thawed

1½ cups frozen corn, thawed

In slow cooker, combine chicken, broth, carrots, wild rice, and onion. Mix well. Cover. Cook on low 8 to 10 hours. Add broccoli and corn. Mix well. Cover. Cook on high an additional 10 minutes. Makes 6 servings.

MEXICAN SPLIT PEA SOUP

1 (16 ounce) package dried split peas, sorted, rinsed

4 cups water

6 ounces smoked chorizo sausage, sliced thin, casings removed

1 (10½ ounce) can chicken broth

1 (11 ounce) can Mexican style whole kernel corn, drained

½ cup sliced green onion

In slow cooker, combine peas, water, sausage, and broth. Mix well. Cover. Cook on low 8 to 9 hours. Add corn and onion. Mix well. Cover. Cook on high an additional 10 minutes. Makes 6 servings.

MARY TYLER MOORE *left dancing because it "lacked the spotlight," and she really wanted to be a star. When she was picked from the world of commercials and minor TV roles for the attractive wife, Laura Petrie, on the Dick Van Dyke Show, it assured her stardom. For that show, Mary Tyler Moore Show, and specials she won six Emmys, and eight other nominations-plus she has two Tony Awards, and an Academy Award nomination. She is active in diabetes research.*

NOODLE LOVERS SOUP

1 pound lean ground beef, browned, drained

1 (14.5 ounce) can diced tomatoes, undrained

1 (1.15 ounce) package dry beefy mushroom soup mix

3 cups water

1 onion, chopped

1 celery stalk, sliced thin

2 cups frozen mixed vegetables, thawed

1 cup uncooked fine egg noodles

In slow cooker, combine beef, tomatoes, soup mix, water, onion, and celery. Mix well. Cover. Cook on low 6 to 8 hours. Add vegetables and noodles. Mix well. Cover. Cook on high an additional 20 minutes. Makes 6 servings.

BEEFY NOODLE SOUP

1 pound ground beef, browned, drained

1 (46 ounce) can V8® juice

1 (16 ounce) package frozen mixed vegetables

1 (1 ounce) package onion soup mix

1 (3 ounce) package beef ramen noodles with flavor packet

In slow cooker, combine all ingredients. Mix well. Cover. Cook over low for 5 to 6 hours. Makes 8 servings.

LORETTA LYNN *had over 70 hits in the '60s and '70s as a country singer. She began writing songs with a feminist viewpoint-unheard of in country music. When she teamed with Conway Twitty, they became one of country music's most successful duos. Sissy Spacek won an Academy Award in 1980 for her portrayal of Lynn in the very successful movie, "Coal Miner's Daughter."*

LOUISIANA SHRIMP GUMBO

1 onion, chopped

1 green bell pepper, chopped

2 cloves garlic, minced

2 tablespoons vegetable oil

3 (10¾ ounce) cans golden mushroom soup

1 (24 ounce) jar salsa with corn and beans

2 pounds frozen peeled small shrimp, thawed

In medium skillet, sauté onion, pepper, and garlic in oil, over medium high heat until lightly golden. Pour mixture into slow cooker. In slow cooker, add soup and salsa. Mix well. Cover. Cook on low 2 hours. Add shrimp. Mix well. Cover. Cook an additional 1 to 2 hours. Makes 6 to 8 servings.

CHICKEN DUMP SOUP

2 (14½ ounce) cans chicken broth

1 (14¾ ounce) can cream style corn

1 (10 ounce) package frozen chopped broccoli

2 (5 ounce) cans chunk chicken, drained

1 (2 ounce) jar diced pimientos, drained

In slow cooker, combine all ingredients. Mix well. Cover. Cook on low 4 hours. Makes 4 servings.

Although she had been a successful performer for decades, **ANGELA LANSBURY** *hit superstardom as senior citizen detective Jessica Fletcher in the TV drama "Murder She Wrote." The English-born actress has won four Tonys, been nominated for three Oscars and ten Emmy Awards.*

BEANS WITH BACON SOUP

10 cups chicken broth

3 (15 ounce) cans great northern beans, drained

1 (14½ ounce) can diced tomatoes, undrained

1 (10 ounce) package frozen diced carrots

1 pound bacon, cooked, crumbled

1 onion, chopped

2 cloves garlic, minced

In slow cooker, combine all ingredients. Mix well. Cover. Cook on low 6 to 8 hours. Makes 8 to 10 servings.

BLACK BEAN SOUP

3 (15 ounce) cans black beans, rinsed, drained

2 (14½ ounce) cans chicken broth

1 (14½ ounce) can diced stewed tomatoes, undrained

2 cups chopped onion

2 cups chopped green bell pepper

2 cloves garlic, minced

In slow cooker, combine all ingredients. Mix well. Cover. Cook on low 8 to 10 hours or high 5 hours. Makes 8 servings.

KITTY WELLS
was the first major female country singer. Her hits, beginning in the 1950s earned her the title "Queen of Country Music." In 1952 her pro-feminist "It Wasn't God Who Made Honky Tonk Angels" was her first hit. She joined the Grand Ole Opry in that year. She was inducted into the Country Music Hall of Fame in 1974.

ALPHABET SOUP

½ pound beef stew meat, diced

1 (14½ ounce) can Italian style diced tomatoes

1 (8 ounce) can tomato sauce

3 cups water

1 (16 ounce) packaged frozen mixed vegetables

3 teaspoons instant beef bouillon

½ cup alphabet noodles, uncooked

In slow cooker, combine all ingredients, except noodles. Mix well. Cover. Cook on low 6 to 8 hours. Add noodles. Cover. Cook on high 20 minutes. Makes 3 to 4 servings.

LEFTOVER CHICKEN AND VEGETABLE SOUP

3 (14 ounce) cans chicken broth

2 cups cooked diced chicken

2 cups frozen whole kernel corn

1 (10 ounce) package frozen cut green beans

2 tomatoes, diced

1 stalk celery, chopped

¼ teaspoon garlic powder

In slow cooker, combine all ingredients. Mix well. Cover. Cook on low 4 to 6 hours. Makes 6 servings.

JEAN STAPLETON *was a character actress who had quite a stage career. Then she became the beloved "dingbat," Edith Bunker, on the 1970's TV series, "All In The Family." She and Archie became pop icons. She won three Emmys and three Golden Globes for her portrayal, but never had another successful TV series. She turned down the lead role in "Murder She Wrote."*

SAUSAGE SOUP

4 (14½ ounce) cans chicken broth

8 red potatoes, diced

1 (1 ounce) package Italian salad dressing mix

1 pound Italian sausage, browned, drained

2 cups frozen chopped spinach, thawed

In slow cooker, combine broth, potatoes, and dressing mix. Cover. Cook on low 8 to 10 hours. Add sausage and spinach. Mix well. Cover. Cook an additional 15 minutes. Makes 8 to 10 servings.

NEW MEXICO STEW

1 pound lean ground beef, browned, drained

1 pound Velveeta® Mexican style cheese, cubed

1 (15 ounce) can Ranch style beans, undrained

1 cup frozen whole kernel corn

1½ cups water

In slow cooker, combine all ingredients. Cover. Cook on low 4 to 6 hours. Makes 4 to 6 servings.

TAMMY WYNETTE dominated the country music charts in the late '60's and early '70s with 17 number one hits. She married George Jones—a stormy relationship—but they recorded a number of successful duets, before and after their divorce. She began having health problems in the 1980s and died in 1998.

GREEN CHILE STEW

6 medium potatoes, peeled, cubed

2 pounds lean pork roast, cubed

2 teaspoons salt

1 teaspoon pepper

⅛ cup minced onion

1 (7 ounce) can chopped green chile

4 cloves garlic, minced

Water

In slow cooker, layer potatoes then pork. Sprinkle with salt and pepper. Top with onion, green chile, and garlic. Add enough water to cover ingredients. Cover. Cook on low 10 to 12 hours. Makes 8 to10 servings.

BEEF GREEN CHILE STEW

2 pounds round steak, cubed

1 clove garlic, minced

2 large onions, chopped

2 (7 ounce) cans chopped green chile

5 (10 ounce) cans tomatoes with green chile

2 cups water

¼ cup beef broth

In large skillet with little oil, combine steak, garlic, and onions, cook over low heat until lightly browned. Pour in slow cooker. Add remaining ingredients. Mix well. Cook on low 10 to 12 hours. Serve with warm tortillas. Makes 8 servings.

FAYE ABDELLAH was the first nurse to hold the rank of Rear Admiral and the title Deputy Surgeon General of the U.S. She spent most of her career in the U.S. Public Health Service. She helped change the focus of nursing from disease centered to patient centered.

HOT TEX-MEX STEW

1½ pounds stewing beef, cubed

2 cups salsa

1 cup barbeque sauce

½ cup chopped onions

2 cups corn

1 (15 ounce) can pinto beans, rinsed, drained

¼ cup chopped cilantro

In slow cooker, combine all ingredients. Mix well. Cover. Cook on low 8 to 10 hours or high 4 to 5 hours. Makes 6 servings.

SAUSAGE & BEANS STEW

1 (16 ounce) package smoked sausage, cut in 1-inch slices

⅓ cup diced onion

2 (15 ounce) cans kidney beans, undrained

1 (15 ounce) can pinto beans, undrained

1 (10 ounce) can diced tomatoes undrained

1 (10¾ ounce) can minestrone soup

In slow cooker, combine all ingredients. Mix well. Cover. Cook on low 6 to 8 hours or high 3 to 4 hours. Makes 6 to 8 servings.

BELLA ABZUG (1920–1998) was a civil rights and labor attorney who was elected as a Democrat from New York to the U.S. House of Representatives, and served from 1971–1977. She gained fame for her support of the women's rights movement. She helped establish Women Strike for Peace, a nuclear disarmament group.

FIX & GO STEW

2½ pounds stewing beef, cubed

3 carrots, sliced

1 small onion, sliced

3 large potatoes, sliced

3 stalks celery, sliced

2 cups chopped tomatoes

2 (10¾ ounce) cans tomato soup

In slow cooker, combine all ingredients. Mix well. Cover. Cook on low 8 to 10 hours. Salt and pepper to taste. Makes 6 servings.

CABBAGE PATCH STEW

2 pounds stewing beef, cubed, browned

6 cups shredded cabbage

½ cup corn

3 carrots, sliced

1 small onion, chopped

1½ cups beef broth

2 (15 ounce) cans chopped tomatoes, undrained

Salt and pepper

In slow cooker, combine all ingredients. Mix well. Cover. Cook on low 8 to 10 hours or high 3 to 4 hours. Makes 4 to 6 servings.

LOUISA MAY ALCOTT *was an author whose book "Little Women" has been in print continuously since being published in 1868. It was the first book for the mass market of juvenile girls in the 19th century. Her family friends and neighbors when she grew up in Massachusetts were writers such as Nathaniel Hawthorne, Henry David Thoreau and Ralph Waldo Emerson.*

STEW ON IT

2 pounds boneless beef chuck, cut into 1-inch cubes

¼ cup flour

1⅓ cups sliced carrots

1 (16 ounce) can whole tomatoes, undrained, chopped

1 (1 ounce) package onion soup mix

½ cup water

1 cup sliced mushrooms

In slow cooker, toss beef with flour. Add carrots, tomatoes, soup mix, and water. Cover. Cook on low 8 to 10 hours. Add mushrooms. Cover. Cook an additional 10 minutes. Makes 8 servings.

BEEF STEW

1 pound stew meat, cut into bite sized pieces

2 potatoes, peeled, cubed

3 carrots, sliced

1 onion, sliced

1½ teaspoons Italian seasoning

2 cups beef broth

In slow cooker, combine all ingredients. Cover. Cook on low 8 to 10 hours. Makes 4 to 6 servings.

JUNE CARTER CASH was the daughter of Mother Maybelle Carter of the legendary country music Carter Family. She performed with her family and toured with Elvis Presley in the 1950s. She began successfully recording with Johnny Cash, and they were married in 1968. Johnny gave her credit for getting him off drugs and alcohol and turning his life around.

BEEFY MUSHROOM STEW

1½ pounds beef stew meat, cut into bite size pieces

1 (10¾ ounce) can cream of mushroom soup

3 (4 ounce) cans sliced mushrooms, drained

½ cup beef broth

1 (1 ounce) package dry onion soup mix

In slow cooker, combine all ingredients. Mix well. Cover. Cook on low 6 to 8 hours. Makes 6 servings.

TEXAS BEEF STEW

2 pounds stew meat

1 (28 ounce) can whole tomatoes, undrained

1 cup small frozen whole onions

1 teaspoon chili powder

1 (1¼ ounce) package taco seasoning mix

1 (15 ounce) can black beans, rinsed, drained

1 (11 ounce) can corn with red and green bell peppers, drained

In slow cooker, combine beef, tomatoes, onions and chili powder. Cover. Cook on low 8 to 10 hours. Stir in taco seasoning, beans and corn. Cover. Cook on high 30 minutes. Makes 6 servings.

LINDA G ALVARADO *is an Hispanic-American businesswoman who started a very successful construction company (a male dominated field) in 1976. She is the first Hispanic-American (man or woman) to own a major league baseball franchise—she is co-owner of the Colorado Rockies.*

HEARTY BEEF STEW

1 pound ground beef

2 cloves garlic, minced

1 (16 ounce) package frozen vegetables

2 cups southern style hash brown potatoes

1 (14 ounce) jar marinara sauce

1 (10½ ounce) can beef broth

1 tablespoon Worcestershire sauce

In large skillet, brown beef with garlic, over medium heat. Drain. In slow cooker, add beef, vegetables, potatoes, sauce, beef broth, and Worcestershire sauce. Cover. Cook on low 4 to 6 hours or high 1½ to 2 hours. Makes 4 to 6 servings.

BEEF SIRLOIN STEW

1 tablespoon vegetable oil

1 pound beef sirloin, cut into thin strips, browned

1 (16 ounce) package frozen potatoes, carrots, celery, and onions

1 (12 ounce) jar beef gravy

In slow cooker, combine all ingredients. Mix well. Cover. Cook on low 3 to 4 hours or high 1½ to 2 hours.

Over 30,000 children and young adults in the U.S. suffer from cystic fibrosis, which affects the lungs. Pediatrician and pathologist **DOROTHY H. ANDERSON** *was the first to identify cystic fibrosis and developed a simple diagnostic test for it. One in twenty Caucasians is a carrier for the disease.*

PORK STEW

1½ pounds boneless pork shoulder roast, cut into bite sized pieces, browned

8 small red potatoes, quartered

2 cups halved baby carrots

1 (12 ounce) jar pork gravy

¼ cup ketchup

½ teaspoon poultry seasoning

1½ cups frozen green beans, thawed

In slow cooker, combine all ingredients, except green beans. Mix well. Cover. Cook on low 8 to 10 hours. Add green beans. Mix well. Cover. Cook an additional 20 minutes. Makes 6 servings.

CHICKEN STEW

1 pound skinless, boneless chicken pieces, cut into bite size pieces

4 medium potatoes, peeled, cubed

1 (14½ ounce) can Italian style tomatoes

2 onions, chopped

1 green bell pepper, chopped

2 cloves garlic, minced

½ cup chicken broth

1 teaspoon Italian seasoning

In slow cooker, layer chicken and potatoes. In large bowl, combine remaining ingredients. Mix well. Pour mixture over chicken and potatoes. Cover. Cook on low 8 to 10 hours. Makes 6 servings.

OVETA CULP HOBBY (1905-1995) was a woman of firsts: First director of Women's Army Corps (WAC); first Secretary of Department of Health, Education and Welfare; first woman to obtain the rank of U.S. Colonel; first woman to receive the Distinguished Service Medal. She was the only woman in President Eisenhower's cabinet.

CHICKEN CHILI

2 pounds chicken, cut into bite sized pieces

2 (14½ ounce) cans Mexican style diced tomatoes, undrained

1 (15 ounce) can tomato sauce

1 (1¼ ounce) package mild chili seasoning mix

2 (15½ ounce) cans hominy

Place chicken in slow cooker. In medium bowl, combine tomatoes, tomato sauce, and seasoning. Pour over chicken. Cover. Cook on low 8 to 10 hours. Add hominy, stir well. Cover. Cook an additional 20 minutes. Makes 6 servings.

HURRY UP CHILI

½ pound ground beef, browned, drained

2 (14.5 ounce) cans stewed tomatoes, undrained, chopped

2 (15 ounce) cans spicy chili beans, undrained

2 teaspoons chili powder

In slow cooker, combine all ingredients. Mix well. Cover. Cook on low 3 to 4 hours or high 1½ hours. Makes 6 servings.

DONNA DE VARONA was a versatile swimmer who won national championships in three events. In the 1964 Olympics she was a gold medalist in the 400 meter individual medley and the 4 x 100 meter relay. She was named the 1964 A.P. female athlete of the year. She set 18 world records in her career. In 1965 she became the first woman sportscaster on network television.

EVERYDAY CHILI

1 pound ground beef, browned, drained

½ cup chopped onions

2 (15 ounce) cans chili with beans

1 (10 ounce) can diced tomatoes and green chiles

In slow cooker, combine all ingredients. Mix well. Cover. Cook on low 4 to 6 hours or on high 1½ to 2 hours. Makes 6 servings.

QUICK DRAW CHILI

1½ pounds lean ground beef, browned, drained

3 links sausage with cheddar, sliced

2 (15 ounce) cans Cajun style mixed vegetables, undrained

1 (14½ ounce) can diced tomatoes, undrained

2 (10¾ ounce) cans tomato soup

In slow cooker, combine all ingredients. Mix well. Cover. Cook on low 4 to 6 hours or high 2 hours. Makes 8 to 10 servings.

DOLLY PARTON *began singing country music on TV at age 12. She became a regular on the Porter Waggoner Show and their duets became famous. She created the image of the dumb blonde (which she is not). She moved successfully from country roots to international fame- a country superstar who crossed over to the pop mainstream. She has appeared in a number of movies, such as "9 to 5." She is an astute businesswoman with ventures such as Dollywood theme park in Tennessee.*

OUT ALL DAY CHILI

1 pound ground beef

1/2 pound Italian sausage

1/2 cup chopped onion

1 (28 ounce) can tomato sauce

1 teaspoon chili powder

1 (15 ounce) can spicy chili beans, undrained

1 (15 ounce) can kidney beans, rinsed, drained

1 teaspoon honey

In large skillet, combine beef and sausage, cook over medium heat until brown. Drain. Pour mixture into slow cooker. Add remaining ingredients. Mix well. Cover. Cook on low 6 to 8 hours. Makes 6 servings.

SLOW COOKED CHILI

2 pounds ground beef

2 tablespoons chili powder

1 tablespoon cumin

1/2 cup diced onion

1 (28 ounce) can crushed tomatoes

1 cup water

2 (15 ounce) cans red kidney beans, rinsed, drained

2 tablespoons hot pepper sauce

In large skillet, combine beef, chili powder, cumin, and onions, cook over medium heat until browned. Drain. Pour mixture into slow cooker. Add remaining ingredients. Mix well. Cover. Cook on low 6 to 8 hours. Makes 6 to 8 servings.

ETHEL PERCY ANDRUS founded the American Association of Retired Persons (AARP). It has over 36 million members over 55 years of age and is a strong political lobbying force. It publishes a magazine, offers health and auto insurance and discounts for senior citizens.

CHICKEN CHILI MADE SPECIAL

1 (18 ounce) package barbeque sauce with shredded chicken

2 (15 ounce) cans black beans, rinsed, drained

1 (28 ounce) can crushed tomatoes, undrained

1 (14 ounce) can beef broth

1 (1.25 ounce) package taco seasoning

1 teaspoon chili powder

In slow cooker, combine all ingredients. Mix well. Cover. Cook on low 4 to 6 hours. Top with sour cream or cheese (optional). Makes 6 to 8 servings.

CHILI CON CARNE

1 pound lean ground beef, browned, drained

½ cup chopped onion

1½ teaspoon chili powder

1 (15 ounce)can Mexican style stewed tomatoes

1 (15 ounce) can kidney beans, undrained

In slow cooker, combine all ingredients. Mix well. Cover. Cook on low 4 to 6 hours. Makes 4 servings.

MADONNA *was the first female pop star to have complete control of her music and image. She manipulated the media with her music, videos, publicity and sexuality. Hit records have received less attention than her mode of dress, her lifestyle, and her turbulent marriage to Sean Penn. She has had seven albums go multi-platinum, and received a Golden Globe for the movie "Evita."*

CHILI DOGS 'N ONE POT

1 (16 ounce) package hot dogs

2 (15 ounce) cans no bean chili

½ cup chopped onion

In slow cooker, combine all ingredients. Mix well. Cover. Cook on low 3 to 4 hours. Serve with hot dog buns. Makes 10 servings.

CHUNKY CHILI

2 (15 ounce) cans chili without beans

1 (16 ounce) package small hot dogs

1 (8 ounce) package American cheese, cubed

½ cup thick and chunky salsa

In slow cooker, combine all ingredients. Mix well. Cover. Cook on low 4 to 6 hours or high 1½ to 2 hours. Makes 6 to 8 servings.

WILLA CATHER (1873-1947) *was a newspaper woman who became one of America's finest novelists with the publication of "O Pioneer" in 1913. She won a Pulitzer Prize in 1922. Her novels about Nebraska and the American Southwest showed a deep love of the land and traditional values.*

Vege-
tables,
Pasta, Rice,
& Casseroles

Infamous Women

9. Biblical DELILAH was asked by five Philistine princes to learn the secret of Samson's great strength. For this secret they would each give her 1100 pieces of silver. Samson loved Delilah, but resisted her efforts to discover his source of strength. Finally he tells her that he must keep his hair long to maintain his strength. While he sleeps, she has his hair cut off and hands him over to his enemies.

10. JEZEBEL has gone down in Bible history as the very worst example of evil. As Queen of Israel she forced the worship of the heathern idol Baal on the Israelites in a ruthless and deadly manner. Her vile and perverted behavior included having infants presented as burnt offerings to her god of stone, and murdering many of the Israel prophets. After her husband Ahab's death in battle, she was thrown from an upper story window, then trampled to bits by horses in the street. Dogs came and ate her body. Her name is synonymous with a wicked, painted woman.

11. BELLE STARR (1848-1889) was known as the Bandit Queen. She has been considered one of the few female outlaws in this country. Legend has her as a horse and cattle rustler and robber in the Southwest. She married Jim reed, a Texas outlaw. He was killed in a gunfight. Belle moved to Indian Territory (Eastern Oklahoma) and married a Cherokee Indian, Sam Starr. Their home became a famous outlaw hideout for Jesse James and other fugitives. She served nine months in prison when she and Sam were convicted of horse stealing. After Starr was shot to death in a fight, Belle lived with Bill July, a horse thief. Belle was shot from ambush while July was appearing in court. Although she married and lived with outlaws, most of the stories about her are exaggerations or outright false.

12. Two girls known as CATTLE ANNIE (McDougal) and LITTLE BRITCHES (Jennie Stevens) ran with the Dalton Gang. They helped steal horses and carried messages for the Oklahoma gang of robbers. Famed Marshall Bill Tilghman captured them near Pawnee, Oklahoma, in 1894, and they were sent to the Federal Reformatory in Massachusetts. In 1980 a star studded movie was made of their exploits.

CAULIFLOWER & BROCCOLI

1 (12 ounce) package frozen cauliflower, thawed

1 (10 ounce) package frozen broccoli, thawed

1 (10¾ ounce) can cheddar cheese soup

4 slices bacon, cooked, crumbled

In slow cooker, place cauliflower and broccoli. Pour soup over vegetables. Sprinkle bacon on top. Cover. Cook on low 2½ to 3 hours. Makes 6 servings.

BROCCOLI, CAULIFLOWER & CHEESE

1 (16 ounce) package frozen cauliflower

2 (10 ounce) packages frozen broccoli

½ cup water

1 tablespoon butter or margarine

2 cups shredded cheddar cheese

In slow cooker, combine all ingredients. Mix well. Cover. Cook on low 3 to 4 hours. Makes 6 to 8 servings.

ANN BANCROFT, one of the world's preeminent polar explorers was named "Woman of the Year" in 2001 by Glamour Magazine, and 1987 "Woman of the Year" by Ms. Magazine. She is the only woman to cross the ice to both the North Pole and the South Pole.

CHEDDAR & BROCCOLI

6 cups cooked broccoli cuts

2 (10¾ ounce) cans cheddar cheese soup

¾ cup milk

1 cup French fried onions

In slow cooker, combine all ingredients. Mix well. Cover. Cook on low 3 to 4 hours. Makes 6 to 8 servings.

CHEESE & BROCCOLI

1 (10¾ ounce) can cheddar cheese soup

¼ cup milk

4 cups frozen broccoli cuts

In slow cooker, combine all ingredients. Mix well. Cover. Cook on low 3 to 4 hours or high 1½ hours. Makes 4 servings

BROCCOLI

6 cups fresh broccoli florets

1½ cups water

1 (1 ounce) package onion soup mix

1 tablespoon olive oil

In slow cooker, combine all ingredients. Mix well. Cover. Cook on low 3 to 4 hours. Makes 4 servings.

PEARL S. BUCK (1892–1973) grew up in China where her parents were missionaries. She is best known for her books dealing sympathetically with life in that country. She won the 1932 Pulitzer Prize for her novel "Good Earth," which dealt with a peasant's life in China. In 1938 she was the first American woman to receive a Nobel Prize in Literature for her body of work.

EASY VEGETABLE DISH

2 (16 ounce) packages frozen mixed
   vegetables, thawed

1 cup French fried onions

1 (16 ounce) package shredded American
   cheese

¼ cup milk

In slow cooker, combine all ingredients. Mix
well. Cover. Cook on low 3 to 4 hours. Makes 6
to 8 servings.

PEAS AU GRATIN

3 cups peas

1 (2.5 ounce) can water chestnuts,
   drained, sliced

1 (10¾ ounce) can cream of mushroom
   soup

1 cup grated cheddar cheese

Coat inside slow cooker with cooking spray. In
slow cooker, combine all ingredients. Mix well.
Cover. Cook on low 4 to 6 hours. Makes 6 servings.

*To save for
graduate studies
in science,*
**STEPHANIE J.
KWOLEK**, *a
graduate of
Carnegie Institute
of Technology, took
a job at Dupont
Chemicals. She
loved her work,
stayed at Dupont,
and discovered a
fiber that led to
the development
of Kevlar, a
bulletproof material
five times stronger
than steel.*

ITALIAN ZUCCHINI

1 red onion, sliced

1 green bell pepper, sliced

4 medium zucchini, sliced

1 (14.5 ounce) can chopped Italian style tomatoes

¼ cup grated Parmesan cheese

1 tablespoon butter or margarine, melted

In slow cooker, layer onion, pepper, zucchini, and tomatoes. Sprinkle cheese over zucchini mixture. Drizzle butter over cheese. Cover. Cook on low 3 hours or high 1½ hours. Makes 6 servings.

SAUCY STUFFED PEPPERS

1 pound lean ground beef, browned, drained

⅔ cup bread crumbs

1 egg

½ teaspoon Italian seasoning

1 (32 ounce) jar spaghetti sauce, divided

5 green bell peppers, halved

In large bowl, combine beef, bread, egg, seasoning, and 1 cup spaghetti sauce. Mix well. In slow cooker, arrange peppers. Spoon beef mixture into pepper halves. Pour remaining spaghetti sauce over peppers. Cover. Cook on low 6 to 8 hours. Makes 5 servings.

MARY WALKER, *the first female U.S. Army surgeon, crossed the lines during the Civil War to treat civilians. She was taken prisoner in Richmond. After the war she was the first woman to receive the Congressional Medal of Honor. It was taken away in 1919 when qualifications were changed. She refused to return the medal and wore it until her death. It was awarded to her posthumously.*

SIDE DISH CABBAGE

1 medium head cabbage, cut in chunks

3 slices raw bacon

⅓ cup butter or margarine

½ cup hot water

Salt and pepper

In slow cooker, combine all ingredients. Mix well. Cover. Cook on high 1 hour. Uncover. Mix well. Cover, reduce heat to low, cook 2 hours. Makes 6 servings.

CABBAGE & HAM

¼ cup water

1 medium size cabbage, cut into quarters

¼ cup melted butter or margarine

4 pounds fully cooked ham

Salt and pepper

In slow cooker, pour water. Place cabbage on top of water. Drizzle butter over cabbage. Add ham. Cover. Cook on low 6 to 8 hours. Salt and pepper to taste. Makes 6 servings.

EMILY WARNER *was hired by Frontier Airlines as the first American female commercial airline pilot in 1973. She later became the first woman airline captain, also at Frontier.*

SOUTHERN STYLE CABBAGE

1 medium head green cabbage, thinly sliced

1 small onion, thinly sliced

½ teaspoon salt

2 slices bacon

½ cup water

In slow cooker, combine all ingredients, except water. Mix well. Pour water over mixture. Cover. Cook on low 4 to 6 hours. Makes 6 servings.

CABBAGE

1 head cabbage, chopped

¼ cup water

2 tablespoons olive oil

1 clove garlic, minced

1 teaspoon soy sauce

In slow cooker, place cabbage. In small bowl, combine remaining ingredients. Pour over cabbage. Cover. Cook on low 4 to 6 hours. Makes 4 to 6 servings.

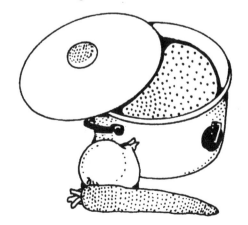

Yale University awarded **FLORENCE WALD** *an honorary Doctorate of Medical Sciences in 1995 for being the founder of the Hospice movement in America. It is to help families, caregivers and patients who are terminally ill. She was a former dean of the Yale School of Nursing.*

CREAMED CORN

2 (16 ounce) packages frozen whole
    kernel corn

4 (3 ounce) packages cream cheese, cubed

1 cup milk

½ cup butter or margarine, melted

2 teaspoons sugar

½ teaspoon salt

¼ teaspoon pepper

In slow cooker, place corn. Top with cream
cheese. In small bowl, combine remaining ingredients. Mix well. Pour mixture over corn.
Cover. Cook on high 3 to 4 hours. Makes 8 to
10 servings.

CORN &
GREEN CHILE DISH

1 (15 ounce) can corn, drained

1 (15 ounce) can creamed corn, undrained

1 (8 ounce) package cream cheese,
    softened

1 (4 ounce) can green chiles, undrained

Coat inside slow cooker with cooking spray. In
large bowl, combine all ingredients. Mix well.
Pour mixture into slow cooker. Cover. Cook on
low 3 to 4 hours. Makes 8 servings.

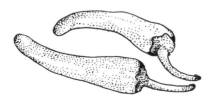

GERTI CORI
*was the first
American woman
to receive the Nobel
Prize in medicine.
She and her
husband received
it in 1947 for
what became the
foundation for
understanding how
cells use food and
convert it to energy.*

DON'T BAKE IT GREEN BEANS

2 (10¾ ounce) cans cream of mushroom soup

¾ cup milk

2 teaspoons soy sauce

8 cups green beans

1 cup French fried onions

In slow cooker, combine all ingredients. Mix well. Cover. Cook on low 4 to 6 hours. Makes 8 servings.

BIT SPECIAL GREEN BEANS

1 (12 ounce) package frozen cut green beans

1 (8 ounce) can sliced water chestnuts, drained

½ cup roasted bell pepper strips (from a jar)

1 (10 ounce) container refrigerated Alfredo sauce

1 cup French fried onions

In slow cooker, combine all ingredients. Mix well. Cover. Cook on low 3 hours. Uncover. Mix well. Cover. Cook an additional 1 hour. Makes 6 to 8 servings.

The Literacy Volunteers of America has taught half a million people to read. It was started in the upstate New York home of **RUTH COLVIN**. *She devised the approach of using community tutors.*

JUST BEEF & BEANS

1 pound lean ground beef, browned, drained

2 (10¾ ounce) cans cream of mushroom soup

1 cup shredded cheddar cheese

2 (15 ounce) cans green beans, drained

In slow cooker, combine all ingredients. Mix well. Cover. Cook on low 4 to 6 hours. Makes 4 to 6 servings.

VEGGIE DISH

4 cups green beans

4 cups corn

½ cup sour cream

1 (10¾ ounce) can cream of chicken soup

½ cup shredded mild cheddar cheese

In large bowl, combine all ingredients. Mix well. Pour mixture into slow cooker. Cover. Cook on low 4 to 6 hours. Makes 8 to 10 servings.

MUSTARD GLAZED CARROTS

12 carrots, sliced

½ cup packed brown sugar

⅓ cup Dijon mustard

In slow cooker, combine all ingredients. Cover. Cook on low 4 to 6 hours or high 2 to 3 hours. Makes 8 to 10 servings.

The first American woman to pilot a spacecraft was a test pilot and math instructor at the Air Force Academy, **EILEEN COLLINS.** *She piloted the space shuttle Discovery in 1995 on a flight to dock with the space station Mir. In 1999 she became NASA's first female commander in space.*

SWEET ORANGE CARROTS

1½ pounds carrots, peeled, sliced

1½ cups orange juice

1 tablespoon sugar

3 tablespoons maple syrup

⅓ cup butter, melted

In slow cooker, place carrots. In medium bowl, combine juice, sugar, syrup, and butter. Mix well. Pour mixture over carrots. Cover. Cook on low 4 to 6 hours. Makes 6 servings.

CANDIED CARROTS

2 (16 ounce) packages frozen sliced carrots

1 (6 ounce) bottle maple syrup

¼ cup packed brown sugar

In slow cooker, combine all ingredients. Mix well. Cover. Cook on low 6 to 7 hours. Makes 8 to 10 servings.

MAPLE GLAZED SQUASH

1 large butternut squash, cut into chunks

2 tablespoons butter, melted

⅓ cup maple syrup

¼ cup packed brown sugar

In slow cooker, place squash. Drizzle butter, pour syrup and sprinkle brown sugar over squash. Cover. Cook on low 6 to 8 hours. Makes 6 servings.

BESSIE COLEMAN earned her international pilot's license in 1921 to become the first licensed black female flyer. She became famous for her stunts and air acrobatics.

I'LL BRING THE CAULIFLOWER

8 cups cauliflower florets

1 large onion, thinly sliced

1 (16 ounce) jar cheddar cheese pasta sauce

In slow cooker, combine all ingredients. Mix well. Cover. Cook on low 6 to 8 hours or high 3 hours. Makes 10 to 12 servings.

GEE WHIZ HOMINY

2 (15½ ounce) cans hominy, drained

1 onion, chopped

1 (10¾ ounce) can cream of mushroom soup

1 (8 ounce) jar jalapeno Cheese Whiz®

½ cup evaporated milk

2 cups crushed corn chips

In slow cooker, combine all ingredients, except corn chips. Mix well. Cover. Cook on low 4 to 6 hours. Top with corn chips. Cover. Cook 15 minutes. Makes 6 servings.

TASTY CORN ON THE COB

6 medium ears corn

½ cup melted butter

Place each ear of corn on a piece of heavy duty aluminum foil. Brush butter over corn, wrap. Place corn in slow cooker. Cover. Cook on high 2 hours, low 4 to 6 hours. Makes 6 servings.

MARY ANN SHADD CARY *was the first African American woman to enroll and graduate from Howard University Law School. She became the first black female lawyer upon her graduation in 1870. The educator and abolitionist worked for women's suffrage and to improve education of blacks.*

SAUCY CORN & BROCCOLI

1 (16 ounce) package frozen cut broccoli

1 (16 ounce) package frozen corn

1 (10¾ ounce) can cream of chicken soup

1½ cups shredded American cheese

¼ cup milk

Spray inside of slow cooker with cooking spray. In slow cooker, combine all ingredients. Mix well. Cover. Cook on low 3 to 4 hours or high 2 hours.. Makes 8 to 10 servings.

GARLIC VEGETABLES

4 medium potatoes, thinly sliced

4 medium carrots, sliced

1 (1 ounce) package herb and garlic soup mix

⅓ cup water

1 tablespoon olive oil

In slow cooker, combine all ingredients. Cover. Cook on low 6 to 8 hours. Makes 4 servings.

STEWED TOMATOES

6 large tomatoes, skinned, diced

½ cup butter

1 teaspoon salt

½ teaspoon pepper

½ cup fresh basil

In slow cooker, add tomatoes. Cover. Cook on high 1 hour. Add remaining ingredients. Mix well. Cover, reduce heat to low, cook 1½ hours. Makes 6 to 8 servings.

In 1904 **MARY MCLEOD BETHUNE** *began a school for African-American women in Daytona Beach, FL, and it later became a coeducational college. She became president of the National Association of Colored Women, and was appointed to various government posts by every president from Coolidge to Truman.*

NOW THAT'S A BAKED POTATO

8 to 10 medium unpeeled potatoes

2 tablespoons vegetable oil

Pierce potatoes with fork. Place potatoes and oil in large plastic food storage bag. Toss to coat with oil. Wrap potatoes individually in aluminum foil. Place in slow cooker without water. Cover. Cook on low heat 8 to 10 hours or until potatoes are tender. Makes 8 to 10 servings.

ALFREDO TOPPED BAKED POTATOES

6 baking potatoes

1 (4.5 ounce) jar sliced mushrooms

2 cups frozen green peas, thawed

1 (7 ounce) jar roasted red peppers, drained, sliced

2½ cups Alfredo sauce

¾ cup milk

Scrub and pierce potatoes. Wrap each potato in aluminum foil. Place in slow cooker without water. Cover. Cook on low 7 to 10 hours or high 3 to 4 hours. In medium saucepan, combine remaining ingredients. Mix well. Cook over medium heat until hot and bubbly. Cut and open potatoes. Put mixture on top of potatoes. Makes 6 servings.

MARY S. CALDERONE, *M.D.(1904–1998), a pioneer in the field of human sexuality, co-founded the Sex Information and Education Council of the United States. The "mother of sex education" authored several books and articles, and was listed by World Almanac as one of the 200 Most Influential People In the World.*

POTATOES SURPRISE

5 medium baked potatoes, cooked, sliced

2 (10¾ ounce) cans broccoli cheese soup

¾ cup milk

1 small onion, sliced

1 cup shredded cheddar cheese

In slow cooker, combine all ingredients. Mix well. Cover. Cook on low 4 to 6 hours. Makes 6 servings.

SATURDAY NIGHT POTATO SKINS

6 to 8 potatoes

½ cup butter, melted

6 to 8 strips bacon, cooked, crumbled

½ cup salsa

1 (8 ounce) package shredded cheddar cheese

Prick potatoes with fork and wrap in aluminum foil. Place in slow cooker without water. Cover. Cook on low 8 to 10 hours. Scoop out potato leaving ¼ of potato on skin. Drizzle butter. Top potato with bacon, salsa and cheese. Place on cookie sheet. Broil 10 to 15 minutes or until cheese melts. Makes 6 to 8 servings.

*In 1849 **AMELIA BLOOMER** was the first woman to own, operate and edit a newspaper for women. The "Lily" was a forum for women's right issues. Amelia wore full cut Turkish pantaloons under a skirt just below the knee when she lectured, and they became known as "bloomers."*

SAUSAGE & POTATOES DINNER

1 (20 ounce) package refrigerated new potato wedges

1 medium green bell pepper, chopped

1 (16 ounce) package smoked sausage, sliced

1 cup barbeque sauce

In slow cooker, combine all ingredients. Mix well. Cover. Cook on low 4 to 6 hours. Makes 4 servings.

CHEDDAR POTATOES

2 pounds russet potatoes, peeled, diced

1 cup water

⅓ cup butter

½ to ¾ cup milk

½ cup finely chopped green onions

3 ounces shredded cheddar cheese

Salt and pepper

In slow cooker, add potatoes and water. Dot potatoes with butter. Cover. Cook on low 6 to 8 hours or high 3 hours. In large bowl, place potatoes and remaining ingredients. Salt and pepper to taste. Mix with electric mixer. Makes 8 servings.

Through wise investments, **LYDIA MOSS BRADLEY** *(1816–1908) increased her husband's estate and established Bradley University as a monument to her deceased children. She was a noted philanthropist and was the first female member of a national bank board in the U.S.*

MASHED RED POTATOES

3 pounds small (2 to 3 inches) red potatoes, halved

4 cloves garlic, minced

½ cup water

2 tablespoons olive oil

1 teaspoon salt

½ cup chives and onions cream cheese, softened

¼ to ½ cup milk

In slow cooker, place potatoes, garlic, water, olive oil, and salt. Mix well. Cover. Cook on low 8 to 10 hours or high 4 to 5 hours or until potatoes are tender. Mash potato mixture with fork or potato masher. Add cream cheese and enough milk for desired consistency. Serve immediately, or reduce heat to low for up to 2 hours. Makes 6 servings.

CHEESY TATERS

4 medium potatoes, peeled, sliced thin

1 cup shredded cheddar cheese

1 (10¾ ounce) can cream of mushroom soup

½ teaspoon pepper

½ teaspoon paprika

In slow cooker, place potatoes. Sprinkle cheese over potatoes. In small bowl, mix soup, pepper and paprika. Pour over potatoes and cheese. Cover. Cook on low 6 to 8 hours or high 3 to 4 hours. Makes 4 to 6 servings.

DR. VIRGINIA APGAR in 1951 *developed a system of simple tests that is used to determine if a newborn child requires special medical attention. It is known as the Apgar Score and has saved thousands of lives.*

CHEESY STEAK FRIES

2 (10¾ ounce) cans cheddar cheese soup

½ cup milk

½ teaspoon garlic powder

¼ teaspoon onion powder

8 cups frozen steak fries

In slow cooker, combine all ingredients. Mix well. Cover. Cook on low 3 to 4 hours or high 1½ to 2 hours. Makes 6 to 8 servings.

DELICIOUS CREAMY POTATOES

2½ pounds small red potatoes, quartered

1 (8 ounce) container sour cream

1 (0.4 ounce) package buttermilk ranch dressing mix

1 (10¾ ounce) can cream of mushroom soup

½ cup water

In slow cooker, combine all ingredients. Mix well. Cover. Cook on low 8 to 10 hours or high 3½ hours. Makes 6 servings.

ELLA BAKER (1903–1986) was an organizer and co-founder of the Southern Christian Leadership Conference (SCLC), which was headed by Dr. Martin Luther King, Jr. She also helped establish the student civil rights organization, the Student Non-Violent Coordinating Committee.

EXTRA CHEESY HASH BROWNS

1 (32 ounce) package frozen hash brown
   potatoes

1 cup shredded cheddar cheese

2 (10¾ ounce) cans cheddar cheese soup

1 (2.8 ounce) can French fried onion rings

Coat inside slow cooker with cooking spray.
Add all ingredients. Mix well. Cover. Cook on
low 4 to 6 hours or high 2 to 3 hours. Makes 8
servings.

IT'S SO CHEESY POTATO HASH BROWNS

1 (2 pounds) package frozen hash brown
   potatoes

2 (10¾ ounce) cans Mexican style
   cheddar cheese soup

1 (12 ounce) can evaporated milk

2 cups crushed cheddar cheese flavored
   crackers, divided

2 cups shredded cheddar cheese

In slow cooker, combine potatoes, soup, milk,
and half of crackers. Mix well. Cover. Cook on
low 6 to 8 hours. Sprinkle remaining crackers
and cheese over potato mixture. Cover. Cook
an additional 15 minutes. Makes 4 to 6 servings.

*LADY BIRD
(Claudia Alta)
JOHNSON
became known
during her tenure as
First Lady for her
"beautification"
program, beginning
in1965. She
worked to improve
the appearance of
areas throughout
the country. Her
efforts resulted in
planting of trees
and flowers , and
she helped push
through Congress
the Highway
Beautification Act,
which limited
billboards along the
Interstate Highway
System.*

SOUPER HASH BROWNS

2 (16 ounce) packages frozen shredded
   hash browns

2 cups shredded cheddar cheese

2 cups diced ham

1 (12 ounce) can evaporated milk

1 (10¾ ounce) can cream of potato soup

Coat inside slow cooker with cooking spray. In
large bowl, combine all ingredients. Mix well.
Pour mixture in slow cooker. Cover. Cook on
low 6 to 8 hours or high 2½ to 3 hours. Makes 4
to 6 servings.

CLASSIC POTATOES

1 (10¾ ounce) can cheddar cheese soup

¾ cup milk

½ cup grated Parmesan cheese

4 medium potatoes, cut in 1-inch pieces

½ cup French fried onions

In slow cooker, combine all ingredients. Mix
well. Cover. Cook on low 6 to 8 hours or high 3
to 4 hours. Makes 4 servings.

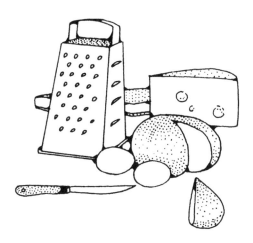

J.K. ROWLING
*was a poor
struggling single
mom who sneaked
off to cafes in
Edinburgh,
Scotland, to find
solitude to write.
She began what is
to be a seven
volume epic about
the boy wizard,
Harry Potter. The
astounding world-
wide success of the
books and the three
successful movies
made from them
have made her
wealthy and Harry
Potter a character
known everywhere.*

RANCH POTATOES

2 (24 ounce) packages frozen hash brown potatoes, partially thawed

2 (8 ounce) packages cream cheese, softened

2 (⅞ ounce) packages Ranch dressing mix

2 (10¾ ounce) cans cream of potato soup

In slow cooker, place hash browns. In medium bowl, combine remaining ingredients. Pour mixture over hash browns. Cover. Cook on low 6 to 8 hours. Stir before serving. Makes 8 to 12 servings.

SOUTHERN STYLE POTATOES

1 (32 ounce) package frozen southern style hash brown potatoes

2 (10¾ ounce) cans cheddar cheese soup

1 (12 ounce) can evaporated milk

1 (2.8 ounce) can French fried onions, divided

In slow cooker, combine hash browns, soup, milk, and half French fried onions. Mix well. Cover. Cook on low 4 to 6 hours. Top with remaining onions before serving. Makes 8 servings.

CONDOLEZZA RICE, an expert on Russian affairs and fluent in Russian, was Senior Director of Soviet and East European Affairs in the National Security Council in President Bush, Sr.'s term in 1989-1991. For six years she served as Stanford University Provost. On January 22, 2001, she became National Security Advisor for President George W. Bush, and was one of his closest advisors. Upon his reelection, President Bush named Dr. Rice his choice for Secretary of State.

POTATOES & GRAVY WITH CHOPS

4 to 6 medium potatoes, quartered

4 to 6 pork chops

2 (12 ounce) jars brown gravy

In slow cooker, place potatoes. Arrange chops on potatoes. Pour gravy over top. Cover. Cook on low 8 to 10 hours. Makes 4 to 6 servings.

SCALLOPED POTATOES & HAM

8 medium potatoes, peeled, thinly sliced

2 cups cubed ham

2 onions, diced

1 (10¾ ounce) can cream of mushroom soup

2 cups grated cheddar cheese

In slow cooker, place half of potatoes, ham, onions, soup, and cheese. Repeat process. Cover. Cook on low 8 to 10 hours. Makes 8 to 10 servings.

SCALLOPED POTATO BAKE

5 medium potatoes, sliced thin

1 small onion, sliced thin

2 (10¾ ounce) cans cream of celery soup

1 cup evaporated milk

1 tablespoon butter or margarine

In slow cooker combine all ingredients. Mix well. Cover. Cook on low 8 to 10 hours. Makes 6 servings.

LAURA BUSH, a former teacher and a popular First Lady, has supported the President's work to ensure that no child is left behind in school or life. She created Ready to Read, Ready to Learn about early childhood education and the importance of reading aloud to young children. She hosts regional conferences across the country about how infants learn and preparing children for lifetime learning.

SOUR CREAM SCALLOPED POTATOES & HAM

1 (28 ounce) bag frozen diced potatoes

1 cup shredded cheddar cheese

1 cup cubed American cheese

1 (10¾ ounce) can celery soup

2 (8 ounce) containers sour cream

1½ cups cubed ham

In slow cooker, combine all ingredients. Mix well. Cover. Cook on low 4 to 6 hours. Makes 8 servings.

SANTA FE STYLE SCALLOPED POTATOES & HAM

1 (32 ounce) package hash browns

2 tablespoons butter or margarine, melted

½ pound cooked diced ham

1 (12 ounce) container chive and onion sour cream potato topper

1 (11 ounce) can Mexican style whole kernel corn, undrained

1 (10¾ ounce) can cream of mushroom soup

2 cups water

1½ cups shredded cheddar cheese

In slow cooker, combine potatoes and butter. Mix well. Add remaining ingredients. Mix well. Cover. Cook on low 6 to 8 hours. Makes 6 servings.

JANE CUNNINGHAM CROLY, a journalist, created in 1857 what was probably the first syndicated women's column and signed it "Jennie June." She was a contributor to many papers and publications on topics ranging from fashions to equal rights for women. She was active in women's clubs, and was the first president of the Women's Press Club of New York in 1889.

SCALLOPED POTATOES & HAM

5 medium potatoes, sliced

2 cups chopped ham

4 tablespoons butter or margarine

3 tablespoons flour

1 teaspoon salt

2 cups milk

1 cup shredded cheddar cheese

In slow cooker, place potatoes and ham. In medium saucepan melt butter over medium low heat, add flour and salt, cook until bubbly. Add milk slowly, stirring until smooth and thickened. Add cheese. Mix well. Pour mixture over potatoes. Cover. Cook on low 8 to 10 hours or high 3 to 4 hours. Makes 6 servings.

SCALLOPED POTATOES & CHOPS

1 box scalloped potatoes

½ cup shredded cheddar cheese

4 pork chops, fat trimmed

In slow cooker add ingredients required on package to make potatoes. Add cheese to potatoes. Mix well. Place chops on potatoes. Cover. Cook on low 6 hours. Makes 4 servings.

GLORIA YERKOVICH *did not see her daughter for ten years, following her abduction by her natural father in 1974. There was no national organization to help. In 1981 she started Child Find which developed a national registry of missing children, a photographic directory of them and a toll-free number for children to find parents. Her efforts led to the Omnibus Victims Protection Act and the Missing Children Act.*

SWEET POTATOES & HAM

4 sweet potatoes, sliced in half lengthwise

2 pounds boneless ham, cubed

1 cup maple syrup

In slow cooker, place potatoes. Top with ham. Pour syrup over ham and potatoes. Cover. Cook on low 8 to 10 hours. Makes 6 servings.

ORANGE SWEET POTATOES & PORK

4 medium sweet potatoes, sliced

6 boneless pork loin chops, browned

1 cup orange juice

⅓ cup packed brown sugar

In slow cooker, place sweet potatoes and pork loin. In small bowl, combine orange juice and brown sugar. Mix well. Pour mixture over top. Cover. Cook on low 8 to 10 hours. Makes 6 servings.

SWEET POTATOES

2 pounds sweet potatoes, peeled, diced

½ cup butter

½ cup packed dark brown sugar

1 teaspoon ground cinnamon

½ teaspoon ground nutmeg

1 teaspoon vanilla

In slow cooker, combine all ingredients. Cover. Cook on low 8 to 10 hours. Makes 8 servings.

MARIAN DE FOREST *was one of the first female reporters in Western New York. In 1919 she started a service organization of executives and professionals, Zonta International, which today has 35,000 members in 70 countries. She was a strong proponent of the arts and was inducted into the National Women's Hall of Fame.*

CANDIED SWEET POTATOES

1½ cups packed brown sugar

⅓ cup butter

¼ cup maple syrup

¼ cup water

8 sweet potatoes, cooked

In small saucepan, combine sugar, butter, syrup and water, mix well, cook over medium heat until mixture starts to boil. Place sweet potatoes in slow cooker. Pour mixture over potatoes. Cover. Cook on low 4 to 6 hours or high 1½ to 2 hours. Makes 8 servings.

PEACHY PIE SWEET POTATOES

2¼ pounds sweet potatoes, peeled, cut into ½ inch slices

1 cup peach pie filling

3 tablespoons butter or margarine, melted, divided

½ teaspoon salt

2 tablespoons brown sugar

⅛ teaspoon cinnamon

½ cup chopped pecans

In slow cooker, combine potatoes, pie filling, 2 tablespoons butter, and salt. Mix well. Cover. Cook on low 8 to 10 hours or high 3 to 3½ hours. In small nonstick skillet, over medium heat, sauté brown sugar, add cinnamon, 1 table-spoon butter and pecans for 3 minutes. Set aside to cool. Just before serving, stir potatoes. Add pecan mixture to top and serve. Makes 8 to 10 servings.

MARJORY STONEMAN DOUGLAS dedicated her life to the preservation of the Everglades. Due to her efforts, President Truman dedicated Everglades National Park in 1947. In 1993 President Clinton presented her the Medal of Freedom and called her "Mother of the Everglades."

REFRIED BEANS DISH

1 (15 ounce) can refried beans

½ cup chopped onion

⅓ cup chopped green bell pepper

3 eggs

1½ cups shredded cheddar cheese

½ teaspoon chili powder

In large bowl, combine all ingredients. Mix well. Pour mixture into slow cooker. Cover. Cook on low 3 to 4 hours. Makes 6 to 8 servings.

PORK & BEANS SUPPER

2 (15 ounce) cans pork and beans

2 cups cooked chopped pork

⅓ cup ketchup

¼ cup packed brown sugar

1 teaspoon dry mustard

In slow cooker, combine all ingredients. Mix well. Cover. Cook on low 4 to 6 hours or high 1½ to 2 hours. Makes 6 to 8 servings.

SHORTCUT BUTTER BEANS

2 (15 ounce) cans butter beans

2 slices uncooked bacon

1 tablespoon butter or margarine

In slow cooker, combine all ingredients. Mix well. Cover. Cook on high 1½ to 2 hours. Makes 4 to 6 servings.

JULIA WARD HOWE (1819–1910) *was a lecturer, playwright, poet and author best known as the author of "Battle Hymn of the Republic." She was an organizer of the women's peace movement and was co-founder of the New England Suffrage Association.*

SHORTCUT BEANS & HAM

2 medium carrots, diced

1 onion, chopped

2 tablespoons butter or margarine

2¼ cups water

2 (15½ ounce) cans great northern beans, divided, rinsed, drained

1½ cups cubed cooked ham

In slow cooker, combine carrots, onion, butter, and water. Cover. Cook on low 5 to 6 hours. Mash 1 can of beans, add to slow cooker. Add remaining beans and ham. Mix well. Cover. Cook an additional 2 to 3 hours. Makes 6 servings.

BEANS, HAM & BUTTER

1 pound butter beans

5 cups water

2 cups chopped fully cooked ham

⅓ cup butter or margarine

1 teaspoon salt

In large pan, place beans, cover with cold water, soak overnight. Drain and rinse beans. Pour beans in slow cooker. Pour water over beans. Add ham. Cover. Cook on low 8 to 10 hours. Add butter and salt. Let sit 5 minutes. Makes 6 to 8 servings.

DELORES HUERTA co-founded the United Farm Workers of America with Cesar Chavez. As an advocate for farm worker rights, she has been arrested 22 times for non-violent union activities. She was named to Ladies Home Journal's 100 Most Important Women of the 20th Century.

NAVY BEANS & HAM HOCK

2½ cups navy beans

6 cups water

1 ham hock

1 teaspoon salt

In slow cooker, add beans and water. Let set 2 hours. Add ham hock. Cover. Cook on low 8 to 10 hours. Add salt. Makes 6 to 8 servings.

CAJUN BEANS & SAUSAGE

2 (15 ounce) cans kidney or pinto beans

1 pound smoked sausage, cut into 2-inch pieces

2 teaspoons Cajun seasoning

In slow cooker, combine all ingredients. Mix well. Cover. Cook on low 3 to 4 hours or high 1½ to 2 hours. Serve with white rice. Makes 4 to 6 servings.

PATSY MINK *was the first Asian American woman to practice law in Hawaii. In 1965 she was the first Asian American woman to be elected to Congress, and served six consecutive terms in the House of Representatives. She played a key role in Title IX, assuring equal treatment of women in classrooms and the playing fields. She ran unsuccessfully for the Senate in 1977, but was reelected to the House in 1990.*

CHUCK WAGON BBQ BEANS

2 pounds boneless pork stew meat, cubed

½ cup chopped onion

1 (16 ounce) bottle barbeque sauce, divided

2 (16 ounce) cans baked beans, drained

1 (14½ ounce) can chopped stewed tomatoes

½ cup packed brown sugar

¼ teaspoon chili powder

In slow cooker, combine pork, onion, and 1 cup barbeque sauce. Cover. Cook on low 6 to 8 hours or high 4 to 5. Add remaining ingredients. Mix well. Cover. Cook on high 30 additional minutes.

QUICK TRICK BAKE BEANS

2 (15 ounce) cans pork 'n beans

¼ cup ketchup

¼ cup maple syrup

½ cup sliced onion

2 tablespoons brown sugar

In slow cooker, combine all ingredients. Mix well. Cover. Cook on low 3 to 4 hours. Makes 6 to 8 servings.

BEVERLY SILLS was one of the most popular operatic sopranos of the 1960's and 1970's. She joined the New York City Opera in 1955 and retired as a performer in 1980. She was the first woman General Director and then President of the NYC Opera, and was the first woman chair of the Lincoln Center for the Performing Arts, from 1994– 2004.

TOUCHDOWN BAKED BEANS

1 (16 ounce) package dried navy beans, sorted, rinsed

11 cups water

½ cup molasses

½ cup chopped onion

⅓ cup packed brown sugar

3 teaspoons dry mustard

1 teaspoon salt

½ teaspoon liquid smoke

In large soup pot, over high heat, combine beans and 10 cups water. Bring to boil. Reduce heat. Cover and simmer 2 hours. Drain. In slow cooker, combine beans, 1 cup water, molasses, onion, brown sugar, dry mustard, salt, and liquid smoke. Cover. Cook on low 10 to 12 hours. Makes 10 servings.

ANTONIO NOVELLA, a pediatrician, was the first woman and the first Hispanic named Surgeon General of the United States. She was appointed by President George H. Bush on March 9, 1990, and served until June 30, 1993. She was very outspoken about underage drinking and tobacco use by young people.

ROUTE 66 BAKED BEANS

2 (15 ounce) cans pork and beans

3½ tablespoons Worcestershire sauce

½ cup barbeque sauce

½ teaspoon dry mustard

¼ cup diced onion

In slow cooker, combine all ingredients. Mix well. Cover. Cook on low 4 to 6 hour or high 1½ to 2 hours. Makes 6 to 8 servings.

SALSA BEANS

2 (15½ ounce) cans great northern beans, rinsed, drained

2 (15 ounce) cans black beans, rinsed, drained

1 (15 ounce) can butter beans, rinsed, drained

1¼ cups barbecue sauce

¾ cup salsa

⅓ cup packed brown sugar

In slow cooker, combine all ingredients. Mix well. Cover. Cook on low 6 to 8 hours. Makes 8 servings.

NEW TWIST BAKE BEANS

3 slices bacon

½ cup chopped onion

½ cup ketchup

½ cup packed brown sugar

1 teaspoon mustard

1 (28 ounce) can pork 'n beans

¼ cup maple syrup

In slow cooker, combine all ingredients. Mix well. Cover. Cook on low 4 to 6 hours or high 2 to 3 hours. Makes 4 to 6 servings.

DOROTHEA LANGE (1895–1965) *was a photographer who is best known for her photographs of the poor conditions of the migrant workers who traveled to California during the Depression. Her pictures brought attention to their plight and motivated agencies and individuals to improve the situation.*

LASAGNA

1 (16 ounces) package wide egg noodles, cooked, drained

1 (16 ounce) carton cottage cheese

1 pound lean ground beef, cooked, drained

1 (12 ounce) jar spaghetti sauce

1 (16 ounce) package shredded mozzarella cheese

In slow cooker, layer ⅓ noodles. Place ⅓ cottage cheese. In skillet, combine beef with spaghetti sauce. Place ⅓ meat mixture over cottage cheese. Top with ⅓ cheese. Repeat process two more times. Cover. Cook on low 4 to 5 hours. Makes 4 to 6 servings.

TERRIFIC TORTELLINI

1 pound mild Italian sausage, browned, drained

1 (15 ounce) jar marinara sauce

1 (14½ ounce) can Italian stewed tomatoes, undrained

1 cup sliced mushrooms

1 (9 ounce) package tortellini, thawed if frozen

1 cup shredded mozzarella cheese

In slow cooker, combine sausage, marinara sauce, tomatoes, and mushrooms. Mix Well. Cover. Cook on low 7 to 8 hours. Add tortellini. Mix Well. Top with cheese. Cover. Cook an additional 20 minutes. Makes 6 to 8 servings.

EDITH NOURSE ROGERS was Presidential inspector of veterans hospitals in 1922-23. As a U.S. Congresswoman from Massachusetts after World War II she was a leading advocate of the GI Bill of Rights, which gave returning veterans the opportunity to go to college and receive low interest housing loans.

GREEK PASTA

2 pounds beef stew meat

1 cup sliced onions

1 (6 ounce) jar pitted Greek olives, drained

¾ cup sun dried tomatoes, chopped

1 (28 ounce) jar marinara sauce

6 cups hot cooked pasta

In slow cooker, place beef. Top with onions, olives, and tomatoes. Pour sauce over ingredients. Cover. Cook on low 8 to 10 hours. Serve with pasta. Makes 6 servings.

PIZZA CHICKEN PASTA

1 (16 ounce) package bow tie pasta, cooked

1 (26 ounce) jar spaghetti sauce

1 teaspoon pizza seasoning

3 skinless, boneless chicken breast, cut into cubes

2 cups shredded mozzarella cheese

In slow cooker, combine all ingredients, except cheese. Cover. Cook on low 6 to 8 hours. Sprinkle cheese over top. Cover, let set 10 minutes. Makes 4 to 6 servings.

KATHERINE SIVA SAUBEL is an internationally respected scholar of Cahuilla Indians. She helped establish the Malki museum, the first non-profit tribal museum on a reservation in California. A major focus of her work has been the Indian knowledge of useful plants, and her efforts to preserve the Cahuilla language.

MEAT LOVERS PIZZA PASTA

1 pound corkscrew pasta, cooked

1½ pounds lean ground beef, cooked, drained

1 pound Italian sausage, cooked, drained

2 (3 ounce) packages sliced pepperoni

4 (14 ounce) jars pizza sauce

2 (16 ounce) packages shredded mozzarella cheese

½ cup chopped green bell pepper

½ cup chopped onion

In slow cooker, combine all ingredients. Mix well. Cover. Cook on low 4 to 6 hours or high 2 hours. Makes 6 servings.

PIZZA TASTING PASTA

1 pound ground beef, browned, drained

1 small onion, chopped

2 (15 ounce) cans pizza sauce

1 (8 ounce) package pepperoni slices

2 cups macaroni, cooked, drained

In slow cooker, combine all ingredients. Mix well. Cover. Cook on low 3 to 4 hours. Makes 6 servings.

KATIE COURIC
is one of the most recognizable and popular TV news personalities. She has been co-anchor of Today Show since April 5, 1991. She has interviewed world leaders, national political figures, actors and pop icons. For her work she has received six Emmys, a George Peabody Award and numerous other awards. In 2001 she signed a 4½ year contract with NBC worth a reported sixty-five million dollars.

SPINACH & CHICKEN PASTA

2 cups cooked egg noodles

1 (10 ounce) package frozen chopped spinach, thawed, drained

2 tablespoons butter or margarine, melted

1½ cups diced cooked chicken

1 cup chicken gravy

1 (4 ounce) package cream cheese with onions and chives, softened

2 tablespoons grated Parmesan cheese

In slow cooker, place noodles. Spread spinach over noodles. Drizzle butter over spinach. In medium bowl, combine chicken, gravy, and cream cheese. Mix well. Pour mixture over spinach. Sprinkle cheese on top of mixture. Cover. Cook on low 3 to 4 hours. Makes 6 servings.

NACHO PASTA

1 (7 ounce) package macaroni, cooked, drained

1 (15 ounce) can black beans, rinsed, drained

1 (10¾ ounce) can nacho cheese soup

⅓ cup evaporated milk

½ cup crushed tortilla chips

½ cup shredded cheddar cheese

In slow cooker, combine macaroni, beans, soup, and milk. Mix well. Cover. Cook on low 3 to 4 hours. During last 20 minutes, stir, top with chips and cheese. Cover. Cook additional 20 minutes. Makes 4 to 6 servings.

SHIRLEY ANN JACKSON *was the first black woman to receive a doctorate in any subject from MIT. She was the first black woman to receive a doctorate in physics in the U.S. She was nominated by President Clinton and became Chairman of the U.S. Nuclear Regulatory Commission in 1995. In 1999 she became president of Rensselar Polytechnic Institute. In 2002 Discover Magazine named her one of the top 50 women in science.*

CHEESE PASTA BAKE

4 cups cooked corkscrew pasta

1 (10¾ ounce) can cream of mushroom soup

1 (8 ounce) package shredded two cheese blend

½ cup grated Parmesan cheese

1 cup milk

In slow cooker, combine all ingredients. Mix well. Cover. Cook on low 3 to 4 hours. Makes 4 to 6 servings.

BEEF & MAC

1 pound ground beef

1 small onion, chopped

1 (10¾ ounce) can tomato soup

¼ cup water

1 tablespoon Worcestershire sauce

1 cup shredded cheddar cheese

3 cups cooked macaroni

In medium skillet, brown beef and onion over medium heat. Drain. In slow cooker add beef mixture, soup, water, Worcestershire sauce, cheese, and macaroni. Mix well. Cover. Cook on low 3 to 4 hours. Makes 4 to 6 servings.

GLORIA STEINEM *is a writer and leading supporter of the women's liberation movement in the U.S. In 1972 she co-founded Ms, a magazine published and edited by women that featured articles about women's careers and ways of life. She helped found the National Women's Political Caucus.*

IS IT GOULASH

1 pound lean ground beef, browned, drained

4 cups cooked macaroni

1 (15 ounce) can chopped tomatoes

1 cup tomato sauce

1 teaspoon salt

In slow cooker, combine all ingredients. Mix well. Cover. Cook on low 2½ to 3 hours. Makes 4 servings.

BEST BOW TIE PASTA

1 (8 ounce) package bow tie pasta, cooked, drained

1 (16 ounce) jar spaghetti sauce with meat

1 (⅞ ounce) package Italian salad dressing mix

1 (8 ounce) package shredded mozzarella cheese

In slow cooker, combine pasta, sauce, and dressing mix. Mix well. Cover. Cook on low 3 to 4 hours. Sprinkle cheese over pasta during last 20 minutes of cooking. Cover. Cook 20 minutes or until cheese melts. Makes 6 to 8 servings.

NETTIE STEVENS *was one of the first females to make a name for herself in the biological sciences. The biology professor at Bryn Mawr College identified the "X" and "Y" chromosomes which determine whether an individual is male or female.*

BOW TIE PASTA

1 pound Italian sausage links, sliced into 1-inch pieces

2 red bell peppers, chopped

½ cup vegetable broth

½ teaspoon Italian seasoning

8 ounces bow tie pasta, cooked

In slow cooker, combine sausage, pepper, broth, and seasoning. Mix well. Cover. Cook on low 4 to 6 hours. Add cooked pasta. Mix well. Makes 4 servings.

CHICKEN N' NOODLES

2½ to 3½ pounds broiler chicken

2 cups water

1 teaspoon salt

1 cup chicken broth

2 tablespoons butter or margarine

1 (8 ounce) package egg noodles, cooked

In slow cooker, place chicken. Add remaining ingredients, except noodles. Cover. Cook on low 8 to 10 hours or high 4 to 5 hours. Remove chicken. Slice into chunks. Add chicken and noodles to slow cooker. Mix well. Cover. Cook on low 1 hour. Makes 6 to 8 servings.

EUDORA WELTY lived in Mississippi all her life and wrote about small town life in the south. One of the most important authors of the 20th century, she combined delicacy with humor, realism with fantasy. She won the Pulitzer Prize for "The Optimist's Daughter" in 1973, and was the first living author published in the Library of America series.

CHICKEN NOODLE CASSEROLE

1 (8 ounce) package noodles, cooked

4 cups chopped cooked chicken

2 (10¾ ounce) cans cream of chicken soup

1 cup milk

1 cup shredded cheddar cheese

In slow cooker, combine all ingredients. Mix well. Cover. Cook on low 3 to 4 hours. Makes 6 servings.

GREEN CHILE CHICKEN ALFREDO

1¼ pounds chicken breast, cut into bite sized pieces

1 (16 ounce) jar Alfredo sauce

2 (4.5 ounce) cans chopped green chiles

1 (10 ounce) package rigatoni noodles, cooked, warm

2 cups shredded mozzarella cheese

In slow cooker, place chicken. Pour Alfredo sauce over chicken. Top with green chiles. Cover. Cook on low 4 to 6 hours. Add rigatoni noodles to slow cooker. Mix well. Sprinkle cheese over top. Cover. Cook on high 25 minutes. Makes 6 servings.

*With a large head, vast mascaraed eyes, kissable lips, and baby doll voice, **BETTY BOOP** was a rather sexy, scantily clad figure near the end of the "roaring '20s." Musicians such as Cab Calloway and Louis Armstrong played torrid jazz in many of her cartoons. Around 1935 the Hays Act censored movies and cartoons and transformed Betty into a wholesome character.*

CHICKEN AND BROCCOLI ALFREDO

1¼ pounds chicken, cut into bite size pieces

1 (4.5 ounce) can sliced mushrooms, drained

1 (16 ounce) jar Alfredo sauce

3 cups frozen broccoli, thawed

1 (10 ounce) package fettuccine noodles, cooked warm

In slow cooker, place chicken and mushrooms. Pour Alfredo sauce over top. Cover. Cook on low 4 to 6 hours. Add broccoli. Mix well. Cover. Cook on high 20 minutes. Add noodles. Mix well. Makes 5 servings.

FETTUCCINE NOODLES

2 (12 ounce) packages fettuccine noodles, cooked, drained

1 cup grated Parmesan cheese

¾ cup half and half

3½ tablespoons butter or margarine

3 tablespoons parsley

In slow cooker, combine all ingredients. Mix well. Cover. Cook on low 2 to 3 hours or high 1½ hours. Makes 6 to 8 servings.

HILLARY CLINTON is either much admired or much disliked. She was twice named one of the nation's top 100 lawyers by the National Law Journal. She stood by her husband, President Bill Clinton, during the effort to impeach him from office. In the most expensive Senate election in history, Mrs. Clinton was elected U.S. Senator from New York in 2000, the first former First Lady to ever be elected to public office. There is much speculation that she will be the 2008 Democratic presidential candidate.

CORNED BEEF PASTA

1 (7 ounce) package small shell pasta, cooked, drained

1 (12 ounce) can cooked corned beef

1 (10¾ ounce) can cream of chicken soup

1 (8 ounce) package cubed cheddar cheese

1 cup evaporated milk

½ cup diced onion

In slow cooker, combine all ingredients. Mix well. Cover. Cook on low 4 to 6 hours. Makes 4 servings.

CHILI SPAGHETTI

1 pound lean ground beef, browned, drained

1 medium onion, chopped

1 (15 ounce) can spicy chili beans

1 (14.5 ounce) can tomatoes with green chiles

1 (8 ounce) can tomato sauce

½ teaspoon cumin

In slow cooker, combine all ingredients. Mix well. Cover. Cook on low 4 to 6 hours or high 1½ to 2 hours. Serve over spaghetti. Makes 4 servings.

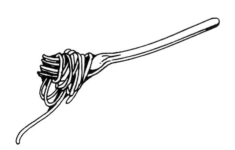

JANE PAULEY was a newswoman on NBC for over 27 years. In 1976 she became co-anchor of NBC "Today," on which she interviewed newsmakers from locations all over the world. She also co-anchored the primetime newsmagazine "Dateline NBC." Among her dozens of awards, including multiple Emmys, she was inducted into the Broadcasting and Cable Hall of Fame in 1998.

IMITATION CRAB PASTA

1 (8 ounce) package spiral pasta, cooked, drained

2 (8 ounce) packages imitation crabmeat, chopped

½ pound shredded Velveeta® cheese

1 onion, chopped

2 cups sliced fresh mushrooms

½ cup chopped green bell pepper

1 tablespoon butter

In slow cooker, place pasta, crabmeat, and cheese. In large skillet, sauté onions, mushrooms, green pepper, and garlic in butter until lightly golden. Pour mixture into slow cooker. Mix well. Cover. Cook on low 4 to 6 hours. Makes 4 to 6 servings.

PASTA & SMOKED SAUSAGE

1 (16 ounce) package smoked sausage, sliced ¼ inch thick

2 (10¾ ounce) cans cream of mushroom soup

2 cups milk

6 cups cooked penne pasta

1½ cups mozzarella cheese

2 cups frozen peas, thawed

In slow cooker, combine all ingredients. Mix well. Cover. Cook on low 4 to 6 hours or high 1½ to 2 hours. Makes 6 servings.

ALICE EVANS (1881–1975) was a scientist who discovered the organism which caused the deadly disease, undulant fever. Her discovery led to mandatory milk pasteurization and has saved countless lives all over the world.

WHAT'S COOKIN MACARONI

1 pound ground beef, browned, drained

1 small onion, sliced

2 tablespoons diced green bell pepper

4 cups slightly cooked macaroni

1 (10 ounce) can tomato sauce

1 cup grated American cheese

In slow cooker, combine all ingredients. Mix well. Cover. Cook on low 4 to 6 hours. Makes 6 to 8 servings.

MAC N' CHEESE FOR LUNCH

4 cups hot cooked macaroni

1 cup milk

2 (10¾ ounce) cans cheese soup

4 hot dogs sliced

1 tablespoon butter

In slow cooker, combine all ingredients. Mix well. Cover. Cook on low 3 to 4 hours. Makes 4 to 6 servings.

MARTHA MATILDA HARPER, *a former servant girl, is credited with creating the modern retail franchising method. She started a beauty products system that had over 500 franchises world-wide in the 1920s. Her floor length hair was an advertising tool for the Harper Method. She would not use permanents or hair dyes in her salons because of the chemicals.*

HOT DOG MACARONI

3½ cups cooked macaroni

5 hot dogs, sliced

2 cups frozen peas

1½ cups milk

1 tablespoon butter or margarine

3 cups shredded cheddar cheese

In slow cooker, combine all ingredients. Mix well. Cover. Cook on low 3 to 4 hours. Makes 4 servings.

MACARONI & CHEESE

1 (8 ounce) package macaroni, cooked, drained

¼ cup butter, melted

1 (12 ounce) can evaporated milk

1 cup milk

½ teaspoon salt

3½ cups shredded American cheese

Coat inside of slow cooker with cooking spray. In large bowl, combine all ingredients. Mix well. Pour mixture into slow cooker. Cover. Cook on low 3 to 4 hours. Makes 4 to 6 servings.

BEATRICE A. HICKS *was an engineer and business owner who worked to get recognition for women engineers. In 1942 she became the first female engineer employed by Western Electric, a division of Bell Telephone. She founded the Society of Women Engineers in 1950 with only 60 members, and it now has over 16,000 members.*

JUST MAC & CHEESE

1 (10¾ ounce) can cheddar cheese soup

1 cup milk

4 cups cooked medium shell macaroni

1 cup shredded cheddar cheese

1 tablespoon butter

In slow cooker, combine all ingredients. Mix well. Cover. Cook on low 3 to 4 hours or high 1½ to 2 hours. Makes 5 servings.

RAVIOLI LASAGNA

1 (28 ounce) jar pasta sauce, divided

1 (25 ounce) package frozen cheese ravioli, partially thawed, divided

1 (16 ounce) carton small curd cottage cheese, divided

1 (16 ounce) package shredded mozzarella cheese, divided

¼ cup grated Parmesan cheese

In slow cooker, pour ½ pasta sauce and ½ ravioli. Mix well. Spread ½ cottage cheese. Sprinkle ½ mozzarella over cottage cheese. In small bowl, combine remaining sauce and ravioli. Mix well. Pour over mozzarella. Spread remaining cottage cheese. Sprinkle with remaining mozzarella cheese and Parmesan cheese. Cover. Cook on low 4 to 6 hours. Makes 6 to 8 servings.

WILHAMENA COLE HALLIDAY *was the founder of the National Museum of Women In the Arts in Washington, DC. Its purpose is to bring national and international attention to the achievements of women in the arts.*

RANCH RAVIOLI

1 (25 ounce) package frozen chicken
ravioli

1 cup roasted red peppers, rinsed, drained,
chopped

3 cups ranch dressing

½ cup grated Parmesan cheese

In slow cooker, combine all ingredients. Cover.
Cook on low 4 to 6 hours. Makes 6 servings.

ALMOST BAKED RAVIOLI

1 (28 ounce) jar tomato pasta sauce

1 (10¾ ounce) can cheddar cheese soup

1 (25 ounce) package frozen sausage
filled ravioli

1½ cups shredded mozzarella cheese

Coat inside of slow cooker with cooking spray.
In slow cooker, combine all ingredients, except
cheese. Mix well. Cover. Cook on low 4 to 6
hours or high 1½ to 2 hours. Sprinkle cheese
over mixture. Makes 4 to 6 servings.

**MAJOR
GENERAL
JEANNE
HOLM**, *USAF
(Ret.) rose from a
private to a two star
general in her 33
years in the Armed
Forces from 1942–
1975. In 1973 she
became the first
woman in the
history of the US
Armed Forces to
become a major
general. That year
she was appointed
director of the
Secretary of the Air
Force Personnel
Council.*

RAVE ABOUT RAVIOLI

1 tablespoon olive oil

½ cup chopped onion

1 clove garlic, minced

2 (26 ounce) jars four cheese flavored tomato pasta sauce

2 (25 ounce) packages frozen beef ravioli

2 cups shredded mozzarella cheese

In large skillet over medium high heat with oil, sauté onion and garlic until golden brown. Add pasta sauce. Mix well. In slow cooker, place 1 cup of sauce mixture. Add 1 package ravioli. Top with 1 cup cheese. Add remaining package of ravioli. Top with remaining cheese. Pour remaining sauce over top. Cover. Cook on low for 5 to 6 hours. Makes 8 to 10 servings.

MEXICAN PASTA SAUCE

2 (12 ounce) packages mild Mexican cheese

4 tablespoons milk

2 cups chopped plum tomatoes

Favorite pasta

In slow cooker, combine cheese and milk. Cover. Cook on low 2 hours or until cheese has melted. Add tomatoes. Mix well. Pour mixture over favorite pasta. Makes 6 to 8 servings.

BERTHA HOLT *led efforts to adopt abandoned Korean-American war orphans. She and her husband convinced Congress to pass the "Holt Bill," making international adoptions more accessible. Grandma Holt adopted eight Korean children and began the Holt International Childen's Service, a highly regarded adoption agency.*

PIZZA SAUCE FOR PASTA

2 (15 ounce) cans pizza sauce

2 cups chopped tomatoes

1 cup diced pepperoni

½ cup sliced green onion

In slow cooker, combine all ingredients. Mix well. Cover. Cook on low 3 to 4 hours or high 1½ to 2 hours. Serve over hot pasta. Makes 6 to 8 servings.

SPAGHETTI SAUCE

1 pound Italian sausage, browned, drained

1 (28 ounce) jar spaghetti sauce

½ cup chopped onions

1 clove garlic, diced

1 cup chopped tomatoes

1 teaspoon sugar

In slow cooker, combine all ingredients. Mix well. Cover. Cook on low 3 to 4 hours or high 1½ to 3 hours. Makes 4 servings.

ANNE HUTCHISON (1591–1643) held religious meetings in her home, the first woman in the New World to do so. Her insistence on practicing her religious beliefs as she chose led her to run afoul of the Puritan leaders and she was banished from the Massachusetts Bay Colony. Her only sin was being able to think for herself at a time when women were considered inferior beings with inferior minds.

SAUSAGE TOPPER FOR FETTUCCINI

1 pound fully cooked polish sausage, cut into ½-inch pieces

2 (15 ounce) cans chunky garlic and herb tomato sauce

1 (16 ounce) package frozen stir fry bell pepper and onion, thawed

In slow cooker, combine all ingredients. Mix well. Cover. Cook on low 3 to 4 hours. Serve mixture over cooked fettuccine. Makes 4 servings.

DON'T PASS UP TOPPER

2 pounds ground beef, browned, drained

1½ cups chopped onion

1 (12 ounce) can beer

2½ tablespoons chili powder

1 (15 ounce) can tomato sauce

2 cups ketchup

¼ cup mustard

In slow cooker, combine all ingredients. Mix well. Cover. Cook on low 3 to 4 hours. Serve over spaghetti. Makes 6 to 8 servings.

JOAN RIVERS got her big break in an appearance as a comedienne on the Tonight Show with Johnny Carson. In 1983 she became a permanent guest host on that show. When she signed with Fox for the unsuccessful Late Night Show with Joan Rivers opposite his show, Carson never spoke to her again, and her career plummeted. She rebounded and now, among other activities, has her own line of jewelry on QVC.

QUICK BEEF TOPPER

2 pounds beef, cubed

2 (10¾ ounce) cans cream of mushroom soup

1 (4 ounce) can mushrooms, with liquid

½ cup wine

In slow cooker, combine all ingredients. Cover. Cook on low 6 to 8 hours. Serve over rice or noodles. Makes 4 to 6 servings.

BEEF STROGANOFF

1 pound beef stew meat, cut into 1-inch cubes

1 medium onion, chopped

2 cups sliced mushrooms

1 (14½ ounce) can beef broth

1 (8 ounce) tub chive and onion cream cheese

London born **CHRISTINE AMANPOUR** *won the 1998 George Peabody Award for reporting and received additional recognition for heroic television journalism for filing reports from the world's trouble spots. She is CNN's chief international correspondent.*

In slow cooker, place meat, onion, mushrooms, and broth. Cover. Cook on low 6 to 8 hours or low 3 to 4 hours. Add cream cheese before serving, stir well. Serve over noodles. Makes 4 servings.

OUT ALL DAY BEEF STROGANOFF

4 pounds stewing beef, cut into 1-inch cubes

2 (10¾ ounce) cans cream of mushroom soup

1 (1 ounce) package onion soup mix

1 (8 ounce) container sour cream

In slow cooker, combine all ingredients except sour cream. Cover. Cook on low 8 hours. Add sour cream. Mix well. Serve over noodles. Makes 6 to 8 servings.

SHORT STEPS STROGANOFF

2 pounds ground beef, browned, drained

2 (10¾ ounce) cans cream of mushroom soup

⅓ cup evaporated milk

¼ cup ketchup

½ cup sour cream

In slow cooker, combine all ingredients, except sour cream. Mix well. Cook on low 4 to 6 hours. Add sour cream. Mix well. Serve over noodles. Makes 4 to 6 servings.

EDNA BUCHANAN became a police beat reporter for the Miami Herald at a time when Miami was becoming an international drug trade center. She covered over 5,000 murders. She won a Pulitzer Prize in 1986 and became one of the best known crime reporters in the country. She now writes mystery novels for which she has received two Edgar Award nominations.

STEAK CASSEROLE

2 pounds round steak, cut into bite sized pieces

4 potatoes, peeled, diced

1 onion, thinly sliced

1 (16 ounce) can French cut green beans, drained

1 (10¾ ounce) can tomato soup

1 (14½ ounce) can stewed tomatoes, drained

In slow cooker, layer steak, potatoes, onion, green beans, soup, and tomatoes. Cover. Cook on low 8 hours. Makes 6 to 8 servings.

SOUPED UP BEEF CASSEROLE

2 pounds stew beef, cut into bite size pieces

1 (10¾ ounce) can cream of mushroom soup

1 (4 ounce) can sliced mushrooms, drained

1 (1⅜ ounce) package dry onion soup mix

½ cup beef broth

In slow cooker, combine all ingredients. Mix well. Cover. Cook on low 8 to 10 hours or high 4 to 5 hours. Makes 6 to 8 servings.

NEVADA BARR *worked intermittently as a National Park Service ranger, and drew upon these experiences when she began writing mystery novels. Her books are very descriptive of the parks and feature a female ranger. She won an Agatha Award and an Anthony Award in 1994 for a novel set in the Guadalupe Mountains National Park. She has written 12 Anna Pigeon mysteries.*

POTATOES & SAUSAGE CASSEROLE

8 to 10 large potatoes, peeled, sliced

1 pound sausage links

2½ cups shredded cheddar cheese

1 (10¾ ounce) can cream of mushroom soup

1 cup milk

In slow cooker, combine all ingredients. Mix well. Cover. Cook on low 8 to 10 hours. Makes 8 to 10 servings.

NOT JUST BEANS 'N WIENERS

1 pound wieners, cut in fourths

3 (15 ounce) cans pork 'n beans in tomato sauce

½ cup ketchup

½ cup diced onion

¼ cup molasses

1 teaspoon mustard

In slow cooker, combine all ingredients. Mix well. Cover. Cook on low 4 to 6 hours. Makes 8 servings.

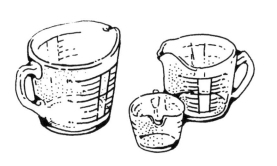

FRANCES WISBART JACOBS is the only woman of 16 pioneers honored in the Colorado Capitol Rotunda. She was the only woman and only Jewish member of the five founders of the Community Chest, now known as United Way. She was a founder of the National Jewish Hospital for Immunology and Respiratory Diseases in 1889, a hospital open to anyone destitute and suffering from tuberculosis.

ALOHA BEANIE WIENNIE CASSEROLE

2 (16 ounce) packages hot dogs, cut into pieces

2 (16 ounce) cans baked beans

2 (8 ounce) cans pineapple chunks, drained

½ cup packed brown sugar

In slow cooker, combine all ingredients. Cover. Cook on low 3 to 4 hours. Makes 6 to 8 servings.

BEANIE WIENNIE CASSEROLE

2 (16 ounce) cans baked beans

1 (16 ounce) package hot dogs, cut into pieces

1 cup barbeque sauce

¼ cup packed brown sugar

In slow cooker, combine all ingredients. Cover. Cook on low 2 to 3 hours. Makes 4 servings.

PORK & VEGGIE SUPPER

4 boneless pork loin chops, cubed, browned

2 (12 ounce) jars pork gravy

3 tablespoons ketchup

2 cups chopped potatoes

2 cups mixed vegetables

In slow cooker, combine all ingredients. Mix well. Cover. Cook on low 8 to 9 hours. Makes 6 servings.

MAE JEMISON, astronaut and physician, once worked for the Peace Corps in Africa. When she traveled on the Endeavor in 1992 she became the first black woman astronaut in space. She works today to encourage women and blacks to pursue careers in science and engineering.

ROLLED UP ENCHILADAS

2 pounds ground beef, browned, drained

2 (17.5 ounce) jars enchilada sauce

4 cups shredded cheddar cheese

8 flour tortillas

In slow cooker, combine all ingredients except tortillas. Cover. Cook on low 2½ to 3 hours. Spoon 2 tablespoons of mixture on each tortilla. Roll up and place seam side down in baking dish. Top with remaining mixture. Bake at 350 degrees, for 20 minutes. Makes 8 servings.

ENCHILADA CASSEROLE

2 (10¾ ounce) cans creamy ranchero soup

1 cup water

3 cups cubed cooked chicken

5 flour tortillas, cut into strips

1 cup shredded cheddar cheese

In slow cooker, combine all ingredients, except cheese. Mix well. Cover. Cook on low 4 to 6 hours. Add cheese during last 15 minutes of cooking. Makes 6 to 8 servings.

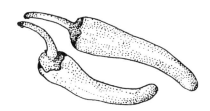

FRANCES KATHLEEN OLDHAM KELSEY, M.D., refused to approve the use of thalidomide in the U.S. when she was a researcher for the Food and Drug Administration, and saved countless children from deformities. She helped get Congress to pass the 1962 drug act which gave the FDA greater control over the manufacture, testing and distribution of drugs.

131

TACO CASSEROLE

1 pound lean ground beef

1 cup salsa

1 teaspoon chili powder

2 cups crushed tortilla chips, divided

1 cup shredded Mexican style cheese

2 cups shredded lettuce

1 tomato, chopped

In large skillet, brown beef over medium heat. Drain. Add salsa and chili powder. Mix well. In slow cooker, place half of meat mixture. Layer 1 cup chips and ½ cup cheese. Place remaining beef mixture over cheese. Layer remaining chips and cheese. Cover. Cook on low 4 to 6 hours. Serve with lettuce and tomato. Makes 6 servings.

LAYERED MEXICAN CASSEROLE

1 pound lean ground beef

1 medium onion, chopped

1 (10¾ ounce) can cream of mushroom soup

1 (11 ounce) can Mexican style whole kernel corn, drained

1 (10½ ounce) package corn chips, crushed

1 (10 ounce) can enchilada sauce

2 cups shredded Mexican style cheese

In large skillet, brown beef and onions over medium heat. Drain. In slow cooker, add beef mixture, soup, and corn. Mix well. Layer with corn chips then enchilada sauce. Cover. Cook on low 4 to 6 hours. Add cheese. Cover. Cook 20 minutes. Makes 6 servings.

SUSETTE LA FLESCHE, a member of the Omaha tribe, was a lecturer, artist and the first American Indian woman published author. She worked tirelessly for Native American rights, especially the Ponca tribe. She helped secure the passage of the Dawes Act in 1887, which was supposed to improve conditions for Indian tribes. Her sister, SUSAN LA FLESCHE, was the first Native American woman to become a doctor in the U.S.

MEXICAN CASSEROLE

6 corn tortillas, cut in strips

1 pound lean ground beef, browned, drained

1 (10¾ ounce) can cream of mushroom soup

1 (10¾ ounce) can cream of chicken soup

1 (14.5 ounce) can chopped tomatoes with green chile

8 ounces Velveeta® cheese, cubed

In slow cooker, place tortilla strips. Layer beef, soup, and tomatoes over tortilla strips. Top with cheese. Cover. Cook on low 3 to 4 hours. Makes 6 to 8 servings.

CHILI & TAMALE CASSEROLE

2 (14 ounce) cans chili con carne

6 tamales

½ cup chopped onions

2 cups crushed corn chips

1 cup shredded cheddar cheese

In slow cooker, cover bottom with chili. Add tamales, onions, chips, and cheese. Cover. Cook on low 4 to 6 hours or high 1½ to 2 hours. Makes 4 to 6 servings.

*Mt. Holyoke, the first college for women, was founded by **MARY LYON** in 1837, and she was its president until her death in 1849. It became the model for women's colleges nationwide. She wanted to provide high quality education, especially in fields other than teaching and homemaking.*

SOUTHWEST TACO PIE

1 pound ground beef, browned, drained

1 (10¾ ounce) can tomato soup

1 cup salsa

½ cup milk

8 corn tortillas, cut into 1 inch pieces

1½ cups shredded cheddar cheese

In slow cooker, combine all ingredients. Mix well. Cover. Cook on low 4 to 6 hours or high 1½ to 2 hours. Makes 4 servings.

CABBAGE WITH BEEF

1 pound lean ground beef, browned, drained

5 cups shredded cabbage

1 cup shredded carrots

¼ cup beef broth

½ cup tomato sauce

Salt and pepper

In slow cooker, combine all ingredients. Mix well. Cover. Cook on low 4 to 6 hours or high 1½ to 2 hours. Makes 4 to 6 servings.

CHERYL MILLER *averaged over 32 points and 15 rebounds and once scored 105 points in a game to become the only basketball player, male or female to be named a high school Parade All-American four straight years. In 1986 Sports Illustrated named her the best male or female player in college basketball. She was All-American four times and Naismith Player of the Year three times at USC. She was a member of the 1984 Olympic gold medal team. She has been a coach at USC and in the WNBA and a television analyst.*

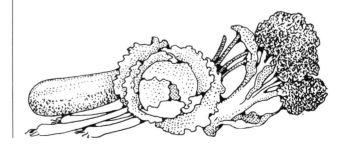

ON THE RUN TUNA CASSEROLE

2 (10¾ ounce) cans cream of mushroom soup

1 cup milk

3 (6 ounce) cans tuna, drained

4 cups hot cooked medium noodles

2 tablespoons butter

In slow cooker, combine all ingredients. Cover. Cook on low 4 to 6 hours or high 1½ to 2 hours. Makes 6 to 8 servings.

POTLUCK TATER CASSEROLE

1 (32 ounce) bag frozen tater tots

1 pound ground beef, browned, drained

½ teaspoon salt

2 (14.5 ounce) cans green beans, drained

1 (10¾ ounce) can cream of mushroom soup

¼ cup milk

In slow cooker, cover bottom with tater tots. In medium bowl, combine beef, salt, green beans, mushroom soup, and milk. Mix well. Pour over tater tots. Cover. Cook on low 4 to 6 hours or high 3 hours. Makes 6 to 8 servings.

GLADYS TOUTAQUID-GEON did not want there to ever be "the last of the Mohegans," and spent her life preserving their ways. As a girl she learned the ways and stories of her people from the elder women of her tribe. In 1947 she returned home to help run the family Mohegan museum. When the U.S. government in the 1970's refused to recognize the Mohegans as an autonomous tribe, she produced hundreds of documents she had stored under her bed in Tupperware to get the government to award tribal recognition.

135

MEATBALL & HASH BROWN CASSEROLE

1 (30 ounce) package frozen shredded hash brown potatoes, thawed

1 (10¾ ounce) can cream of chicken soup

1 cup shredded cheddar cheese

1 cup sour cream

1 onion, chopped

20 pre-made fully cooked meatballs

In slow cooker, combine hash browns, soup, cheese, sour cream, and onions. Mix well. Top with meatballs. Cover. Cook on low 6 to 8 hours. Makes 8 servings.

LAYERED CASSEROLE

2 pounds potatoes, sliced thin

2 cloves garlic, minced

1 green bell pepper, diced

1 onion, diced

3 stalks celery, diced

1 pound smoked sausage, sliced

In slow cooker, place potato slices. In large bowl, combine garlic, bell pepper, onion and celery. Add half of mixture to slow cooker. Add half of sausage over vegetables. Add remaining vegetables. Add remaining sausage. Cover. Cook on low 10 to 12 hours. Makes 8 servings.

ROSIE THE RIVETER was not a real woman, but was the embodiment of all the women working in the war industry during World War II. The number of working women in the U.S. went from 12 million in 1940 to 18.2 million in 1944. Rosie was a Norman Rockwell painting on the cover of Saturday Evening Post in 1943, sporting goggles and a rivet gun with a flag backdrop. She was celebrated in songs, movies and posters. Unfortunately, many of the women who would liked to have continued in their jobs lost them when the soldiers returned from the war.

CABBAGE & CORNED BEEF CASSEROLE

1 medium head cabbage, shredded

¾ pound corned beef, cubed

1 small onion, chopped

1 (15½ ounce) can white hominy, drained

1 cup water

¼ teaspoon hot pepper sauce

In slow cooker, combine all ingredients. Mix well. Cover. Cook on low 4 to 6 hours. Makes 6 servings.

TUNA CASSEROLE

7 ounces wide egg noodles, cooked

1 (10¾ ounce) can cream of mushroom soup

1 (12 ounce) can evaporated milk

2 (6 ounce) cans water packed tuna, drained

1½ cups frozen sweet peas

1 tablespoon minced onion

1 (2.8 ounce) can French fried onions

In slow cooker, combine all ingredients, except French fried onions. Mix well. Cover. Cook on low 4 to 5 hours. Top with French fried onions before serving. Makes 6 servings.

MAYA LIN was a 21 year old student at Yale when she and over 1400 others entered a competition for the design of a memorial honoring Vietnam War veterans. Her entry won, and her shiny black wall with 57,661 names of Americans who died in the war created considerable controversy. Her monument does not glorify war, but touches the heart with its harsh reality. The Vietnam Veterans Memorial was dedicated in 1982 and is the most visited National Park Service site in Washington, DC.

KIDS LOVE IT CHEESEBURGER CASSEROLE

2 pounds lean ground beef, browned, drained

2 (10¾ ounce) cans cheddar cheese soup

1 (20 ounce) package frozen crinkle-cut French fries

In slow cooker, combine beef and soup. Mix well. Top with French fries. Cover. Cook on low 6 to 8 hours. Makes 6 to 8 servings.

SAUSAGE AND HASH BROWN CASSEROLE

1½ pounds Polish sausage, sliced

1 (16 ounce) package frozen hash brown potatoes

1 (10¾ ounce) can cheddar cheese soup

1 cup evaporated milk

1 green bell pepper, diced

1 bunch green onions, diced

Coat inside of slow cooker with cooking spray. In slow cooker, place all ingredients. Mix well. Cover. Cook on low 4 to 6 hours. Makes 6 servings.

MERL STREEP, a Vassar College and Yale School of Drama graduate, has been nominated for ten Academy Awards and has won two Oscars— "Kramer vs. Kramer" and "Sophie's Choice." She has played a great assortment of complex women. She won an Emmy for the miniseries "Holocaust", and dominated the movies box office during the 1980s.

BACON POTATO CASSEROLE

2 eggs

2 tablespoons flour

½ cup evaporated milk

1 pound bacon, cooked, crumbled

1 (16 ounce) package hash brown
  potatoes

1 small onion, diced

2 cups shredded cheddar cheese

Coat inside of slow cooker with cooking spray.
In small bowl, combine eggs, flour and milk.
Mix well. In slow cooker, combine all ingredients. Mix well. Cover. Cook on low 4 to 6
hours. Makes 6 servings.

ITALIAN SAUSAGE POTATO CASSEROLE

1 pound Italian sausage, browned, drained

1 (16 ounce) package hash brown
  potatoes with peppers and onions

2 cups shredded cheddar cheese.

1 teaspoon salt

½ teaspoon pepper

Coat inside of slow cooker with cooking spray.
In slow cooker, combine all ingredients. Cover.
Cook on low 4 to 6 hours. Makes 6 servings.

CHARLAYNE HUNTER-GAULT wanted to be a journalist ever since she was a little girl. Unfortunately, the only journalism program in the state was at the University of Georgia, which did not admit blacks. The courts ordered her admission and she suffered slurs, taunts and riots. Twenty-five years after she graduated she was the first black commencement speaker at the university. She won two Emmys as the MacNeil-Lehner News Hour national correspondent on PBS.

COWBOY CHILI CASEROLE

1 (40 ounce) can chili with beans

1 (8 ounce) package shredded cheddar cheese

2 cups crushed nacho cheese flavored tortilla chips

1 (4 ounce) can chopped green chiles

1 (2¼ ounce) can sliced black olives, drained

In slow cooker, combine all ingredients. Cover. Cook on low 4 to 6 hours. Makes 6 servings.

ONE DISH CHICKEN CASSEROLE

2 (10¾ ounce) cans cream of mushroom soup

2 cups water

¾ cup uncooked white rice

½ teaspoon paprika

4 skinless, boneless, chicken breasts halves

In slow cooker, combine soup, water, rice, and paprika. Mix well. Place chicken on mixture. Cover. Cook on low 8 to 10 hours or high 4 to 6 hours. Makes 4 servings.

ROSEANNE BARR went from being a mother of three in a trailer park, to comedy clubs, to "domestic goddess." Her big break came as a guest on the Tonight Show. In 1988 she began a nine year run on her own show, hilariously dealing with everyday family life of average people. She wrestled control of her show from the executives and became one of the most powerful and wealthiest women in Hollywood. Her tumultuous and stormy marriage to and divorce from Tom Arnold filled tabloid pages and was perfect material for late night comedians.

STIR FRY CHICKEN CASSEROLE

2 cups uncooked instant rice

1 (8 ounce) can sliced water chestnuts, drained

2 cups cooked chicken

1 (16 ounce) package frozen stir fry vegetables, thawed

1 (14½ ounce) can chicken broth

¼ cup soy sauce

½ teaspoon garlic powder

½ teaspoon ground ginger

In slow cooker, layer rice, chestnuts, chicken, and vegetables. In small bowl combine broth, soy sauce, garlic, and ginger. Mix well. Pour over vegetables. Cover. Cook on low 6 to 8 hours. Makes 4 servings.

ONE FOR ALL CHICKEN DINNER

3 pounds whole chicken, cut up

4 carrots, peeled, sliced

4 potatoes, peeled, sliced

2 celery stalks, sliced

1 cup Italian dressing

½ cup chicken broth

In slow cooker, place chicken. Add carrots, potatoes, and celery. Pour dressing and broth over vegetables. Cover. Cook on low 8 to 10 hours. Makes 6 servings.

ANITA HILL maintained her composure under intense questioning by the U.S. Senate Judiciary Committee in the 1991 televised hearings on the nomination of Clarence Thomas to the U.S. Supreme Court. The poised black woman told of her boss, Hill's sexual harassment, but he was confirmed by a 52-48 vote. However, her testimony inspired thousands of women to come forward and tell their story. Within a year the number of women filing sexual harassment charges with the EEOC increased by 50 per cent.

PLAY 'N EAT CHICKEN DINNER

4 skinless, boneless chicken breasts

1 (10¾ ounce) can cream of chicken soup

⅓ cup milk

1 (6 ounce) package stuffing mix

1⅔ cups hot water

In slow cooker, place chicken. In small bowl, combine soup and milk. Mix well. Pour mixture over chicken. In medium bowl, combine stuffing and water. Spoon stuffing over chicken. Cover. Cook on low 6 to 8 hours. Makes 4 servings.

CHICKEN & DROP DUMPLINGS

3 pounds skinless, boneless chicken thighs, cut into bite size pieces

3 (14 ounce) cans chicken broth

1 pound small red potatoes, cubed

2 cups sliced carrots

1 onion, chopped

2 cups Bisquick®

½ cup water

In slow cooker, combine chicken, broth, potatoes, carrots, and onion. Mix well. Cover. Cook on low 9 to 10 hours. In small bowl, combine Bisquick and water. Mix well. Drop dough onto chicken mixture in slow cooker. Cover. Cook on high an additional 45 to 55 minutes or until dumplings are dry in center. Makes 5 servings.

TWYLA THARP is one of the most popular and imaginative choreographers in the world. Her clever, original and irreverent choreography has delighted audiences all over the world. She created the ballet "Push Comes to Shove" for Mikhail Barishnikov at the American Ballet Theatre, and has choreographed the films "Hair," "Ragtime," "Amadeus," and "White Knights."

EASY SUPPER

2 pounds ground beef, browned, drained

3 stalks celery, chopped

½ green bell pepper, chopped

1 small onion, chopped

1 teaspoon sugar

½ teaspoon salt

1 (10¾ ounce) can cream of mushroom soup

In slow cooker, combine all ingredients. Cover. Cook on low 4 to 6 hours. Serve over biscuits or with cheddar cheese. Makes 6 to 8 servings.

AMAZING ASPARAGUS & CHICKEN CASSEROLE

2 cups cooked cubed chicken

1 (8 ounce) package frozen chopped asparagus, thawed

1 (10¾ ounce) can cream of chicken soup

1 (2.8 ounce) can French fried onions

¼ cup water

In slow cooker, combine all ingredients. Mix well. Cover. Cook on low 4 to 6 hours. Makes 4 servings.

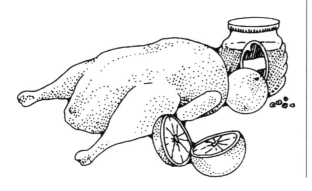

LOIS GIBBS, *a mother and housewife, learned that her son's school was built atop a toxic chemical dump and that Love Canal had been used as a chemical dumping ground. Her children had various health problems as did many others in the neighborhood. She became active and helped organize the Love Canal Homeowners Association, and they eventually persuaded President Jimmy Carter to order the relocation of 900 families, making Love Canal a household term.*

JUST AHEAD POTATOES & BEEF

1 (17 ounce) package fully cooked beef tips with gravy

2 cups frozen chunky style hash brown potatoes

1 red bell pepper, cut in 1 inch strips

1 green bell pepper, cut in 1 inch strips

1 small onion, cut in wedges

½ cup water

In slow cooker, combine all ingredients. Cover. Cook on low 4 to 6 hours. Makes 4 servings.

TUNA & SPINACH CASSEROLE

2 (10 ounce) packages frozen chopped spinach, thawed, drained

2 (6 ounce) cans tuna, drained

1 cup crushed seasoned bread crumbs

1 cup mayonnaise

½ cup sour cream

1 teaspoon lemon juice

¼ cup Parmesan cheese

In slow cooker, combine all ingredients, except cheese. Mix well. Cover. Cook on low 4 to 6 hours. Add cheese. Cover. Cook 20 minutes. Makes 4 servings.

As a child **YOSHIKO UCHIDA** *found almost no books about Asian families. She devoted her career to telling the stories of her people. She wrote her first book on brown wrapping paper at the age of ten. She and her family were among 120,000 people of Japanese ancestry who were interred after Pearl Harbor. She told this painful story through the eyes of an 11 year old girl in "Journey to Topaz" (1971) and "Journey Home" (1978).*

CHEESY TUNA CASSEROLE

2 (7.25 ounce) boxes macaroni and cheese

1 tablespoon butter

1 (15 ounce) can peas, drained

3 (6 ounce) cans tuna, drained

1 cup grated American cheese

Prepare macaroni and cheese according to package directions. In slow cooker combine macaroni mixture and remaining ingredients. Mix well. Cover. Cook on low 4 to 6 hours or high 3 to 4 hours. Makes 6 servings.

BEEF & TATER-TOTS CASSEROLE

1½ pounds ground beef, browned, drained

1 (16 ounce) package frozen green beans

1 cup shredded American cheese

1 (10¾ ounce) can mushroom soup

1 (21 ounce) package frozen tater tots

In slow cooker, combine all ingredients, except tater tots. Mix well. Place tater tots on mixture. Cover. Cook on low 4 to 6 hours. Makes 6 servings.

NADIA BOULANGER is considered one of the greatest teachers of music and composing of modern times. She inspired such greats as Aaron Copland and George Gershwin. She was the first woman to conduct the Boston Symphony Orchestra (1938) and the New York Philharmonic (1939). She selected and conducted the musical program at the wedding of the Prince of Monaco and Grace Kelly in 1956.

ONE POT CHICKEN DINNER

6 skinless, boneless chicken breasts

2 (6 ounce) packages one step dressing

½ cup chicken broth

2 cups jar chicken gravy

2 (15 ounce) cans green beans, drained

In large skillet, brown chicken lightly. Place in slow cooker. In large bowl, combine dressing, broth, and gravy. Mix well. Cover chicken with half of dressing. Spread green beans over dressing. Top with rest of dressing. Cover. Cook on low 6 to 8 hours. Makes 4 servings.

FANNIE LOU HAMER, the youngest of 20 children of a sharecropper, got her family kicked off the Mississippi farm for registering to vote in 1962. She went to work for the Student Nonviolent Coordinating Committee to get blacks registered to vote. For this she was shot, jailed and beaten. Her nationally televised speech at the 1964 Democratic Convention led the party to no longer recognize delegations that were not integrated.

SHOESTRING CASSEROLE

2 (4 ounce) cans shoestring potatoes

2 (10¾ ounce) cans cream of mushroom soup

2 (6 ounce) cans tuna, drained

½ cup evaporated milk

1 (4.5 ounce) jar sliced mushrooms, drained

In slow cooker, combine all ingredients. Mix well. Cover. Cook on low 4 to 6 hours. Makes 6 to 8 servings.

CARROT CASSEROLE

8 cups sliced carrots

1 onion, chopped

1 (10¾ ounce) can cream of mushroom soup

1 (4 ounce) can sliced mushrooms, drained

¼ cup evaporated milk

1 cup crushed butter flavored crackers

In slow cooker, combine all ingredients, except crackers. Mix well. Cover. Cook on low 8 to 10 hours. During last 30 minutes of cooking, stir, sprinkle cracker crumbs over carrot mixture. Cover. Cook remaining 30 minutes. Makes 8 servings.

KIND OF A HAM PASTA

2 cups cubed cooked ham

2 cups cooked macaroni noodles

1 (10¾ ounce) can cheddar cheese soup

1 cup frozen peas

1 cup crushed potato chips

In slow cooker, combine all ingredients, except chips. Mix well. Cover. Cook on low 3 to 4 hours. Stir, top with chips. Cover. Cook 30 minutes. Makes 4 servings.

FANNIE WATTLETON *witnessed firsthand at Harlem Hospital the terrible effects of illegal abortions. She began a crusade for reproductive freedom, saying, "Women can't control their lives unless they can control their fertility." In her 14 years as president of Planned Parenthood she traveled widely, appeared on television shows and before Congress. Her fundamentalist preacher mother once asked for prayers for Fannie's salvation.*

VEGGI & SAUSAGE CASSEROLE

2 medium potatoes, sliced

3 tablespoons Italian dressing

1 tablespoon Dijon Mustard

2 onions, sliced

2 medium carrots, sliced

2 cups chopped cabbage

1 pound Polska Kielbasa, sliced

1 (14½ ounce) can Italian style chopped tomatoes

In slow cooker, place potatoes. In small bowl, mix dressing and mustard. Drizzle $^1/_3$ of dressing mixture over potatoes. Arrange onions and carrots over potatoes. Drizzle $^1/_3$ of dressing mixture over carrots. Place cabbage over carrots. Drizzle remaining dressing mixture over cabbage. Top with sausage. Pour tomatoes over sausage. Cover. Cook on low 7 to 8 hours. Makes 4 to 6 servings.

CHICKEN & RICE DISH

3 pounds skinless, boneless chicken pieces, browned, cubed

1½ cups diced cooked ham

1 onion, chopped

1 red bell pepper, chopped

1 (14 ounce) can chicken broth

1 (8 ounce) package wild rice mix

In slow cooker, combine all ingredients. Mix well. Cover. Cook on low 8 to 10 hours. Makes 6 to 8 servings.

*In 1951 **LILLIAN VERNON** placed an ad in Seventeen magazine hoping to sell monogrammed matching purse and belt sets to make extra money. In three months she had $32,000 in orders. In a few years she expanded and offered combs, towels, bookmarks, etc., all with free monogramming. Now the Lillian Vernon Corporation is a catalog company that sells affordably priced gifts, household and decorative products amounting to $240 million a year.*

CHICKEN AND RICE

4 skinless, boneless chicken breasts, cut
into bite size pieces

3 (10¾ ounce) cans cream of chicken
soup

1 cup instant rice, uncooked

In slow cooker, place chicken. In small bowl,
combine soup and rice. Pour over chicken.
Cover. Cook over low heat 6 to 8 hours. Makes
4 servings.

RICE & SHRIMP DISH

3 boil in bags rice

2 (12 ounce) jars Alfredo sauce

2 (10 ounce) cans diced tomatoes with
basil

2 pounds cooked shrimp

1 cup shredded Parmesan cheese

Prepare rice according to package directions. In
slow cooker, combine Alfredo sauce and tomatoes. Cover. Cook on low 3 to 4 hours. Add
shrimp. Pour mixture over rice. Sprinkle cheese
over mixture. Makes 6 to 8 servings.

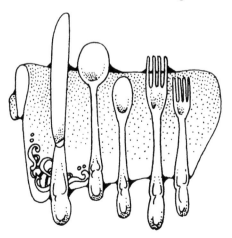

*In 1942 **CHIEN-
SHIUNG WU**, a
physicist who was
unable to find a job
in California
because of Anti-
Asian feelings,
joined the
Manhattan Project
which developed the
atomic bomb.
Later, her
experiment
disproved the law
of parity-that like
nuclear particles
always act alike-
and astonished the
world of physics.
However in 1957
the Nobel Prize
went to Lee and
Yang, who had the
theory, not Wu
who proved it first.*

JUST SPAM IT RICE

2 (12 ounce) cans Spam®, cubed

1 medium onion, chopped

1 teaspoon butter

3 (15 ounce) cans green beans, drained

1½ cups tomato sauce

1 teaspoon garlic powder

In large skillet, brown Spam and onions in butter over medium high heat. In slow cooker, combine Spam mixture, green beans, tomato sauce, and garlic powder. Mix well. Cover. Cook on low 4 to 6 hours or high 1½ to 2 hours. Serve over rice. Makes 6 to 8 servings.

BEEF MIXTURE ON RICE

2 pounds beef, cubed, browned

1 cup beef broth

1 small onion, chopped

2 (10¾ ounce) cans of cream of
    mushroom soup

3 tablespoons dry onion soup mix

In slow cooker, combine all ingredients. Mix well. Cover. Cook on low 6 to 8 hours or high 2 to 3 hours. Serve over rice. Makes 6 to 8 servings.

BARBARA MANDRELL *began playing the accordion at age five. By age 12 she was playing steel guitar on TV with major country music artists. In 1980 she and her sisters* **LOUISE** *and* **IRLENE** *had their own variety show on NBC. It featured musical guests, comedy sketches and Barbara showing her tremendous musical talents by performing on a number of instruments. She gave up the show in 1982 due to vocal strain. She had many hit records and won over 20 major industry awards.*

CREAMY GREEN CHILE RICE

1½ cups uncooked instant rice

1 (10¾ ounce) can cream of celery soup

1½ cups evaporated milk

1 cup shredded cheddar cheese

1 (4 ounce) can chopped green chiles

In slow cooker, combine all ingredients. Mix well. Cover. Cook on low 6 to 8 hours. Makes 4 to 6 servings.

WILD RICE DISH

1 pound lean ground beef, browned, drained

1 (6.2 ounce) package fast cooking wild rice mix, prepared

1 (10¾ ounce) can tomato soup

¼ cup evaporated milk

1 cup shredded cheddar cheese

In slow cooker, combine all ingredients, except cheese. Mix well. Cover. Cook on low 4 hours. Mix, top with cheese. Cover. Cook an additional 15 minutes. Makes 4 servings.

ANNE MORROW LINDBERGH, the wife of famed aviator Charles Lindbergh, became well known in her own right as a writer. After the kidnapping of their son in 1932 and the resultant media craze about it, the couple went on a five month around the world flight, surveying airlines for transatlantic flights. She wrote and published books about their journeys and continued to write until her death in 2001.

CHICKEN & WILD RICE

8 skinless chicken breast halves

1½ cups water

1 (6 ounce) package seasoned long grain wild rice mix

2 (10¾ ounce) cans cream of celery soup

In slow cooker, place chicken. In large bowl, combine remaining ingredients. Mix well. Pour mixture over chicken. Cover. Cook on low 8 to 10 hours. Makes 8 servings.

JAMBALAYA

1 small onion, chopped

⅓ cup diced green bell pepper

⅓ cup diced celery

1 cup chicken broth

1 (14½ ounce) can diced tomatoes

1 (16 ounce) package smoked sausage, cut into 1-inch slices

1 teaspoon Cajun seasoning

1 cup uncooked long grain rice, cooked

In slow cooker, combine all ingredients. Mix well. Cover. Cook on low 6 to 8 hours. Makes 4 servings.

JULIA TUTTLE convinced the Florida East Coast Railroad to extend its line to the wilderness area that was then known as Bay Biscayne in 1896. With the land she received and already owned, and with other property owners, they incorporated Miami, FL, the only major U.S. city founded by a woman.

CHIPPED BEEF ON TOAST

2 ($10^{3}/_{4}$ ounce) cans potato soup

1 tablespoon butter

$^{1}/_{4}$ cup evaporated milk

2 cups jar chipped beef, rinsed, chopped

In slow cooker, combine all ingredients. Mix well. Cover. Cook on low 2½ to 3 hours. Serve over toast. Makes 4 servings.

AFTER THE GAME TACOS

2 pounds lean ground beef, browned, drained

$^{1}/_{2}$ cup chopped onion

2 ($11^{1}/_{4}$ ounce) cans Fiesta® chili beef soup

$^{1}/_{2}$ cup water

In slow cooker, combine all ingredients. Mix well. Cover. Cook on low 3 to 4 hours. Serve with cheese, lettuce, tomatoes, sour cream, and taco shells. Makes 10 to 15 servings.

EASY TO MAKE DRESSING

2 (6 ounce) packages one step dressing

1 cup chicken broth

2 cups chicken gravy

1 cup diced onion

$^{3}/_{4}$ cup diced celery

In large bowl, combine all ingredients. Mix well. Pour mixture in slow cooker. Cover. Cook on low 4 to 6 hours. Makes 6 to 8 servings.

*Artist **JUDY BACA** got the aid of scholars, kids, artists and other helpers to complete the "Great Wall of Los Angeles," which is a brilliantly colored mural depicting California ethnic history and is half a mile long. She has directed programs that have created hundreds of murals in Los Angeles.*

NO BAKE DRESSING

15 cups dried bread crumbs

2 cups chopped celery

1 cup diced onions

1½ cups chicken broth

1 (10¾ ounce) can cream of chicken soup

¼ cup melted butter

2 teaspoons sage

1 teaspoon salt

Coat inside of slow cooker with cooking spray. In slow cooker, combine all ingredients. Mix Well. Cook on low 4 to 6 hours. Makes 8 to 10 servings.

GAME TIME JOES

2 pounds lean ground beef

1 cup chopped onion

½ cup chopped green bell pepper

2 (14 ounce) jars pizza sauce

¾ cup sliced pepperoni, chopped

1 cup shredded mozzarella cheese

In medium skillet, combine beef, onions and pepper, cook over medium heat until browned. Drain. Pour mixture into slow cooker. Add pizza sauce and pepperoni. Mix well. Cover. Cook on low 4 to 6 hours. Serve with cheese and hamburger buns. Makes 10 to 12 servings.

HELENA RUBENSTEIN was born in Poland where she studied medicine. She moved to Australia in 1902 and opened a beauty salon that featured her own face cream. She studied with the leading dermatologists in Europe to further perfect it. She opened salons in London, Paris and the U.S. featuring medicated skin care products and waterproof mascara. She turned the focus in 1917 to distribution and devoted her fortune to philanthropy.

TURKEY SLOPPY JOES

2 pounds lean turkey, browned

2 small onions, chopped

2 (15½ ounce) cans sloppy Joe sauce

4 cups corn

In slow cooker, combine all ingredients. Mix well. Cover. Cook on low 4 to 6 hours. Serve with hamburger buns. Makes 6 to 8 servings.

FIXIN BEEF BURGERS

2½ pounds ground beef, browned, drained

½ cup ketchup

¼ cup diced onion

2 (10¾ ounce) cans cream of mushroom soup

½ cup milk

In slow cooker, combine all ingredients. Cover. Cook on low 4 to 6 hours. Serve with hamburger buns. Makes 6 servings.

BBQ HAMBURGERS

2 pounds lean ground beef, lightly browned, drained

1½ tablespoons brown sugar

1 cup tomato soup

½ cup ketchup

1 teaspoon dry mustard

¼ cup diced onion

In slow cooker, combine all ingredients. Mix well. Cover. Cook on low 4 to 6 hours or high 1½ to 3 hours. Serve with hamburger buns. Makes 6 to 8 servings.

HANNA HOLBORN GRAY came to the U.S. from Germany with her family when the Nazis came to power in 1934. Her father was an eminent historian and she became a top scholar. She became the first woman to head a major American university when she became president of the University of Chicago (1978–1993).

BARBEQUE SANDWICHES

2 pounds lean ground beef, browned, drained

½ cup diced celery

⅓ cup diced green bell pepper

¼ cup diced onion

½ cup barbeque sauce

In slow cooker, combine all ingredients. Cover. Cook on low 4 to 6 hours or high 1½ to 2 hours. Serve with hamburger buns. Makes 6 servings.

WAKE UP TO BREAKFAST

1½ cups oatmeal

3 cups water

2 cups sliced apples

½ teaspoon cinnamon

Coat inside of slow cooker with cooking spray. In slow cooker, combine all ingredients. Mix well. Cover. Cook on low 8 to 9 hours. Can add ½ cup raisins. Makes 4 to 6 servings.

NELL MERLINO *was named New Woman magazine Woman of the Year in 1993, and received the Fulbright Award for Outstanding Achievement in 1994. She created and produced the "Take Our Daughter to Work Day" for the Ms. Foundation for Women in 1993. It received extensive newspaper and TV coverage, and is now an annual event in the U.S. and in dozens of countries worldwide. She is co-founder and CEO of Count Me In for Women's Economic Independence.*

Beef, Pork, Poultry, & Seafood

Women's Rights

1. On July 2, 1776, the colony of New Jersey was the first to grant female suffrage in the current United States. The legislation was repealed in 1807.

2. In the early 1800's women in Kentucky were allowed to vote in school elections. Nineteen states allowed women to vote in school politics by 1890. Many West and Midwest states gave women general voting rights in the early 1900's.

3. The National Woman Suffrage Association and the National Women's Party mounted an early 20th Century claim to the rights of citizenship for one-half of the population.

4. In 1912 Abigail Scott Duniway was the first Oregon woman to cast her ballot. She had been active for over 40 years campaigning for women's rights.

5. The Women's Franchise Bill granted suffrage to women in federal elections in Canada on May 24, 1918.

6. The 19th Amendment to the Constitution of the United States was ratified on August 18, 1920, giving women the right to vote.

7. The League of Women Voters was founded in 1920.

8. An act of Congress on October 7, 1975, made women eligible to enter the United States Military Academy at West Point, N.Y., the U.S. Naval Academy at Annapolis, MD, and the U.S. Air Force Academy at Colorado Springs, CO, for the class beginning in the calendar year 1976.

9. In August, 1996, The Citadel, a military academy in Charleston, SC, admitted four women for the first time to its formerly all male student body. Virginia Military Institute was also ordered to admit women.

POT ROAST DINNER

3 potatoes, sliced

3 carrots, sliced

1 small onion, sliced

1 teaspoon salt

3 to 4 pounds chuck roast

¼ cup beef broth

In slow cooker, add all vegetables. Salt roast, place on vegetables. Pour broth over roast. Cover. Cook on low 10 to 12 hours or high 4 to 5 hours. Makes 6 to 8 servings.

AMERICA'S POT ROAST

1 teaspoon salt

3 to 4 pounds chuck roast, browned

4 medium potatoes, cut in quarters

3 carrots, sliced

2 stalks celery, sliced

1 medium onion, sliced

½ cup hot water

Salt roast. In large skillet with oil, brown roast over medium heat. In slow cooker, place vegetables. Add roast and water. Cover. Cook on low 10 to 12 hours. Makes 6 to 8 servings.

As First Lady, **ROSELYN CARTER** *focused national attention on the performing arts and invited to the White House leading classical artists from around the world, as well as traditional American artists. Mental health became her focus, while her husband, Jimmy Carter, was President, and she currently leads a program at the Carter Center in Atlanta to diminish stigma against mental illness and promote mental health care.*

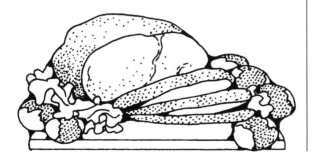

POT ROAST ON THE GO

3¼ to 4 pound chuck pot roast

1 (10¾ ounces) can cream of mushroom soup

1 (1 ounce) envelope dry onion soup

¼ cup water

In slow cooker, place roast. In medium bowl, combine mushroom soup, onion soup, and water. Mix well. Pour mixture over roast. Cover. Cook on low 8 to 10 hours. Makes 8 servings.

MARY BRECKIN-RIDGE, *descendant of a U.S. Vice President, went into nursing after the early death of her two children and her husband. She founded the Frontier Nursing Service. In the 1920s nurses rode horses and brought medical care to a wide area of remote rural Kentucky in all kinds of weather. Mary and the FNS trained hundreds of midwives. A hospital named for her and operated by the FNS is in the Kentucky mountain town of Hyden.*

CHUCK ROAST

3 to 4 pounds beef chuck roast

2 tablespoons oil

⅓ cup creamy horseradish

½ cup water

In large skillet, brown roast in oil over medium heat. In slow cooker, place roast. Spread top of roast with horseradish. Add water. Cover. Cook on low 8 to 10 hours. Makes 6 to 8 servings.

MIX IT & GO ROAST

3 pounds roast

2 (⅞ ounce) envelopes brown gravy mix

1½ cups water

In slow cooker, place roast. In medium bowl, combine gravy mix and water. Mix well. Pour gravy mixture over roast. Cover. Cook on low 6 to 8 hours. If frozen 8 to 10 hours. Makes 6 servings.

OH SO DELICIOUS ROAST

3 to 4 pounds chuck beef roast

1 (6 ounce) jar sliced dill pickles, undrained

1 medium onion, chopped

1 teaspoon mustard seed

4 garlic cloves, chopped

1(14 ounce) can crushed tomatoes with Italian seasoning

In slow cooker, place roast. Pour pickles with juice over top of beef. Add onions, mustard seed, garlic, and tomatoes. Cover. Cook on low 8 to 10 hours. Shred beef. Pile beef onto toasted rolls or buns. Makes 6 to 8 servings.

ITALIAN BEEF ROAST

3 to 4 pounds rump roast

1 (14 ounce) can beef broth

2 cups mild giardiniera

In slow cooker, place roast. Add broth and giardiniera. Cover. Cook on low 8 to 10 hours. Shred beef. Serve with crusty rolls. Makes 8 servings.

CICELY TYSON *got an Oscar nomination for "Sounder" in 1972, but is most remembered for her Emmy winning performance in the TV movie, "Autobiography of Miss Jane Pittman." She was in "Roots," and won another Emmy for the miniseries "Oldest Living Confederate Widow Tells All" in 1994.*

ITALIAN STYLE BEEF ROAST

3 to 4 pounds rump roast

1 cup water

1 (⅞ ounce) package Italian dressing mix

1 (1 ounce) package au jus gravy mix

2 teaspoons Italian seasoning

In slow cooker, place roast. In small bowl, combine water, dressing mix, gravy mix, and seasoning. Mix well. Pour mixture over roast. Cover. Cook on low 8 to 10 hours. Makes 8 to 10 servings.

BEEF CHUCK ROAST

2 medium green bell peppers, cut into strips

½ cup chopped onion

1 teaspoon salt

3 pounds chuck roast, browned

2 (14.5 ounce) cans stewed tomatoes

In slow cooker, add peppers and onions. Place roast on mixture. Sprinkle salt over roast. Pour tomatoes over top of roast. Cover. Cook on low 8 to 10 hours or high 4 to 6 hours. Makes 6 servings.

MARY DECKER SLANEY won the 1500 and 3000 meter races at the 1983 World Championships. She has held every American track and field record from the 800 to 10,000 meter runs, but never won an Olympic medal. In the 1984 Olympic 3000 meter finals she got tangled up with Zola Budd and took a heartbreaking fall, injuring her hip.

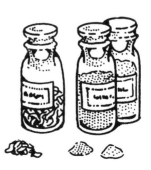

DELICIOUS CHUCK ROAST

1 teaspoon salt

2½ to 3 pounds chuck roast

1 cup flour

⅓ cup oil

2 tablespoons butter or margarine

2 (10¾ ounce) cans cream of mushroom soup

½ cup evaporated milk

Salt roast, dredge in flour. In large skillet with oil and butter, brown roast on both sides. Place in slow cooker. In medium bowl, combine soup and milk. Mix well. Pour mixture over roast. Cover. Cook on low 8 to 10 hours. Makes 6 to 8 servings.

HOME-STYLE ROAST

4 to 6 pounds potatoes, peeled, quartered

4 carrots, sliced

1 small onion, sliced

2 (14 ounce) cans stewed tomatoes

3 pounds chuck roast, browned

1 teaspoon salt

In slow cooker, place vegetables. Add stewed tomatoes. Mix well. Place roast on mixture. Sprinkle salt over roast. Cover. Cook on low 10 to 12 hours or high 3 to 4 hours. Makes 6 to 8 servings.

BUTTERFLY MCQUEEN *became part of film history with her role in "Gone with the Wind" in 1939. Movie roles were scarce, and she was out of films by 1950. She worked as a waitress and as a dance instructor between small roles on Broadway. At age 64 she received a bachelors degree in political science from New York City College.*

SOUTHWEST BEEF ROAST

1½ cups thick and chunky salsa

1 cup beer or water

1 (16 ounce) can tomato paste

2 tablespoons taco seasoning

3 pounds rump roast

In medium bowl, combine all ingredients except roast. Mix well. Place roast in slow cooker. Pour mixture over roast. Cover. Cook on low 8 to
10 hours or high 3 to 4 hours. Makes 6 to 8 servings.

BEYOND EASY BEEF ROAST

1 (3 to 4 pounds) beef roast

1 (24 ounce) jar yellow banana peppers, with juice

2 cloves garlic, minced

In slow cooker, place roast. Pour peppers over roast. Sprinkle garlic on top. Cover. Cook on low 10 to 12 hours. Makes 6 to 8 servings

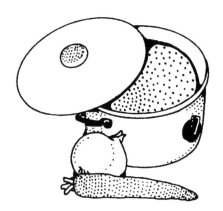

GUDRID THORBJARN-DOTTIR was born in Iceland about 985. According to Iceland folklore, Gudrid "the traveler" and her husband sailed to North America and founded the Vinland settlement. Her son, Snorri, was the first European born in North America. They returned to Iceland due to the dangers of the new settlement.

SUNDAY SUPPER ROAST

2 pounds boneless beef roast

4 potatoes, peeled, quartered

3 carrots, peeled, cut into 1½ inch pieces

1 (14 ounce) can stewed tomatoes

1 (1 ounce) package onion soup mix

In slow cooker, place roast. Add potatoes and carrots. In small bowl, combine tomatoes and soup mix. Pour over roast. Cover. Cook on low 8 to 10 hours. Makes 4 to 6 servings.

ANYTIME ROAST

4 pounds chuck roast

4 potatoes, peeled, quartered

½ pound baby carrots

1 (16 ounce) jar beef gravy

1 (10¾ ounce) can tomato soup

1 (1 ounce) package stew seasoning mix

In slow cooker, place roast. Add potatoes and carrots. In small bowl, combine gravy, soup, and seasoning mix. Pour over roast. Cover. Cook on low 10 to 12 hours.

TERIYAKI ROAST

3 pound roast, browned on all sides

¼ cup sliced onion

2 cups teriyaki baste and glaze sauce

Place roast in slow cooker. Sprinkle onion over roast. Cover with sauce. Cover. Cook on low 8 to 10 hours. Makes 6 to 8 servings.

DALE EVANS *became known as "Queen of the Cowgirls" when she starred in movies and on television with her husband, Roy Rogers, "King of the Cowboys." She authored several inspirational books, including "Angel Unaware."*

CRAZY CAJUN POT ROAST

2 pounds beef roast

1 tablespoon Cajun seasoning

1 (9 ounce) package frozen corn

½ cup chopped green bell pepper

½ cup chopped onion

1 (14½ ounce) can diced tomatoes, undrained

Rub beef with Cajun seasoning, place in slow cooker. Top with corn, pepper and onion. Pour tomatoes over vegetables and roast. Cover. Cook on low 6 to 8 hours. Makes 4 to 6 servings.

BBQ ROAST BEEF

3 pounds boneless beef roast

2 (12 ounce) bottles barbeque sauce

½ cup water

1 cup sliced onion

In slow cooker, place roast. In small bowl, combine remaining ingredients. Pour sauce over roast. Cover. Cook on low 8 to 10 hours. Makes 4 to 6 servings.

JULIE KRONE *was the first woman jockey to win a Triple Crown race-in the 1993 Belmont Stakes astride Colonial Affair. She retired as the winningest female jockey with over 3000 victories, and was the first woman jockey elected to the thoroughbred racing hall of fame.*

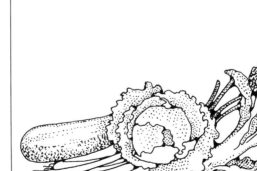

BLACK EYED PEA ROAST

1½ teaspoons garlic salt

1 teaspoon pepper

3 pounds beef roast

1 (14½ ounce) can black eyed peas, drained

1 (12 ounce) can sliced potatoes, drained

2 (3 ounce) packages gravy mix

1 cup water

Salt and pepper roast. In slow cooker, place roast. In large bowl, combine remaining ingredients. Mix well. Pour mixture over roast. Cover. Cook on low 8 to 10 hours. Makes 6 to 8 servings.

BEEF SHORT RIBS

4 pounds beef short ribs, cut into pieces

1 (10¾ ounce) can beef broth

½ cup prepared horseradish

In slow cooker, place ribs. Cover. Cook on high 1½ hours. Drain. In small bowl, combine broth and horseradish. Mix well. Pour mixture over ribs. Cover. Cook on low 8 to 10 hours. Makes 8 servings.

*In 1782 **DEBORAH SAMSON** dressed as a man and enlisted in the Revolutionary War. She earned a reputation as an outstanding soldier. She concealed a wound in her leg, received at Tarrytown, to avoid being discovered. The doctor eventually discovered her secret, but did not immediately reveal it. She was discharged, awarded a small pension, and is the official heroine of the Commonwealth of Massachusetts.*

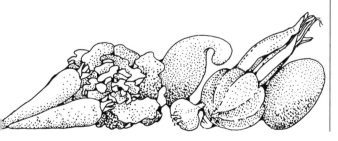

IRISH CORNED BEEF BRISKET

6 potatoes, peeled, halved

1 pound baby carrots

4 pounds corned beef brisket, fat trimmed

3 cloves garlic, minced

6 onions, quartered

1 medium head cabbage, cut into 6
    wedges

In slow cooker, place potatoes and carrots. Add enough water to cover. Place meat over potatoes and carrots. Sprinkle with garlic. Top with onions. Cover. Cook on low 8 hours. Add cabbage. Cover. Cook an additional 2 hours. Makes 10 to 12 servings.

COOK & SLICE BRISKET

4 to 5 pounds beef brisket

1 (1.5 ounce) bottle liquid smoke

¼ cup water

2 cups barbeque sauce

JEAN HARLOW
was the original
platinum blonde.
During the 1930s
she was the model
of feminine
sexuality in the
movies, where her
roles were of the
tough working girl.
She died at the age
of 26 of uremic
poisoning.

In large bowl, place brisket. Pour liquid smoke over meat. Cover, refrigerate over night. In slow cooker, place brisket. Add water. Cover. Cook on low 10 to 12 hours. Last two hours of cooking, pour barbeque sauce over brisket. Makes 8 to 10 servings.

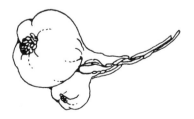

A ROBUST BEEF BRISKET

3 to 3½ pounds trimmed corn beef brisket

¾ teaspoon crushed red pepper

1 cup reduced sodium chicken broth

1 tablespoon Worcestershire sauce

In slow cooker, place beef. Sprinkle red pepper over beef. In small bowl, combine broth and Worcestershire sauce. Pour over beef. Cover. Cook on low 8 to 10 hours. Makes 8 servings.

BRISKET MARINADE

3 to 4 pounds brisket

1 (16 ounce) bottle Italian dressing

In large bowl, place brisket. Pour dressing over meat. Cover, refrigerate overnight. Wrap brisket in aluminum foil. Place in slow cooker. Cover. Cook on low 8 to 10 hours. Makes 8 to 10 servings.

AFTER WORK SWISS STEAK

1½ cups sliced carrots

4 medium potatoes, sliced

1 (14.5 ounce) can diced tomatoes with Italian herbs, undrained

1 (12 ounce) jar beef gravy

2 to 3 pounds round steak, browned, cut into serving pieces

In slow cooker, combine all ingredients except steak. Mix well. Place steak on mixture. Cover. Cook on low 8 to 10 hours. Makes 6 servings.

*On February 23, 1836, **SUSANNA DICKERSON**, her husband and daughter took refuge in the Alamo to avoid advancing Mexican troops. Her husband was killed in the famed siege. After the battle Santa Anna wanted to adopt her daughter, Elizabeth, but Susanna refused. She was sent to Sam Houston with a letter warning against further military action.*

SLOW COOKER SWISS STEAK

1 medium green bell pepper, chopped

2 stalks celery, chopped

1 (14 ounce) can tomatoes

1 (14.5 ounce) can tomato sauce

3 pounds round steak, browned

In slow cooker, combine all ingredients except steak. Mix well. Place steak in mixture. Cover. Cook on low 8 to 10 hours. Makes 6 servings.

CREAMY STYLE SWISS STEAK

3 pounds round steak, browned

2 (10¾ ounce) cans cream of mushroom soup

1 cup evaporated milk

¼ cup water

In slow cooker, place steak. In medium bowl, combine remaining ingredients. Mix well, pour mixture over steak. Cover. Cook on low 8 to 10 hours. Makes 6 servings.

NADIA COMANECI *was a Romanian gymnast who under coach Bela Karolyi won six medals in the 1976 Olympics- three gold, two silver and one bronze. She scored a perfect 10 in two events, the first such scores ever awarded. She defected to the United States and married U.S. Olympic gold medalist Bart Conner.*

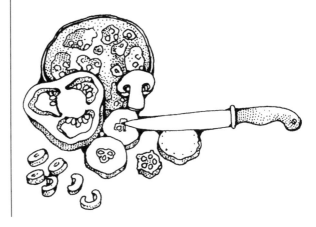

PEPPERS AND SWISS STEAK

4 pounds top sirloin steaks, cut in serving size

2 (14½ ounce) cans diced tomatoes

2 green bell peppers, sliced into ½ inch strips

1 medium onion, chopped

1½ teaspoons salt

1 teaspoon pepper

In slow cooker, place steak. Add tomatoes, bell pepper, onion, salt, and pepper. Cover. Cook on low 8 to 10 hours. Makes 10 servings.

ROUND STEAK AND MUSHROOM GRAVY

3 pounds round steak, cut into pieces

1 tablespoon butter

1 (10¾ ounce) can cream of mushroom soup

1 (1 ounce) package onion soup mix

1¼ cups water

In large skillet over medium high heat, brown steak in butter. In slow cooker, combine all ingredients. Mix well. Cover. Cook on low for 4 to 6 hours. Makes 6 to 8 servings.

*In 1907 **EMILY BISSELL** designed a seal to be sold at Christmas to raise money for a tuberculosis hospital. The seal with a wreath, the Red Cross emblem and saying Merry Christmas sold over 30,000 in two days. All her life she was a leading proponent of Christmas Seals. In 1986 a U.S. postage stamp was printed in her honor.*

ITALIAN STYLE ROUND STEAK

2 pounds round steak, fat trimmed, cut into serving size

2 (15½ ounce) jar spaghetti sauce

1 onion, sliced

1 (4.5 ounce) jar sliced mushrooms, drained

In slow cooker, place steak. Pour sauce over steak. Top with onion and mushrooms. Cover. Cook on low 6 to 8 hours. Makes 6 servings.

MIX IT QUICK MEAT LOAF

2 pounds ground beef

2 eggs

1 package saltine crackers, crushed

1 small onion, chopped

2 cups salsa

Coat inside of slow cooker with cooking spray. In large bowl, combine beef, eggs, crackers, onion, and 1cup salsa. Mix well. Shape mixture into loaf. Place in slow cooker. Top with remaining cup of salsa. Cover. Cook on low 6 to 8 hours. Makes 6 servings.

GRACIE ALLEN was the scatterbrained half of a beloved husband and wife Hollywood team. They performed in vaudeville, radio, movies and their own TV show from 1950–1958. Her straight man husband, venerable George Burns, gave Gracie the credit for their success, saying that all he had to do was ask, "Gracie, how's your bother?", and she did the rest.

MEXI MEAT LOAF

2 pounds ground beef

2 cups crushed corn chips

1 cup grated cheddar cheese

⅔ cup salsa

4 tablespoons taco seasoning

2 eggs, beaten

Coat inside of slow cooker with cooking spray. In large bowl, combine all ingredients. Mix well. Shape mixture into a loaf. Place in crock pot. Cover. Cook on low 6 to 8 hours. Makes 4 to 6 servings.

HEARTY MEAT LOAF

2 pounds ground chuck

½ cup chopped green bell pepper

½ cup chopped onion

1 cup cracker crumbs

1 egg

1 (⅞ ounce) envelope brown gravy mix

1 cup milk

Coat inside slow cooker with cooking spray. In large bowl, combine all ingredients. Mix well. Shape mixture into loaf. Place in slow cooker. Cover. Cook on low 6 to 8 hours. Makes 5 to 6 servings.

PAT SUMMIT, *women's basketball coach at the University of Tennessee, is the all-time leader in career victories-well over 800. Under her guidance the U.S. Women's Olympic basketball team won its first gold medal in 1984. Her Lady Vols have won six national championships.*

LAZY DAY MEAT LOAF

2 pounds lean ground beef

1 cup crushed saltine crackers

1 egg

⅓ cup diced onion

⅓ cup diced celery

½ cup diced tomato

2 (10¾ ounce) cans mushroom soup

Coat inside slow cooker with cooking spray. In large bowl, combine all ingredients except soup. Mix well. Shape mixture into loaf. Place in slow cooker. Pour soup over loaf. Cover. Cook on low 6 to 8 hours. Makes 4 to 6 servings.

TEXAS MEAT LOAF

2 pounds lean ground beef

½ cup salsa

2 eggs

1 cup crushed bread crumbs

1½ cups shredded Mexican blend cheese, divided

Coat inside slow cooker with cooking spray. In large bowl, combine all ingredients except ½ cup cheese. Mix well. Shape mixture into loaf. Place in slow cooker. Cover. Cook on low 6 to 8 hours. Sprinkle cheese over top. Cover. Turn off slow cooker. Let sit 5 minutes. Makes 5 to 6 servings.

Seventeen year old **JOANNA TROUTMAN** *sewed a flag for a Georgia battalion going to fight for Texas independence. In 1836 it became the first flag to fly over free Texas. She never visited Texas in her lifetime, but her remains were re-interred in the State Cemetery in Austin in 1913.*

MEAT LOAF FOR DINNER

2 pounds lean ground beef

½ cup tomato soup

1 egg

2 tablespoons dry onion soup mix

½ cup dry bread crumbs

Coat inside slow cooker with cooking spray. In large bowl, combine all ingredients. Mix well. Shape mixture into loaf. Place in slow cooker. Cover. Cook on low 6 to 8 hours. Makes 4 to 6 servings.

JUST A MEAT LOAF

2 pounds lean ground beef

½ cup stuffing mix

1 small onion, chopped

2 eggs

2 (10 ¾ ounce) cans tomato soup

¼ teaspoon salt

Coat inside slow cooker with cooking spray. In large bowl, combine all ingredients. Mix well. Shape mixture into loaf. Place in slow cooker. Cover. Cook on low 6 to 8 hours. Makes 5 to 6 servings.

NANCY LOPEZ, *a Hispanic American golfer, was the Ladies Professional Golf Association Rookie of the Year in 1977. She won the LPGA championship three times and was LPGA Player of the Year four times. She reached the Hall of Fame at age 30.*

MIX IT UP MEATLOAF

2 pounds ground beef

1 (6 ounce) package stuffing

3 eggs

1 cup catsup

In large bowl, combine beef, stuffing, and eggs. Mix well. Spray inside of slow cooker with non-stick cooking spray. Shape mixture into loaf. Place in slow cooker. Cover. Cook on low 6 to 8 hours or high 4 hours. Spread catsup over meatloaf. Cover. Cook 20 minutes longer. Makes 5 to 6 servings.

MEAT LOAF

DELORES DEL RIO, once described as "one of the most beautiful women to grace the American screen," starred in silent films and then talkies. She appeared in over forty U.S. and Mexican produced films from the 1920's through the 1970s. Although successful here, she tired of Hollywood and made money and critical acclaim in films in her native Mexico in later years.

2 pounds ground beef

5 slices bread, cubed

2 eggs

1 (1 ounce) package onion soup mix

¾ cup water

⅓ cup ketchup

In large bowl, combine all ingredients. Spray slow cooker with cooking spray. Shape mixture into loaf. Place in slow cooker. Cover. Cook on low 6 to 8 hours or high 3 to 4 hours. Makes 5 to 6 servings.

SHREDDED BEEF SANDWICHES

2 pounds beef flank steak

1 small onion, sliced

1 cup sliced mushrooms

2 medium tomatoes, chopped

1 cup barbecue sauce

2 teaspoons Italian seasoning

In slow cooker, place steak, top with remaining ingredients. Cover. Cook on high 5 hours or low 8 to 10 hours. Remove steak, shred. Return to slow cooker, stir well. Serve on buns. Makes 6 to 8 servings.

FRENCH DIP SANDWICHES

4 pounds beef roast, fat trimmed

2 (10¾ ounce) cans French onion soup

1 (10½ ounce) can beef broth

6 French rolls, toasted

6 slices mozzarella cheese

In slow cooker, place roast. Add soup and broth. Cover. Cook on low 8 to 10 hour. Slice beef, place on rolls, top with cheese. Makes 6 servings.

NAMPEYO *(1860–1942), a Hopi Indian from Arizona, was an internationally known potter who specialized in "crackle ware," intricately painted pottery. She integrated prehistoric designs into her work. She taught First Mesa women her technique and created a renaissance in Hopi pottery.*

SANTA FE BEEF FAJITAS

2 pounds beef flank steak, sliced into ½-inch strips

2 (16 ounce) jars salsa

1 cup chopped onion

1 cup chopped green bell pepper

In slow cooker, combine all ingredients. Mix well. Cover. Cook on low 6 to 8 hours or high 3 to 4 hours. Serve with flour tortillas, grated cheddar cheese, sour cream, and guacamole. Makes 6 to 8 servings.

MEATBALL SANDWICHES

3 pounds frozen fully cooked meatballs

1 green bell pepper, chopped

1 onion, chopped

1 (15½ ounce) jar spaghetti sauce

6 French rolls

6 slices mozzarella cheese

In slow cooker, combine meatballs, pepper, onion, and spaghetti sauce. Mix well. Cover. Cook on low 4 to 5 hours. Spoon meatballs on rolls. Top with cheese. Makes 6 servings.

CHRIS EVERT *helped popularize women's tennis. She was a media favorite, noted for her poise and her two-handed backhand. She won at least one Grand Slam title every year from 1974 to 1986. She won seven French Open titles, six U.S. Open titles, three Wimbledon titles, and two Australian Open titles.*

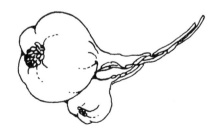

MEATBALLS AND GRAVY SANDWICHES

3 pounds frozen fully cooked meatballs

1 (10 ounce) jar beef gravy

1 (1 ounce) package dry onion soup mix

2 cloves garlic, minced

2 tablespoons water

6 French rolls

6 slices mozzarella

In slow cooker, place all ingredients except rolls and cheese. Mix well. Cover. Cook on low 4 to 5 hours. Spoon meatballs on French rolls. Top with cheese. Serve with remaining sauce. Makes 6 servings.

TASTY BEEF BURGERS

1 (10¾ ounce) can gumbo soup

¼ cup ketchup

1 tablespoon mustard

1½ pounds ground beef, browned

1 teaspoon salt

In slow cooker, combine all ingredients. Cover. Cook on high 1 hour. Reduce heat to low. Cook on low 1 hour.
Makes 4 to 6 servings.

*Petite **OLGA KORBUT**, Soviet gymnast, was the media darling of the 1972 Olympics. She won three gold medals and in 1976 was part of the USSR gold medal winning all-around team. She was the first gymnast to perform a back somersault on the balance beam, and was the first gymnast inducted into the Women's Sports Hall of Fame.*

PIZZA SLOPPY JOES

2 pounds lean ground beef

1 cup chopped onion

2 (14 ounce) jars pizza sauce

1 (3½ ounce) package sliced pepperoni, chopped

½ cup chopped green bell pepper

8 sandwich buns

2 cups shredded mozzarella cheese

In large skillet, brown beef and onion, over medium high heat. Drain. In slow cooker, combine beef and remaining ingredients except for the buns and cheese. Mix well. Cover. Cook on low 3 to 4 hours. Makes 8 servings.

CORNED BEEF RUEBENS

MAUD BOOTH and her husband withdrew from the Salvation Army (founded by the Booth family) and founded the Volunteers of America in 1896. The Volunteers have an extensive program for abused and neglected children youths, homeless and others. They have 12,000 employees and use more than 60,000 volunteers annually.

2 to 3 pounds marinated corn beef

2 garlic cloves, minced

10 peppercorns

In slow cooker, place corned beef. Top with garlic and peppercorns. Cover. Cook on low 8 to 10 hours. To make Rueben sandwiches, slice corned beef thin, use pumpernickel bread, Swiss cheese, sauerkraut, and thousand island dressing on each sandwich. Makes 6 servings.

FLAVOR PACKED PORK ROAST

4 cups herb seasoned stuffing cubes

¾ cup chicken broth

½ cup chopped onions

2 to 2½ pounds boneless pork loin roast

½ cup apricot jam

2 tablespoons vinegar

Coat inside slow cooker with cooking spray. In medium bowl, combine stuffing, broth, and onions. Place mixture in slow cooker. Place roast on top of mixture. In small bowl, combine jam and vinegar. Mix well. Brush mixture over roast. Cover. Cook on low 8 to 10 hours. Stir stuffing before serving. Makes 6 servings.

BONELESS PORK ROAST

3 to 4 pounds boneless pork roast

2 (14.5 ounce) cans crushed tomatoes

2 tablespoons dry onion soup mix

⅓ cup sliced onion

In slow cooker, place roast. In medium bowl, combine remaining ingredients. Mix well. Pour mixture over roast. Cover. Cook on low 8 to 10 hours or high 4 to 5 hours. Makes 6 to 8 servings.

In 1984 the United Methodist Church elected **LEONTINE KELLY** *their first black woman bishop. She was the second female Methodist bishop, behind Marjorie Swank Matthews. She became bishop of the Western Conference, the administrative and spiritual leader of over 100,000 Methodists in California and Nevada. She retired and now works for AIDS awareness and acceptance of gays and lesbians in the church.*

PORK ROAST & CHERRIES

2 to 3 pounds boneless pork roast

¼ cup pineapple juice

1 (20 ounce) can cherries

In slow cooker, place roast. Pour juice over roast. Cover. Cook on low 4 hours. Remove lid. Cover roast with cherries. Cover. Cook an additional 2 to 4 hours. Makes 6 servings.

GARLIC PORK ROAST

2½ pounds boneless pork loin roast

1 tablespoon chopped fresh thyme

½ teaspoon salt

2 tablespoons olive oil

2 cloves garlic, minced

In slow cooker, place roast. In small bowl, combine remaining ingredients. Mix well. Rub mixture over roast. Cover. Cook on low 6 to 8 hours. Makes 6 to 8 servings.

PORK LOIN ROAST

4 pounds pork loin roast

1 cup apple jelly

2 tablespoons cider vinegar

1 cup ketchup

In slow cooker, place roast. In medium bowl, combine remaining ingredients. Mix well. Spoon mixture over roast. Cover. Cook on low 8 to 10 hours. Makes 6 to 8 servings.

EVANGELINE BOOTH, born in England, was an evangelistic preacher from age 17, and became a general of the Salvation Army. She was commander of the Army in Canada and the United States. She was general of the international Salvation Army from 1934–1939.

PORK ROAST

2 tablespoons vegetable oil

4 pounds boneless pork roast

1 onion, sliced

3 cloves garlic, minced

1 (15 ounce) can chicken broth

In large skillet, over medium heat, with oil, brown roast on all sides. In slow cooker, place onions. Top with garlic. Place roast in slow cooker. Pour chicken broth over roast. Cover. Cook on low 10 to 12 hours or high for 6 to 7 hours. Makes 8 servings

ORANGE GLAZED PORK ROAST

3 to 4 pounds pork shoulder roast

1 (6 ounce) can frozen orange juice, thawed

¼ cup brown sugar

½ teaspoon salt

¼ teaspoon pepper

¼ teaspoon allspice

In slow cooker, place roast. In small bowl, combine remaining ingredients. Pour mixture over roast. Cover. Cook on low 8 to 12 hours. Makes 6 to 8 servings.

PEGGY GUGGGENHEIM, an American art patron and collector, inherited a fortune and became a friend, patron and sometimes lover of avant-garde artists and writers. She opened a gallery of abstract and surrealist art in London and then in 1942 in New York. Her superb collection of modern art was installed in her Venice palazzo in 1946, and is now administered by the Solomon R. Guggenheim Foundation.

CRANBERRY ROAST

2 pounds pork loin roast

2 (15 ounce) cans whole cranberry sauce

2 tablespoons sugar

In slow cooker, place roast. In medium bowl, combine cranberries and sugar. Pour mixture over roast. Cover. Cook on low 8 to 10 hours. Makes 4 to 6 servings.

KRAUT & CHOPS

3 pounds pork chops

½ teaspoon garlic powder

½ teaspoon pepper

1 (32 ounce) bag sauerkraut, rinsed

1 cup applesauce

In slow cooker, place chops. Sprinkle with garlic powder and pepper. Pour sauerkraut and then applesauce over chops. Cover. Cook on low 8 to 10 hours. Makes 6 to 8 servings.

PIZZA TASTING PORK CHOPS

6 pork chops, 1 inch thick, fat removed

2 tablespoons oil

2 cups pizza sauce

½ teaspoon dried basil leaves

1 small onion, chopped

In large skillet with oil, brown pork chops over medium heat. In slow cooker, place pork chops. In medium bowl, combine pizza sauce, dried basil, and onion. Mix well. Pour mixture over chops. Cover. Cook on low 8 to 10 hours. Makes 6 servings.

CAROL BURNETT started in show business as a singer and switched to comedy. She was a regular on the Garry Moore Show from 1959–62. She became extremely popular on her own TV variety show from 1967–79, the Carol Burnett Show, which featured musical numbers and tremendous comedy sketches with a great supporting cast. Her show won five Emmy Awards. She has also appeared in feature films and on Broadway.

CELERY AROUND PORK CHOPS

6 pork chops, 1 inch thick

1 (10¾ ounce) can cream of celery soup

¼ cup water

2 stalks celery, chopped

In slow cooker, place chops. In medium bowl, combine soup, water, and celery. Mix well. Pour over chops. Cover. Cook on low 8 to 10 hours. Makes 6 servings.

CRAN-APPLE PORK CHOPS

4 center cut pork loin boneless chops, ¾-inch thick

5 McIntosh apples, peeled, cored, cut into chunks

½ cup dried cranberries

1 cup cranberry apple juice

In slow cooker, place pork chops. Add remaining ingredients. Cover. Cook on low 6 to 8 hours. Makes 4 servings.

MARIE TUSSAUD learned wax modeling from her uncle who owned wax museums in Paris. She was imprisoned during the Reign of Terror, and the heads of many famous people were brought to her for modeling. She inherited her uncle's collection and immigrated to England. In 1835 she opened her own museum in London. Madam Tussaud's Wax Museum is a popular tourist attraction today.

PORK CHOPS & SWEET POTATOES

1 cup chunky applesauce

3 large sweet potatoes, sliced

1 tablespoon brown sugar

6 pork loin chops

1 (15 ounce) can whole cranberry sauce

In slow cooker, place applesauce. Layer sweet potatoes over applesauce. Sprinkle brown sugar over potatoes. Place chops over potatoes. Spoon cranberry sauce over chops. Cover. Cook on low 8 to 10 hours. Makes 6 servings.

NUTTY MAPLE CHOPS

6 boneless pork loin chops, 1-inch thick

1 teaspoon salt

6 tablespoons butter or margarine, melted, divided

3 tablespoons maple syrup

1/2 cup chopped pecans, toasted

Sprinkle chops with salt. Add 1 tablespoon butter in slow cooker. Place chops on butter. Cover. Cook on low 8 to 10 hours. In small bowl, combine butter and syrup. Mix well. Remover chops to platter. Spread mixture over chops. Sprinkle with pecans. Makes 6 servings.

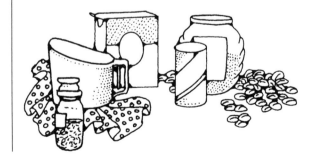

MARLENA DEITRICH *recorded the song "Lili Marleen"— a sad, beautiful German's soldier's song about the sweetheart of a soldier going off to war, and it was as popular with American GI's during World War II as it was with the German soldiers. She was an actress and cabaret singer in Germany, but was established in the movies in the U.S. when the Nazis came to power. They asked her to return to Germany, but she responded by becoming a U.S. citizen.*

SWEET ORANGE PORK CHOPS

6 pork loin chops

1 (12 ounce) jar orange marmalade

⅓ cup orange juice

In slow cooker, place chops. In medium bowl, combine remaining ingredients. Mix well. Pour mixture over chops. Cover. Cook on low 8 to 10 hours. Makes 6 servings.

SWEET & SOUR CHOPS

6 to 8 pork chops, ½-inch thick

2 cups sweet and sour sauce

Spoon sauce over each chop. Place in slow cooker. Cover. Cook on low 8 to 10 hours. Makes 6 to 8 servings.

ORIENTAL CHOPS

1 (16 ounce) package frozen oriental vegetables

6 pork chops

1 (12 ounce) bottle sweet and sour sauce

⅓ cup water

1 cup frozen pea pods

In slow cooker, add vegetables. Arrange chops on top of vegetables. In medium bowl, combine sauce and water. Mix well. Pour over chops. Cover. Cook on low 8 to 10 hours. Turn to high add pea pods. Cover. Cook 20 minutes. Makes 6 servings.

LIZ CLAIBORNE *was born in Belgium, raised in New Orleans and studied in Europe. After 25 years working as a fashion designer in New York, she founded her own company in 1976. She began with sportswear for working women and then expanded into men's clothing and accessories. The company had reached a billion dollars a year in sales before she retired in 1989, and now has sales in excess of $4 billion.*

PORK CHOPS

6 (1-inch thick) pork loin chops

1 tablespoon olive oil

1 onion, chopped

2 cups pasta sauce

In large skillet, over medium high heat, in olive oil, brown chops. In slow cooker, place chops. Sprinkle onions over chops. Pour sauce over chops and onions. Cover. Cook on low 8 to 10 hours. Makes 6 servings.

SHORTCUT PORK CHOPS

1 medium onion, sliced

6 pork chops

2 (10¾ ounce) cans cream of celery soup

½ cup evaporated milk

½ teaspoon salt

In slow cooker, place onions. Arrange chops on onions. In medium bowl, combine remaining ingredients. Mix well. Pour mixture over chops. Cover. Cook on low 8 to 10 hours. Makes 6 servings.

TEXAS STYLE CHOPS

4 to 5 butterfly pork chops

2 (10¾ ounce) cans tomato soup

1 (7 ounce) can green chiles

1 cup shredded Monterey Jack cheese

In slow cooker, place chops. Add soup and chiles. Cover. Cook on low 8 to 10 hours. Sprinkle cheese over mixture. Cover, let set 10 minutes. Makes 4 to 5 servings.

ANN LEE, an illiterate cotton factory worker in England, joined the religious group, the "Shaking Quakers." About 1770 she claimed to have a vision that the second coming of Christ was fulfilled in her, and she became the leader of the Shakers, and became known as Mother Ann. In 1774 she and seven others came to America to found Shaker settlements. They were known for their industriousness and for celibacy. Shaker furniture is still prized today.

SWISS PORK CHOPS

6 to 8 pork chops

2 (14.5 ounce) cans chopped tomatoes

1 cup tomato sauce

1 cup chopped green bell pepper

½ cup chopped onion

1 teaspoon salt

In slow cooker, place chops. In large bowl, combine all ingredients. Mix well. Pour mixture over chops. Cover. Cook on low 10 to 12 hours. Makes 6 to 8 servings.

TERIYAKI PORK

1 pound boneless pork shoulder, cut into 1-inch cubes

1 small onion, sliced

1 (5 ounce) can sliced bamboo shoots, drained

½ cup teriyaki baste and glaze

1 teaspoon gingerroot

1 (16 ounce) package frozen broccoli, carrots and water chestnuts, thawed

In slow cooker, combine pork, onion, and bamboo shoots. In small bowl, combine teriyaki baste and gingerroot. Add to slow cooker. Mix well. Cover. Cook on low 6 to 7 hours. Add vegetables to slow cooker. Cover. Cook on high an additional 15 minutes. Serve over rice. Makes 5 servings.

EVA PERON *was a minor actress in Argentina when she married Juan Peron in 1945. She virtually co-governed the country during his first six years as President, running the ministries of health and labor. She was a fiery orator and had a great political following. The army blocked her 1951 vice-presidential bid. A 1997 musical movie based on her life, "Evita," starred Madonna.*

IN A HURRY PORK CHOPS

4 pork chops

1 (16 ounce) bottle Italian dressing

In slow cooker, place pork chops. Pour dressing over chops. Cover. Cook on low 6 to 8 hours. Makes 4 servings.

GLAZED COVER PORK LOIN

1 (16 ounce) package baby carrots

4 boneless pork loin chops

1 (8 ounce) jar apricot preserves

In slow cooker, place carrots. Top with pork. Brush pork with preserves. Cover. Cook on low 6 to 8 hours. Makes 4 servings.

PORK TENDERLOINS

2 pounds pork loins

1 medium onion, sliced

2 apples, peeled, chopped

2 tablespoons apple jelly

1 tablespoon cider vinegar

In slow cooker, combine all ingredients. Cover. Cook on low 8 to 10 hours. Serve over rice. Makes 4 servings.

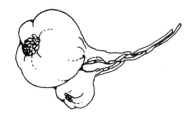

ANNE BANCROFT *was a stage and film actress who became well known for her role of Helen Keller's teacher, Annie Sullivan, in the stage and screen version of "The Miracle Worker," for which she received an Academy Award. "The Graduate," 1967, became a movie classic about a romance between an older woman and a younger man. She is married to comedic actor/director Mel Brooks.*

NUTS ABOUT PORK

1 tablespoon soy sauce

1 tablespoon oil

4 garlic cloves, minced

¼ cup packed brown sugar

1½ pounds lean pork strips

½ cup cashews

In small bowl, combine soy sauce, oil, garlic, and brown sugar. Mix well. In slow cooker, place chops. Top with mixture. Cover. Cook on low 5 to 6 hours, 2½ to 3 hours on high. Makes 4 to 6 servings.

SPOUT ABOUT BBQ PORK

2 to 3 pounds boneless pork loin

1 cup cola

¾ cup barbecue sauce

¼ cup ketchup

In slow cooker, place pork. In small bowl, combine cola, sauce, and ketchup. Mix well. Pour mixture over pork. Cover. Cook on low for 8 to 10 hours. Makes 6 to 8 servings.

SHREDDED PORK FOR TACOS

2 pounds boneless pork roast

1 (4 ounce) can chopped green chiles

½ teaspoon garlic salt

½ teaspoon pepper

In slow cooker, combine all ingredients. Cover. Cook on low 8 to 10 hours or until meat is tender. Use fork to shred pork. Makes 6 servings.

BAN ZHAO *(45–116) was born into a scholarly Chinese family of historians. Upon her husband's death shortly after her marriage, she turned to writing and research. She became imperial historian and completed her brother's history of the Han Dynasty after his death. She tutored women of the imperial court, including the dowager empress. Her best known work outlined the proper behavior for women.*

CHOP STICK RIBS

½ cup sweet and sour sauce

¼ cup soy sauce

1 clove garlic, minced

3 to 4 pounds pork ribs

In small bowl, combine sweet and sour sauce, soy sauce and garlic. Mix well. Brush sauce over ribs. In slow cooker, place ribs. Pour remaining ingredients over ribs. Cover. Cook on low 8 to 10 hours. Makes 6 to 8 servings.

BARBEQUE PORK RIBS

3 to 3½ pounds pork ribs

½ teaspoon salt

½ teaspoon pepper

1 large onion, sliced

2 (16 ounce) jars barbecue sauce

⅓ cup maple syrup

2 tablespoons packed brown sugar

Sprinkle ribs with salt and pepper. Place ribs on cookie sheet. Place under broiler 15 minutes to brown. Drain. Cut ribs into serving pieces. Place onions in slow cooker. In medium bowl, combine barbeque sauce, syrup, and sugar. Mix well. Arrange ribs over onions. Pour mixture over ribs. Cover. Cook on low 8 to 10 hours. Makes 6 servings.

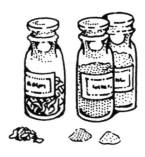

IRMA BOMBECK quit work as a journalist to raise her family. She started a widely syndicated humor column using her experiences as a housewife and mother. The titles of her books struck a chord with every wife or mother: "The Grass Is Always Greener Over the Septic Tank")1976); "Motherhood: The Second Oldest Profession" (1983); "When You Look Like Your Passport Photo, It's Time To Go Home" (1991).

COUNTRY BBQ RIBS

2½ to 3 pounds boneless country style
   pork ribs

½ cup ketchup

½ cup honey

¼ cup soy sauce

2 cloves garlic, minced

In slow cooker, place ribs. In small bowl, combine remaining ingredients. Mix well. Pour mixture over ribs. Cover. Cook on low 8 to 10 hours. Makes 4 servings.

PORK BABY BACK RIBS

1 teaspoon salt

1 teaspoon dried thyme leaves

3 to 3½ pounds pork baby back ribs, cut
   into 4 rib pieces

½ cup ketchup

3 tablespoons brown sugar

1 tablespoon Worcestershire sauce

1 tablespoon soy sauce

Rub salt and thyme over ribs. Place ribs in slow cooker. Cover. Cook on low 8 to 10 hours. Drain. In small bowl, combine remaining ingredients. Mix well. Pour over ribs. Cover. Cook on high 30 to 40 minutes. Makes 6 servings.

ANN-MARGRET *started out as a sex kitten in such movies as "Viva Las Vegas" with Elvis Pressley, and continues as a sexy older woman with Walter Matthau and Jack Lemmon in the "Grumpier Old Men" movies. She has won five Golden Globe Awards for her movie and TV roles. She has made 42 films and is still an attraction in Las Vegas and Atlantic City. She also has two Oscar nominations, "Carnal Knowledge" in 1971 and "Tommy" in 1975.*

EASY BARBEQUE RIBS

2½ to 3 pounds spareribs

¼ cup maple syrup

2 cups barbeque sauce

Place ribs on cookie sheet. Place under broiler for 15 minutes to brown. Drain. Slice ribs into serving pieces. Place ribs in slow cooker. Combine sauce and syrup. Pour mixture over ribs. Cover. Cook on low 8 to 10 hours. Makes 4 to 6 servings.

BARBECUE SPARERIBS

3 to 4 pounds spareribs

1 large onion, sliced

1 (24 ounce) bottle barbecue sauce

In slow cooker, place spareribs. Top with onions. Pour barbecue sauce over onions. Cover. Cook on high 1½ hours. Drain. Turn to low and cook 8 hours. Makes 4 to 6 serving.

FORK TENDER SHORT RIBS

4 pounds beef short ribs

1 medium onion, sliced

1 (12 ounce) jar beef gravy

1 (⅞ ounce) envelope beef gravy mix

In slow cooker, place ribs, cover with onions. In a medium bowl, combine gravy and dry gravy mix. Pour over top. Cover. Cook on low 9 to 11 hours. Makes 6 servings.

Because she was a semi-invalid as a child in England, **ELIZABETH BARRETT BROWNING** *read voraciously and wrote verse. Her first book, "Poems," in 1844 brought her immediate fame, and started a correspondence with poet Robert Browning. They were married and spent most of their lives in Italy. During her lifetime she was considered a better poet than her husband, but today's critics are less enamored of her works.*

PORK RIBS & KRAUT

2½ to 3 pounds country style ribs

2 cups tomato juice

3 tablespoons honey

1 (28 ounce) can sauerkraut, rinsed, drained

In slow cooker, place ribs. In large bowl, combine remaining ingredients. Mix well. Pour mixture over ribs. Cover. Cook on low 8 to 10 hours or high 3 to 4 hours. Makes 6 servings.

TANGY RIBS

1 (8 ounce) bottle French salad dressing

1 onion, chopped

2 cloves, garlic, minced

1½ to 2 pounds pork ribs

In small bowl, combine dressing, onion, and garlic. Mix well. Brush onto ribs. In slow cooker, place ribs. Pour remaining dressing mix over ribs. Cover. Cook on low 6 to 8 hours. Makes 4 to 6 servings.

ORANGE GLAZED HAM

5 pounds ham

⅓ cup orange marmalade

1 tablespoon Dijon mustard

1 large oven roasting bag

In roasting bag, place ham. In small bowl, combine orange marmalade and mustard. Mix well. Spread mixture over ham. Seal bag and poke 4 holes in top of bag to vent. Place bag in slow cooker. Cook on low 8 to 10 hours. Makes 8 servings.

ALICE MUNRO *is known as one of the finest short-story writers. The Canadian author's works deal with daily life, mainly about girls and women and are set in rural Ontario. Themes in her fiction are independence and domesticity, class distinctions, women's sexuality and female artists' problems. Collections of her stories have been published from 1974 to 2001.*

HAM WITH COLA

¹⁄₂ cup packed brown sugar

1 teaspoon cream horseradish

1 teaspoon dry mustard

¹⁄₃ cup cola soda

3 or 4 pounds precooked ham

In small bowl, combine brown sugar, horseradish, mustard, and soda. Mix well. In slow cooker, place ham. Brush mixture on top of ham. Cover. Cook on low 6 hours, high 2 to 3 hours. Makes 10 servings.

GOOD 'N TASTY HAM

2 (1 pound) ham slices, fully cooked

¹⁄₂ cup water

¹⁄₃ cup honey mustard

Cut each ham slice into 4 serving pieces. In slow cooker, combine water and honey mustard. Place ham in mixture. Cover. Cook on low 4 to 6 hours or high 2½ hours. Makes 8 servings.

MOUTH WATERING HAM

3 pounds smoked boneless ham, fully cooked

1½ cups fruit chutney

1 cup sliced onion

1 tablespoon balsamic vinegar

Place ham in slow cooker. In small bowl, combine remaining ingredients, pour over ham. Cover. Cook on low 6 to 8 hours. Makes 8 servings.

DOROTHY PARKER gained a legendary reputation for her bitter, derisive wit while working as drama critic for Vanity Fair and as book critic for the New Yorker. "Enough Rope" (1926), her first volume of poetry, brought her fame. Her satiric verse is concise and well crafted and her short stories are wry and witty. Her "Collected Stories" were published in 1942 and "Collected Poetry" in 1944.

HONEY MUSTARD HAM

3 pounds cooked ham

⅓ cup apple juice

¼ cup packed brown sugar

1 tablespoon Dijon mustard

1 tablespoon honey

In slow cooker, place ham. Add apple juice. In small bowl, combine brown sugar, mustard and honey. Spread over ham. Cover. Cook on low 6 to 8 hours. Makes 6 to 8 servings

HONEY BAKED HAM

3 to 3½ pounds smoked ham

4 pineapple rings

¼ cup honey

2 tablespoons pineapple juice

¼ cup packed brown sugar

In slow cooker, place ham. Arrange pineapple rings on top. In small bowl, combine remaining ingredients. Mix well. Spoon mixture over ham. Cover. Cook on low 7 to 8 hours. Makes 6 servings.

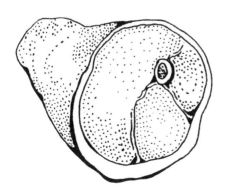

AYN RAND *worked for many years as a screenwriter after she came to the U.S. from Russia, where she was born. Her dramatic and romantic novels serve as a means of expressing her philosophy of Objectivism, based on individualism and self interest. "The Fountainhead," 1943, and "Atlas Shrugged", 1957, are her best known novels.*

PINEAPPLE OVER HAM

3½ to 4 pounds fully cooked ham

½ cup pineapple juice

1 cup crushed pineapple

⅓ cup packed brown sugar

1 teaspoon mustard

In slow cooker, place ham. In medium bowl, combine remaining ingredients. Mix well. Spread mixture over ham. Cover. Cook on low 8 to 10 hours. Makes 6 to 8 servings.

PEACH GLAZED HAM

4 to 5 pounds fully cooked ham

⅔ cup peach preserves

½ cup red raspberry jam

In slow cooker, place ham. Cover. Cook on low 3 to 4 hours. Spread preserves and jam over ham. Cover. Cook an additional 4 to 5 hours. Makes 8 to 10 servings.

BBQ HAM SLICES

1½ pounds ham, cut into ½ inch slices

¾ cup honey mustard barbecue sauce

½ cup orange marmalade

In slow cooker, place ham slices. In small bowl, combine barbeque sauce and marmalade. Pour sauce over ham. Cover. Cook on low 3 to 4 hours. Makes 6 servings.

ANNA FREUD, a British psychoanalyst, born in Austria, was a pioneer in the psychoanalysis of children. She was the daughter of psychoanalysis founder, Sigmund Freud. In 1938 she founded and directed a clinic in England for child therapy. She argued that ego was active in resolving conflict and tension. The seven volumes of "The Writings of Anne Freud" were published in 1973.

ITALIAN SAUSAGE DINNER

1 large green bell pepper, sliced

1 small onion, sliced

3 cloves garlic, minced

1 (16 ounce) package hot or mild Italian sausage, cut into 6 links

2 cups spaghetti sauce

¼ cup red wine

In slow cooker, place bell pepper and onions. In large bowl, combine garlic, sausage, spaghetti sauce, and wine. Mix well. Pour mixture over vegetables. Cover. Cook on low 6 to 8 hours or high 4 to 5 hours. Serve over hot spaghetti. Makes 6 servings.

CITY SLICKER BRATWURST

1 large onion, sliced

2 tablespoons vegetable oil

1½ pounds bratwurst

1 (12 ounce) can beer

In slow cooker, place onion. In large skillet with oil, lightly brown bratwurst. Drain. Place on onions. Pour beer over top. Cover. Cook on low 4 to 6 hours. Makes 4 to 6 servings.

ROSALYN YALOW, a medical physicist, was a researcher at the Bronx Veterans Hospital. She and a colleague developed radioimmunoassay (RIA), a process that made it possible to detect mere traces of biological substances in blood and other fluids. In 1977 she was awarded the Nobel Prize in Physiology or Medicine, along with two others.

LEISURE DAY LAMB CHOPS

2 tablespoons oil

6 lamb chops

½ cup orange juice

3 tablespoons honey

2 tablespoons cornstarch

In large skillet with oil, brown chops over medium heat. Drain. In small bowl, combine juice, honey and cornstarch. Mix well. Brush lamb chops with mixture. In slow cooker, place chops. Cover. Cook on low 10 to 12 hours. Makes 6 servings.

HONEY MUSTARD CHICKEN

4 skinless, boneless chicken breasts

¾ cup Dijon mustard

¼ cup honey

In slow cooker, place chicken. In small bowl, combine mustard and honey. Pour over chicken. Cover. Cook on low 6 to 8 hours. Makes 4 servings

HONEY DIJON CHICKEN

½ cup honey

¼ cup Dijon mustard

¼ cup onion

4 skinless, boneless chicken breasts

In medium bowl, combine all ingredients, except chicken. Mix well. Coat each breast with mixture. Place in slow cooker. Cover. Cook on low 6 to 8 hours. Makes 4 servings.

ANITA BRYANT sang her first solo in church at age two and was recording by 13. In the 1959 Miss America pageant she was second runner-up. She toured with Bob Hope and Billy Graham. Recent years have been concentrated on the gospel music field, and she has written several inspirational books. She was forced out of her job as TV spokesperson for the Florida Orange Growers for leading a fight against a gay rights ordnance in Dade County, FL, in 1977.

PINEAPPLE CHICKEN

4 to 6 skinless, boneless chicken breasts

1 (20 ounce) can pineapple chunks, undrained

1 small green bell pepper, sliced in strips

½ cup packed brown sugar

In slow cooker, place chicken. In medium bowl combine remaining ingredients. Mix well. Pour mixture over chicken. Cover. Cook on low 6 to 8 hours. Makes 4 to 6 servings.

APRICOT GLAZED CHICKEN

4 large skinless, boneless chicken breasts

1 cup apricot preserves

2 tablespoons chili sauce

1 teaspoon Dijon mustard

In slow cooker, place chicken. In small bowl, combine remaining ingredients. Mix well. Spoon mixture over chicken. Cover. Cook on low 7 to 8 hours. Makes 4 servings.

APRICOT CHICKEN

6 skinless, boneless chicken breasts

½ cup apricot preserves

⅓ cup Russian salad dressing

½ (of 1 ounce) package onion soup mix

In slow cooker, place chicken. In small bowl, combine remaining ingredients. Pour mixture over chicken. Cover. Cook on low 8 to 10 hours. Makes 6 servings.

LENA HORNE, singer and actress, began performing at age six, and by 16 was singing with Cab Calloway and Duke Ellington at Harlem's Cotton Club. She was the first African-American woman to sign a long-term contract with a major movie studio (MGM), but her scenes were shot so that they could be cut before being shown in the South. She was blacklisted in the 1950s for condemning racism and associating with Paul Robeson, an actor with communist ties.

GLAZE OVER CHICKEN BREAST

4 large skinless chicken breasts

1/2 cup apricot preserves

1 tablespoon chili sauce

2 teaspoons Dijon mustard

In slow cooker, place chicken. In small bowl, combine apricot preserves, chili sauce, and mustard. Mix well. Pour mixture over chicken. Cover. Cook on low 6 to 8 hours or high 3 to 4 hours. Makes 4 servings.

CRANBERRY LOVER'S CHICKEN

3 pounds whole skinless chicken pieces

1 (15 ounce) can whole cranberry sauce

1 cup French salad dressing

2 tablespoons dry onion soup mix

In slow cooker, place chicken. In medium bowl, combine remaining ingredients. Mix well. Pour mixture over chicken. Cover. Cook on low 10 to 12 hours. Makes 6 servings.

BERRY-LICOUS CHICKEN

6 skinless, boneless chicken breasts

1 (15 ounce) can whole berry cranberry sauce

1 cup maple syrup

1/2 cup soy sauce

In slow cooker, place chicken. In small bowl, combine remaining ingredients. Pour over chicken. Cover. Cook on low 8 to 10 hours. Makes 6 servings

On Chicago's WLS National Barn Dance, John Lair formed the first all girl band in radio. It featured **LILLIE MAY LEDFORD** *and was called The Coon Creek Girls. They played traditional folk and mountain music. She went with Lair to the Renfro Valley Barn Dance in Kentucky (second only to the WSM Grand Ole Opry in country music shows). The Coon Creek Girls performed on the Barn Dance and The Sunday Morning Gathering on CBS radio until retiring in 1957.*

LEMON CHICKEN

3 to 4 pounds roasting chicken
3 tablespoons butter
Juice of 1 lemon
2 teaspoons grated lemon peel
½ teaspoon salt

Clean and pat dry chicken with paper towels. Place in slow cooker. Rub butter over chicken. Pour lemon juice over chicken. Sprinkle lemon peel and salt over chicken. Cover. Cook on low 8 to 10 hours. Makes 6 to 8 servings.

LEMON OVER CHICKEN

4 skinless, boneless chicken breasts
1 lemon, halved
1 teaspoon lemon pepper
1 teaspoon paprika

In slow cooker, place chicken. Squeeze half on lemon over chicken. Sprinkle lemon pepper and paprika over chicken. Slice remaining lemon, arrange over chicken. Cover. Cook on low 6 to 8 hours. Makes 4 servings.

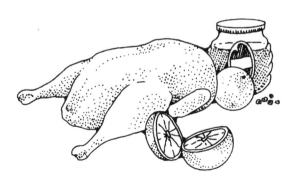

SARAH WINNEMUCCA wrote the first book ever published by a Native American woman. It was her autobiography, "Life Among the Paiutes: Their Wrongs and Claims" (1883), and described the sufferings of the Paiutes caused by corrupt white Indian agents. She gave nearly 300 lectures in East Coast cities in 1883 and 1884 to publicize injustices suffered by Native Americans.

SWEET & SOUR CHICKEN

4 skinless, boneless chicken breasts, cut into 1-inch cubes

½ cup chopped green bell pepper

1 cup pineapple chunks

1 cup orange marmalade

2 teaspoons soy sauce

In slow cooker, combine all ingredients. Mix well. Cover. Cook on low 6 to 8 hours. Makes 4 servings.

SWEET & TASTY CHICKEN

In Boston in 1861 **ELIZABETH PALMER PEABODY** *opened one of the first kindergartens in the country. She studied in Germany, opened the first kindergarten training school in the U.S., then traveled all over the country for the cause of kindergarten training. Elizabeth Peabody House in Boston was established as a memorial to her.*

1½ cups baby carrots

2 pounds skinless chicken breast

1½ cups sweet and sour sauce

1 (20 ounce) can pineapple chunks, drained

1 (16 ounce) package frozen broccoli, bell pepper, and onions, thawed and drained

In slow cooker place carrots, top with chicken. Cover. Cook on low 8 to 10 hours. Drain liquid from slow cooker. Pour sweet and sour sauce over chicken. Add pineapple, broccoli, bell pepper, and onions. Cook on high 60 minutes. Serve over rice. Makes 6 servings.

TASTE OF THE ORIENT CHICKEN

4 skinless, boneless chicken breasts, halved

1 (20 ounce) can pineapple chunks, with juice

¼ cup brown sugar

2 teaspoons soy sauce

In slow cooker, place chicken. In small bowl, combine pineapple, brown sugar, and soy sauce. Pour over chicken. Cover. Cook on low 6 to 8 hours. Makes 6 servings.

CHICKEN IN MUSHROOM GRAVY

3 whole skinless chicken breasts, halved

¼ cup chicken broth

1 (10¾ ounce) can cream of mushroom soup

1 (4.5 ounce) jar sliced mushrooms, drained

In slow cooker, place chicken. In medium bowl, combine remaining ingredients. Mix well. Pour mixture over chicken. Cover. Cook on low 8 to 10 hours or high 3 to 4 hours. Makes 6 servings.

ADA LOUISE HUXTABLE *was architecture critic for the New York Times from 1963–1982. A pioneer of contemporary architectural journalism, her writings went from modernism to post modernism and contributed to the preservation movement. In 1970 she received the first Pulitzer Prize for distinguished criticism.*

MUSHROOM CHICKEN

4 skinless, boneless chicken breasts, cut
　　into bite sized pieces

2 (4½ ounce) cans sliced mushrooms

1 (10¾ ounce) can cream of mushroom
　　soup

In slow cooker, place chicken. Sprinkle mushrooms over chicken. Top with soup. Cover.
Cook on low 6 to 8 hours. Serve over rice or
noodles. Makes 5 to 6 servings.

ROASTED CHICKEN

8 skinless, boneless chicken breasts

1 tablespoon olive oil

1½ teaspoons parsley flakes

1 teaspoon seasoned salt

1 teaspoon garlic pepper

Brush both sides of chicken with oil. Sprinkle
with parsley flakes, seasoned salt and pepper.
Place chicken in slow cooker. Cover. Cook on
low 8 to 10 hours. Makes 8 servings.

**RONA
BARRETT**
*became a
syndicated
newspaper gossip
columnist in 1957.
She edited three
entertainment
industry magazines
and had a radio
show in Los
Angeles. She
appeared regularly
on TV and wrote
three books. She
recently founded a
skin care and food
product company
and started a
foundation to help
the elderly. She still
covers the
entertainment
industry in "The
Rona Report."*

SHOPPING DAY CHICKEN

6 skinless, boneless chicken breasts

1 (15 ounce) can tomato sauce

1 (4.5 ounce) jar sliced mushrooms, drained

⅓ cup water

½ teaspoon Italian seasoning

In slow cooker, place chicken. In medium bowl, combine remaining ingredients. Mix well. Pour mixture over chicken. Cover. Cook on low 8 to 9 hours or high 4 to 6 hours. Makes 6 servings.

ALMOST BBQ CHICKEN

2 pounds skinless, boneless chicken pieces

1 (8 ounce) bottle French dressing

2 tablespoons Worcestershire sauce

2 tablespoons catsup

2 tablespoons brown sugar

¼ teaspoon garlic powder

In slow cooker, place chicken. In small bowl, combine remaining ingredients. Pour over chicken. Mix well. Cover. Cook on low 8 to 10 hours. Makes 4 to 6 servings.

DORIS KEARNS GOODWIN in 1967 wrote an article for New Republic that was critical of President Lyndon Johnson. He saw it and offered her a job as his special assistant. They formed a close bond and he asked her to help him write his memoirs. The historical biographer won a Pulitzer Prize in History for her book on FDR and Eleanor, and her book on the Kennedys was made into an ABC miniseries.

BACKYARD BBQ CHICKEN

6 skinless, boneless chicken breasts

1 onion, sliced

1 (16 ounce) bottle barbecue sauce

In slow cooker, place chicken. Top with onions. Pour barbecue sauce on top. Cover. Cook on low 8 to 10 hours. Makes 6 servings.

BARBEQUE CHICKEN BREASTS

4 whole skinless chicken breasts

2 cups barbecue sauce

¼ cup ketchup

2 tablespoons maple syrup

In slow cooker, place chicken. In medium bowl, combine remaining ingredients. Mix well. Pour mixture over chicken. Cover. Cook on low 6 to 8 hours. Makes 4 servings.

SPUNKY BBQ CHICKEN

4 skinless, boneless chicken breasts

1 cup barbeque sauce

½ cup packed brown sugar

⅓ cup Grey Poupon® mustard

In slow cooker, place chicken. In small bowl, combine barbeque sauce, brown sugar, and mustard. Mix well. Pour mixture over chicken. Cover. Cook on high 2½ to 3 hours or low 6 to 8 hours. Makes 4 servings

ERICA JONG is the author of eight novels. With a comic novel of sex and psychiatry that challenged conventional views of women, she created a sensation with "Fear of Flying" (1973). Several of her novels have been worldwide best sellers, popular in Eastern Europe, China, Asia and Japan. In 1998 she received the U.N. Award for Excellence in Literature.

NEW MEXICO STYLE CHICKEN

6 skinless chicken breasts

2 (10 ounce) cans Festival Rot-tel® tomatoes and green chiles, undrained

4 green onions, sliced

½ teaspoon salt

In slow cooker, place chicken. In medium bowl, combine remaining ingredients. Mix well. Pour mixture over chicken. Cover. Cook on low 8 to 10 hours. Makes 6 servings.

SALSA CHICKEN

6 skinless, boneless chicken breasts

1 (16 ounce) jar salsa

In slow cooker, place chicken. Pour salsa over chicken. Cover. Cook on low 8 to 10 hours. Makes 6 servings.

NACHO CHICKEN

6 skinless, boneless chicken breasts

1 (14½ ounce) can Mexican style stewed tomatoes, chopped

1 (10¾ ounce) can nacho cheese soup

In slow cooker, place chicken. In small bowl, combine tomatoes and soup. Mix well. Pour over chicken. Cover. Cook on low 8 to 10 hours. Makes 6 servings.

EDNA ST. VINCENT MILLAY lived in Greenwich Village and wrote satirical sketches for Vanity Fair in the 1920s. She was one of the most admired poets of her day, and was as admired for her bohemian lifestyle as much as for her verse. Her farm "Steepletop" near Austerlitz, NY, is now an arts colony.

CHICKEN BURRITOS

4 skinless, boneless chicken breasts, diced

1 (16 ounce) jar chunky salsa

1 green bell pepper, diced

1 onion, diced

4 to 6 tortillas

1½ cups shredded cheddar cheese

In slow cooker, combine chicken, salsa, pepper, and onion. Cover. Cook on low 6 to 8 hours. Spoon mixture into center of tortillas. Top with cheese and roll to close. Makes 4 to 6 servings.

CHICKEN CACCIATORE

2 (9 ounce) packages frozen cooked chicken breast strips

2 (28 ounce) jars tomato pasta sauce

2 cups sliced mushrooms

1 cup shredded fresh Parmesan cheese

In slow cooker, combine all ingredients, except cheese. Mix well. Cover. Cook on low 6 to 8 hours. Serve over hot linguine. Sprinkle cheese on top. Makes 6 servings.

GEORGE SAND (1804-1876) was a French novelist who wrote 80 novels which were widely popular in her day. She wore male clothes as a mark of rebellion. Her affairs (Chopin and others) were open and notorious. She demanded for women a freedom in living that was a matter of course for men.

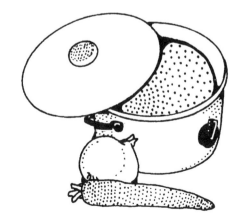

MIXED UP CHICKEN

1 (2½ ounce) jar sliced dried beef, rinsed

4 skinless, boneless chicken breasts

½ pound bacon

2 (10¾ ounce) cans cream of mushroom soup

½ cup chicken broth

In slow cooker, place beef. Wrap chicken breast with bacon, place over beef. In small bowl, combine soup and broth. Mix well. Pour over chicken. Cover. Cook on low 6 to 8 hours. Makes 4 servings.

KEEP IT SIMPLE CHICKEN

4 large skinless, boneless chicken breasts

½ teaspoon salt

2 (10¾ ounce) cans cream of mushroom soup

1 (4.5 ounce) jar sliced mushrooms, drained

½ cup evaporated milk

In slow cooker, place chicken. Sprinkle salt over top of chicken. In medium bowl, combine remaining ingredients. Mix well. Pour mixture over chicken. Cover. Cook on low 6 to 8 hours. Makes 4 to 6 servings.

MARY SHELLEY *fell in love with the poet Percy Bysshe Shelley and married him in 1816. Her most notable work is her novel of terror, "Frankenstein." The widely known story of a German student who infuses life into inanimate matter and creates a destructive monster has been the subject of numerous movies and television shows.*

CHIPPED BEEF CHICKEN

1 (6 ounce) jar dried chipped beef, rinsed, chopped

1 (10¾ ounce) can cream of mushroom soup

½ pint sour cream

6 skinless, boneless chicken breasts

In small bowl, combine beef, soup and sour cream. In slow cooker, place chicken. Pour beef mixture over chicken. Cover. Cook on low 8 to 10 hours. Makes 6 servings.

ITALIAN CHICKEN

6 skinless, boneless chicken breasts

1 green bell pepper, sliced

1 onion, sliced

1 (8 ounce) bottle Italian salad dressing

In slow cooker, place chicken. Top with pepper and onions. Pour dressing over top. Cover. Cook on low 8 to 10 hours. Makes 6 servings.

SIMPLY CHICKEN

5 skinless, boneless chicken breasts

2 tablespoons melted butter or margarine

1 teaspoon seasoned salt

½ teaspoon pepper

In slow cooker, place chicken. Drizzle butter over chicken. Sprinkle seasoned salt and pepper over chicken. Cover. Cook on low 8 to 9 hours. Makes 5 servings.

DANIELLE STEELE had her first romantic novel published in 1973. Her fourth novel, "The Promise," was a best seller and launched a steady stream of successes that made her a publishing phenomenon and very wealthy. Critics pan her, but by 1988 her books had sold over 85 million copies in 42 countries. Twenty-one have been made into television movies.

SWISS SLOW COOKED CHICKEN

4 whole skinless chicken breasts, split in half

8 slices Swiss cheese

2 (10¾ ounce) cans cream of mushroom soup

¼ cup chicken broth

1 cup herb seasoned stuffing mix

In slow cooker, place chicken. Top with cheese slices. In medium bowl, combine soup and broth. Mix well. Pour mixture over chicken. Sprinkle stuffing on top. Cover. Cook on low 8 to 10 hours. Makes 6 to 8 servings.

GARLIC CHICKEN

4 skinless, boneless chicken breasts

1 tomato, chopped

1 (1 ounce) herb and garlic soup mix

⅓ cup water

1 tablespoon olive oil

In slow cooker, place chicken. Arrange tomato over chicken. In small bowl, combine soup mix, water and olive oil. Pour over tomato and chicken. Cover. Cook on low 6 to 8 hours. Makes 4 servings.

Boxing was the category in which **DR. JOYCE BROTHERS** *won the quiz shows $64,000 Question and $64,000 Challenge in the 1950s. This gained her national attention and she became co-host of NBC's Sports Showcase. She went on to appear in syndicated TV shows as a psychologist, and to write a daily syndicated newspaper column and monthly magazine columns. She has appeared many times as herself on TV and in movies.*

CHICKEN CORDON BLEU

4 skinless, boneless chicken breasts pounded thin

4 slices deli ham

4 slices Swiss cheese

1 (10¾ ounce) can cream of mushroom soup

¼ cup milk

On each chicken breast layer ham and cheese. Roll up, secure with a toothpick. In small bowl, combine soup and milk. Place chicken in slow cooker. Pour mixture over chicken. Cover. Cook on low 6 to 8 hours. Makes 4 servings.

PEPPER CHICKEN

8 skinless, boneless chicken breasts

2 green bell peppers, sliced

1 onion, sliced

2 cups pasta sauce

In slow cooker, place chicken. Top with pepper and onion. Pour sauce over ingredients. Cover. Cook on low 10 to 12 hours. Makes 8 servings.

DOROTHY BUFFUM CHANDLER was the wife and mother of publishers and helped the Los Angeles Times gain prominence. She raised $20 million in private donations for the Los Angeles County Music Center, completed in 1967. The 3,197 seat Dorothy Chandler Pavilion, named in her honor, is the home of the Los Angeles Opera and Music Center Dance and has been the venue for the Academy Awards many times.

ANOTHER PEPPER CHICKEN

6 skinless, boneless chicken breasts

2 green bell peppers, sliced

1 (14 ounce) can stewed tomatoes

½ (6 ounce size) bottle Italian salad dressing

In slow cooker, place chicken. Add green bell pepper. In small bowl, combine tomatoes and dressing. Pour mixture over peppers and chicken. Cover. Cook on low 8 to 10 hours. Makes 6 servings.

SWEET POTATO CHICKEN

3 sweet potatoes, peeled, cubed

1 onion, chopped

4 skinless, boneless chicken breasts

2 tablespoons butter, melted

In slow cooker, place sweet potatoes and onions. Place chicken on top of sweet potatoes and onions. Drizzle with butter. Cover. Cook on low 6 to 8 hours. Makes 4 servings.

JULIA CHILD *learned French cooking in the late 1940s while her husband was in the diplomatic service in France. She co-authored the first practical French cooking cookbook in the U.S. She became a star on educational television cooking shows, such as "The French Chef" (1963–1976) for which she won an Emmy. She also authored a number of other cookbooks.*

HUNGRY MAN'S CHICKEN

6 potatoes, peeled, quartered

2 onions, sliced

6 skinless, boneless chicken breasts, halved

2 (10¾ ounce) cans cream of mushroom soup

In slow cooker, layer potatoes, onion, and chicken. Pour soup over top. Cover. Cook on low 8 to 10 hours or high 4 to 6 hours.

OLIVE CHICKEN

6 skinless, boneless chicken breasts

¼ teaspoon garlic salt

2 cups pasta sauce with green olives

½ cup grated Parmesan Cheese

In slow cooker, place chicken. Sprinkle chicken with garlic salt. Pour sauce over chicken. Sprinkle cheese over sauce. Cover. Cook on low 8 to 10 hours. Makes 6 servings.

CONNIE CHUNG *began as a TV reporter in Washington, DC. In 1971 she became a national correspondent for CBS News. She was co-anchor of CBS Evening News from 1993- 95, and later became co-anchor of ABC's 20/20. Her attempt at her own talk show was short lived—less than a year. She is married to talk show host Maury Provich.*

SAUCY CHICKEN SANDWICHES

4 chicken breasts, cut into bite size pieces

1 (8 ounce) can tomato sauce

½ cup water

1 (1¼ ounce) package spaghetti sauce seasoning mix

1 (4.5 ounce) jar sliced mushrooms

6 to 8 buns

4 slices mozzarella cheese, cut in half

In slow cooker, combine chicken, tomato sauce, water, seasoning mix, and mushrooms. Cover. Cook on low 6 to 8 hours. Place chicken mixture on buns. Top with cheese and serve. Makes 6 to 8 servings.

CHICKEN LOAF

1 pound ground chicken

15 saltine crackers, crushed

4 green onions, finely chopped with tops

1 egg

⅓ teaspoon salt

In large bowl, combine all ingredients. Coat inside of slow cooker with cooking spray. Shape meat mixture into loaf. Place in slow cooker Cover. Cook on low 3 to 4 hours. Makes 4 servings.

HEDDA HOPPER *was best known for her Hollywood gossip and her feud with rival Louella Parsons. Her gossip began on radio, then newspaper columns and movie documentaries in the 1940s. Less known is the fact that she was a chorus girl on Broadway and an actress in 120 films from 1916–1939. She also had a famous hat collection.*

TASTY CHICKEN ITALIANO

4 to 6 skinless, boneless chicken breasts

1 (26 ounce) jar pasta sauce

¾ cup Italian seasoned dry bread crumbs

2 cups shredded mozzarella cheese

In slow cooker, place chickens breast. Pour pasta sauce over chicken. Sprinkle bread crumbs over sauce. Cover. Cook on high 3 to 4 hours or low 6 to 8 hours. Sprinkle cheese over mixture last hour of cooking. Makes 4 to 6 servings.

STUFFING TOP CHICKEN

6 skinless, boneless chicken breasts

6 slices Swiss cheese

1 (10¾ ounce) can cream of mushroom soup

¼ cup milk

2 cups herb stuffing mix

½ cup butter, melted

Spray slow cooker with cooking spray. Arrange chicken breasts in slow cooker. Top with cheese. In small bowl, combine soup and milk. Mix well. Spoon mixture over cheese. In a small bowl, combine stuffing mix and butter. Sprinkle stuffing on top. Cover. Cook on low 8 to 10 hours, on high 4 to 6 hours. Makes 6 servings.

LOUELLA PARSONS wrote the first movie column in the country for the Chicago Record Herald in 1914. While working for the New York American, she contracted tuberculosis and was told she had six months to live. She moved to California, recovered, and became the Hearst Newspaper chain's syndicated Hollywood columnist. Her column was in 400 newspapers and she became one of the most influential voices in Hollywood.

FAMILY PLEASING CHICKEN

4 skinless, boneless chicken breasts

⅓ cup apple jelly

1 tablespoon honey

1 tablespoon Dijon mustard

In slow cooker, place chicken. In small bowl, combine jelly, honey, and mustard. Mix well. Brush mixture on chicken. Cover. Cook on high 1½ hours. Remove lid. Brush chicken with mixture. Cover, reduce heat to low. Cook 3 hours. Makes 4 servings.

CREAMY GARLIC CHICKEN

4 boneless, chicken breast halves

1 (10¾ ounce) can cream of garlic soup

½ cup milk

In slow cooker, place chicken. In small bowl, combine soup and milk. Pour mixture over chicken. Cover. Cook on low 6 to 8 hours or high 3 to 4 hours. Makes 4 servings.

EASY TO MAKE TURKEY

4½ to 5 pounds turkey breast

1 teaspoon poultry seasoning

2 (10¾ ounce) cans cream of mushroom soup

½ cup water

Rinse turkey, pat dry. Rub seasoning over turkey. In slow cooker, combine soup and water. Mix well. Place turkey on top of mixture. Cover. Cook on low 10 to 12 hours. Makes 8 servings.

EMILY POST *began as a novelist but became known as the foremost American authority on etiquette. Her best known book, a practical guide to proper social behavior, "Etiquette" (1922), sold over a million copies. She had a radio show and a syndicated newspaper column in over 200 newspapers.*

TURKEY ANYTIME

4 to 6 pounds turkey breast

1 (15 ounce) can whole cranberry sauce

½ cup orange juice

1 (1 ounce) envelope dry onion soup

In slow cooker, place turkey. In medium bowl, combine cranberry sauce, orange juice, and onion soup mix. Mix well. Pour over turkey. Cover. Cook on low 8 to 12 hours. Makes 6 to 8 servings.

TURKEY AND STUFFING

1 tablespoon butter or margarine

½ cup chopped onion

1 tablespoon apple jelly

1 (6 ounce) package chicken flavored one step dressing

¾ cup water

1 (2 to 2½ pounds) skinless, boneless turkey breast half

In medium skillet, over medium high heat with butter, sauté onion until lightly browned. Add jelly, sauté until golden brown. In slow cooker, place stuffing in bottom. Sprinkle with water. Stir well. Place turkey breast on stuffing. Drizzle with onion mixture. Cover. Cook on low 6 to 8 hours. Makes 5 to 6 servings.

DIANE SAWYER came to Washington to help President Nixon write his memoirs. In 1984 she became the first woman correspondent for "60 Minutes." She became co-host of ABC's Good Morning America in 1999, and has won numerous awards, including an Emmy and a George Peabody.

COMPLETE BBQ TURKEY MEAL

6 carrots, cut into 2 inch pieces

3 potatoes, cut into inch pieces

2½ to 3 pounds turkey, cut into bite sized pieces.

1 cup barbeque sauce

¼ cup hot water

In slow cooker, layer carrots, potatoes, then turkey. In small bowl combine barbeque sauce and water. Mix well. Pour sauce over turkey. Cover. Cook on low 8 to 10 hours. Makes 4 to 6 servings.

SEASONED TURKEY

2 pounds skinless, boneless turkey breast, cut into bite-sized pieces

1 onion, chopped

4 cloves garlic, minced

¼ cup chicken broth

½ teaspoon crushed red pepper flakes

1 teaspoon salt

In slow cooker, combine all ingredients. Cover. Cook on low 6 to 8 hours. Makes 8 servings.

DR. LAURA SCHLESSINGER *began working in radio around 1980. She has a doctorate in psychology, and is a licensed marriage, family and child counselor. On her top rated radio talk show she gives advice to callers, often using the Bible for guidance. She has written seven books, writes a weekly newspaper column and is editor of a monthly magazine.*

ROASTED TURKEY BREAST

3½ to 4 pounds skinless turkey breast

3 tablespoons butter or margarine

1 teaspoon salt

½ cup raspberry jam

1 teaspoon Dijon mustard

In slow cooker, place turkey, rub with butter. Sprinkle salt over top. Cover. Cook on low 10 to 12 hours. In small bowl, combine jam and mustard. Mix well. Spoon mixture over turkey last hour of cooking. Makes 6 to 8 hours.

AMY VANDERBILT *published a blockbuster best seller, "Amy Vanderbilt's Etiquette," in 1952. She had worked as a reporter and in advertising and public relations. She hosted a TV show, "It's In Good Taste," and a radio show, "The Right Thing to Do." She wrote books on cooking and was a consultant for several organizations, including the State Department.*

MEDITERRANEAN TURKEY

1½ pounds skinless, boneless turkey, cut into bite sized pieces

¼ cup sliced black olives

¼ cup chopped onions

2 cloves garlic, minced

1 (14½ ounce) can stewed tomatoes

In slow cooker, combine all ingredients. Mix well. Cover. Cook on low 6 to 8 hours. Makes 5 to 6 servings.

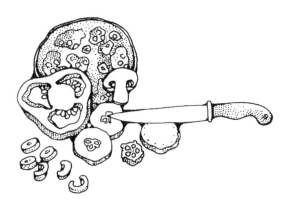

TASTY TURKEY

1 cup chicken broth

5 to 6 pounds turkey breast

4 tablespoons melted butter

In slow cooker, pour chicken broth. Add turkey. Drizzle butter over turkey. Cover. Cook on low 10 to 12 hours. Makes 6 to 8 servings.

TURKEY AND VEGETABLES

4 carrots, cut into 2 inch pieces

3 potatoes, peeled, cut into 8 pieces

2 celery stalks, cut into 1 inch pieces

½ cup chicken broth

3 pound turkey breast

Salt and pepper

In slow cooker, combine vegetables and both. Place turkey on top. Salt and pepper to taste. Cover. Cook on low 10 to 12 hours. Makes 6 to 8 servings.

TURKEY LOAF

1 cup herb seasoned stuffing mix, crushed

2 eggs

1 cup whole berry cranberry sauce, divided

2 pounds ground turkey

In medium bowl, combine all ingredients. Mix well. Coat inside slow cooker with cooking spray. In slow cooker, place meat mixture. Cover. Cook on low 4 to 6 hours. Heat remaining cranberry sauce in microwave for 1 minute. Serve sauce with loaf. Makes 4 servings.

ALICE WALKER, *an African-American novelist and poet, won a Pulitzer Prize for "The Color Purple" in 1982. It was made into a popular movie that helped make Oprah Winfrey known. She writes mainly of African-Americans in the South and of Africans. She has published novels, poetry, shorts stories, and essays.*

CLASSIC MARINARA SHRIMP

2 (15 ounce) jars refrigerated marinara sauce

3 cups frozen cooked shrimp without tails

1 cup sliced green onion

In slow cooker, combine all ingredients. Mix well. Cover. Cook on low 2½ to 3 hours. Makes 4 servings.

SWEET AND SOUR SHRIMP

1 (6 ounce) package Chinese pea pods, partially thawed

1 (13 ounce) can pineapple chucks, drained, juice reserved

1 (10 ounce) jar sweet and sour sauce

2 (4½ ounce) cans shrimp, rinsed, drained

In slow cooker, place pea pods and pineapple. In small bowl combine sweet and sour sauce and 3 tablespoons reserved pineapple juice. Mix well. Add mixture in slow cooker. Mix well. Cover. Cook on low 3 hours. Add shrimp. Mix well. Cover. Cook an additional 15 minutes. Serve with rice. Makes 2 to 3 servings.

PEGGY NOONAN is considered one of the best speech writers in the country. She was a producer at CBS News in NY and wrote daily radio commentary for Dan Rather. She became a speech writer and special assistant to President Ronald Reagan in 1984, and then speech writer for VP George H. Bush in his 1988 bid for the White House. She is author of books and is contributing editor of the Wall Street Journal, Time Magazine and Good Housekeeping.

FRESH COD FILLETS

2 large tomatoes, chopped

4 green onions, chopped

1 cup sliced fresh mushrooms

2 pounds fresh cod fillets

¼ cup butter, melted

1 teaspoon salt

In slow cooker, combine tomatoes, onions, and mushrooms. Place cod on mixture. Drizzle butter and sprinkle salt over cod. Cover. Cook on low 2½ to 3 hours. Makes 4 servings.

RED SNAPPER

2 medium green bell peppers, sliced

1 large onion, sliced

4 (8 ounce each) red snapper fillets

4 tablespoons butter

1 cup shredded Parmesan cheese

In slow cooker, layer green bell pepper and onions. Place red snapper over peppers and onions. Dot each snapper with butter. Sprinkle with cheese over top. Cover. Cook on low 3 to 4 hours or until fish flakes. Makes 4 servings.

THEODORA,
Byzantine empress,
was the daughter of
a circus animal
trainer and was an
actress and a
prostitute. Her
husband, Justinian
I, upon succeeding
to the throne in
527, made her joint
ruler of the empire.
She was stronger
than her husband,
and her actions
helped save the
throne in the Nika
riot over religious
differences.
Mosaics represent
her in the church
of San Vitale in
Ravenna.

FLAVOR OF FLORIDA FISH

1½ pounds cod fish fillets

1 small onion, sliced

2 teaspoons grated orange peel

2 teaspoons grated lemon peel

2 tablespoons butter or margarine, melted

Spray slow cooker with butter flavored cooking spray. In slow cooker, place fish. Add onions. Sprinkle orange and lemon peel. Drizzle butter over fish. Cover. Cook at low 1½ to 2 hours. Makes 5 to 6 servings.

CROCK THAT TUNA

3 pounds tuna, cut into serving size

¾ cup prepared ranch salad dressing

Place tuna on heavy foil. Cover tuna with salad dressing. Seal foil, place in slow cooker. Cover. Cook on high 2 hours or low 4 to 6 hours. Makes 6 servings.

The empire built by **MARGARET I**, *queen of Denmark, Norway and Sweden was one of the largest of Europe, but it did not last. She ruled Denmark and Norway after the death of her husband and son, then in 1389 defeated and captured the Swedish king. She persuaded the diets of the three countries to accept her grandnephew as king, but she remained the actual ruler until her death, ruling rather autocratically.*

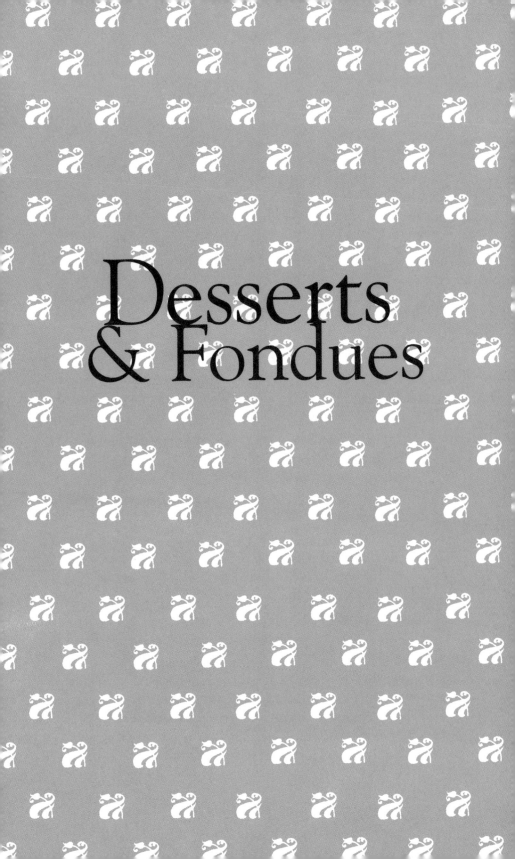

Desserts
& Fondues

Did You Know?

1. HELEN TAFT was the first First Lady to ride seated beside her husband for the inauguration day carriage ride in the Capitol. William H. Taft thought it was her day after all. The presidency had been her dream, not his. His dream was to be Chief Justice, which he realized in 1921.

2. The DIONNE QUINTUPLETS were born May 28, 1934, in Callendar, Ontario, the first recorded case in which all seven babies survived. They became a great tourist attraction, drawing people from all over the United States and Canada to see them.

3. In 1892 ELLA KNOWLES became the first woman in Montana to take the bar exam and passed it with one of the highest scores on record.

4. In 1656 MARY FISHER and ANN AUSTIN, the first Quaker missionaries to North America arrived in Boston. They were arrested and deported to Rhode Island, the only state that did not bar Quakers.

5. On March 12, 1912, the American Girl Guides were founded. In 1913 their name was changed to Girl Scouts.

6. GERTRUDE EDULE became the first woman to swim the English Channel on August 6, 1926. She did it in 14 hours 31 minutes—a new record for either sex.

7. The first monument to a woman financed by women was dedicated May 10, 1894, to Mary Ball Washington, mother of President George Washington. The National Mary Washington Memorial Association raised a fund of $11,500 to replace a neglected monument.

8. ELLA GRASSO was elected governor of Connecticut in 1974, the first woman governor in the United States whose husband had not been governor before her.

9. MARGARET JONES of Charlestown, part of present Boston, was the first person executed as a witch in America. At her 1648 trial she was accused of possessing a "malignant touch" that caused deafness or violent illness. As a result of the Salem witch trials, twenty persons were put to death on testimony of hysterical young women aged 9 to 19.

CHERRY DUMP DESSERT

2 (21 ounce) cans cherry pie filling

1 (18.25 ounce) box yellow cake mix

⅔ cup butter, melted

Coat inside slow cooker with cooking spray. Pour pie filling. Sprinkle with cake mix. Drizzle butter over top. Cover. Cook on high 4 hours. Serve with ice cream.

JUST LIKE PEACH COBBLER

⅓ cup buttermilk baking mix

⅔ cup quick oats

½ cup packed brown sugar

1 teaspoon cinnamon

4 (canned or fresh) cups peaches

½ cup peach juice or water

In medium bowl, combine buttermilk baking mix, oats, sugar, and cinnamon. Mix well. Coat inside slow cooker with cooking spray. Add mixture. Cover mixture with peaches and juice or water, Cover. Cook on low 5 hours. Take off lid. Cook additional 20 minutes. Makes 6 servings.

LADY JANE GRAY was Queen Jane of England for only nine days. Upon the death of the boy king Edward (who had named Lady Jane to follow him on the throne), Lady Jane was named Queen on July 10, 1553. The English people protested in favor of Mary I and the army deserted. Nine days later she was imprisoned and eventually beheaded in 1554.

PEACH TREE PEACHES

2 tablespoons butter or margarine, melted

6 fresh peaches, peeled, halved, seeded

½ cup packed brown sugar

1 teaspoon cinnamon

Whipped topping

In slow cooker, combine butter and peaches. Mix well. Sprinkle brown sugar over peaches. Cover. Cook on low 3 to 4 hours. Sprinkle cinnamon over peaches. Serve with whipped topping. Makes 4 servings.

PEACHES & CREAM

DIANE FEINSTEIN became mayor of San Francisco in 1978 after the assassination of George Muscone. In two full terms she revitalized the city's economy and reduced the crime rate 30%. She was elected to the U.S. Senate, a Democrat from California, in 1992, 1994, and in 2000. She takes a hard stand against crime and sponsored the Assault Weapons Ban and the Gun-Free School Act.

¼ cup water

6 fresh firm peaches, peeled, halved

3 tablespoons butter or margarine, melted

¼ cup packed brown sugar

1 tablespoon sugar

Ice cream

In slow cooker, pour water. Place peaches cut side up in water. Drizzle butter over top. In small bowl, combine brown sugar and sugar. Mix well. Sprinkle over peaches. Cover. Cook on low 3 to 4 hours or until tender. Serve with ice cream. Makes 6 servings.

HAWAII PINEAPPLE DESSERT

4 cups pineapple chunks

1 (11 ounce) can mandarin oranges, drained

⅓ cup packed brown sugar

¼ cup rum

2 tablespoons butter or margarine

$^1/_3$ cup shredded coconut, toasted

In slow cooker, combine pineapple, oranges, brown sugar, rum, and butter. Mix well. Cover. Cook on high 1½ to 2 hours or until bubbly. Sprinkle coconut over mixture. Serve warm. Makes 6 servings.

GLAZED PINEAPPLE

4 (8 ounce) cans pineapple chunks

1¼ cups sugar

½ cup cider vinegar

1 teaspoon cinnamon

¼ teaspoon ground cloves

Drain pineapple, reserving 1 cup. In slow cooker, place pineapple. In medium bowl, combine remaining ingredients. Mix well. Pour mixture over pineapple. Cover. Cook on low 2 to 3 hours.

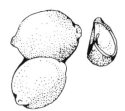

QUEEN ANNE, *the last Stuart ruler, was the first to rule over Great Britain when the Act of Union joined Scotland to England and Wales in 1707. Her reign was a transition to parliamentary government. She was the last English ruler to exercise the royal veto. She was devoted to the Church of England and created a trust fund for poor clerics, known as Queen Anne's Bounty.*

CARAMEL APPLES

2 (14 ounce) packages caramels

¼ cup water

8 medium apples

In slow cooker, combine caramels and water. Cover, and cook on high 1 to 1½ hours, stirring frequently. Insert sticks in stem of each apple. Dip apples in mixture, coat entire surface. Place on greased wax paper to cool. Makes 8 servings.

CARAMELS N' APPLES

4 large cooking apples, cored

½ cup apple juice

¼ cup packed brown sugar

2 tablespoons sugar

¼ teaspoon cinnamon

8 caramel candies

In slow cooker, place apples. Pour juice on top. In small bowl, combine brown sugar and cinnamon. Mix well. Sprinkle mixture over apples. Put 2 caramels in each apple. Cover. Cook on low 4 to 6 hours or until apples are tender. Makes 4 servings.

When she took the throne in 1558, England's fortunes were at a low ebb with religious strife and a huge government debt. During the 45 years reign of **ELIZABETH I,** *Queen of England, her country became a major power with a great navy, commerce and industry prospered, and English colonization was begun. This great period in English history produced William Shakespeare, Francis Bacon, Walter Raleigh, Francis Drake and other notable figures.*

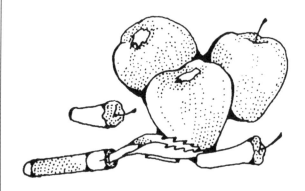

STUFFED APPLES

1/2 cup water

6 apples, cored

1/2 cup brown sugar

2 tablespoons raisins

2 tablespoons chopped walnuts

1 teaspoon cinnamon

2 tablespoons butter or margarine

In slow cooker, pour water. Place apples in water. In small bowl, combine sugar, raisins, walnuts, and cinnamon. Mix well. Fill core of apple with mixture. Dot each apple with butter. Cover. Cook on low 6 to 8 hours.

SLOW COOKED BAKED APPLES

1/2 cup water

1/4 cup sugar

1 teaspoon cinnamon

3 tablespoons raisins

4 large cooking apples, cored

3 tablespoons butter

In slow cooker, add water. In small bowl, combine sugar, cinnamon and raisins. Mix well.
Fill apple holes with mixture. Place in water. Dot with butter. Cover. Cook on low 4 to 6 hours. Serve hot with whipped cream. Makes 4 servings.

HATTIE WYATT CAROWAY *(Arkansas) filled his unexpired term in the U.S. Senate when her husband died in 1932. She became the first woman elected to the U.S. Senate (with the help of Huey Long) later that year. She failed to be re-nominated in 1944 and was appointed by FDR to the Federal Employees Compensation Commission.*

A LITTLE CHUNKY APPLESAUCE

8 large apples, peeled, cored, cubed

⅔ cup sugar

½ cup water

1 teaspoon cinnamon

In slow cooker, combine all ingredients. Cover. Cook on low 8 to 10 hours or high 3 to 4 hours.

APPLE AND CRANBERRY FRUIT DESSERT

8 apples, peeled, sliced

1½ cups fresh cranberries

1 cup boiling water

2 cups sugar, divided

¼ cup cornstarch

In slow cooker, combine apples, cranberries, water, and 1 cup sugar. Cover. Cook on low 6 to 8 hours. In small bowl, combine remaining sugar and cornstarch. Add to slow cooker. Mix well. Cover. Cook additional 20 minutes. Makes 6 servings.

SERENA and VENUS WILLIAMS, African-American *sisters began playing tennis before kindergarten. Unable to afford lessons, they were taught by there father from a book on tennis. They were the first sisters to each win grand slam titles. They are known for their powerful game and flashy outfits. Serena, 18 months younger and three inches shorter (5'10") than her sister, held all four grand slam titles at once in 2003–04.*

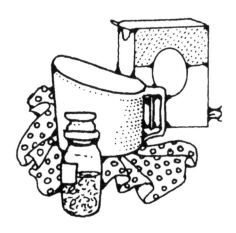

ALMOST APPLE CRISP

¾ cup packed brown sugar

⅔ cup quick cooking oats

⅓ cup sugar

2 tablespoons flour

¼ teaspoon cinnamon

5 cups peeled, sliced apples

⅓ cup raisins

3 tablespoons melted butter or margarine

In large bowl, combine brown sugar, oats, sugar, flour, and cinnamon. Mix well. Add apple slices and raisins. In slow cooker, pour apple mixture. Drizzle butter over mixture. Cover. Cook on low 6 to 8 hours.

CARAMEL ROLLS FOR DESSERT

¼ cup butter or margarine, melted

½ cup brown sugar

1 teaspoon cinnamon

¼ cup chopped walnuts

2 (8 ounce) packages refrigerated biscuits

Place butter in small bowl. In another small bowl, combine brown sugar and cinnamon. Mix well. Place nuts in small bowl. Dip each biscuit in butter. Roll in brown sugar then nuts. Place biscuits in slow cooker. Sprinkle remaining butter, brown sugar mixture and nuts over top of biscuits. Cover. Cook on high 3 to 4 hours.

LILIUOKALANI
was the last
reigning queen
of the Hawaiian
Islands. She
refused to recognize
constitutional
changes, and a
revolt led by
sugar planters
(Americans
mostly) cost her
the throne in 1893.
When she failed to
regain the throne
she moved to the
U.S. and brought
suit against the
government.
The Hawaiian
legislature voted
her a $4,000 per
year pension and
income from a
sugar plantation.
She wrote many
songs including
"Aloha Oe."

RAISIN BREAD PUDDING

6 cups dry French bread cubes

⅔ cup raisins

8 eggs

4 cups milk

⅔ cup sugar

1 teaspoon vanilla

1 teaspoon cinnamon

In slow cooker, spray with butter flavored cooking spray. Place bread cubes in bottom of slow cooker. Top bread with raisins. In large bowl, combine eggs, milk sugar, vanilla, and cinnamon. Mix well. Pour over bread cubes and raisins. Cover. Cook on high 3 hours.

RICE PUDDING

6 cups whole milk

1 cup regular white rice, uncooked

¾ cup sugar

1 teaspoon cinnamon

1 teaspoon vanilla

In slow cooker, combine all ingredients. Mix well. Cover. Cook on high 2 to 3 hours. Stir twice during cooking.

VIOLETA BARRIOS DE CHAMORRO *was the first woman to govern a Central American nation when she was elected President of Nicaragua in 1990. She instituted a program of national reconciliation, ended Sandanista control of the military and brought an end to the U.S. backed Contra war.*

COOK DON'T BAKE BROWNIES

2 (14 ounce) cans sweetened condensed milk

4 (1 ounce) squares unsweetened chocolate, chopped

1½ teaspoons vanilla

4 cups chocolate cookie crumbs

½ cup chopped walnuts

Coat slow cooker with cooking spray. Add milk and chocolate squares. Cover. Cook on high 1 to 1½ hours or until chocolate has melted. Add vanilla and cookies. Mix well. Spread mixture in greased 13 x 9 inch baking pan. Sprinkle nuts over mixture. Press nuts down with a spoon. Cover, chill. Makes 24 large brownies.

PACK-N-GO COOKIES

⅓ cup cocoa

¼ cup sugar

2 cups miniature marshmallows

1 cup peanut butter chips

½ cup butter

1¼ cups quick cooking oats

In slow cooker, combine cocoa and sugar. Add marshmallows, peanut butter chips, and butter. Cover. Cook on high 1½ hours. Reduce Heat to low, stirring often, until mixture is smooth. Add oats. Mix well. Drop by heaping teaspoon on wax paper. If mixture is too soft, let stand a few minutes before you drop mixture. Chill. Makes 24 cookies.

MARY QUEEN OF SCOTS *was executed in 1587 by Elizabeth I of England because of her strong claim to the throne and her Roman Catholic faith. Mary's beauty, charm and courage have made her a romantic figure in history. She is the subject of an opera and a number of plays.*

BUTTERSCOTCH KRISPIES

2 (6 ounce) packages butterscotch bits

1 tablespoon butter or margarine

6 cups rice krispies

In slow cooker, combine butterscotch bits and butter. Cover. Cook on high 1 hour. Mix well. Cook on low until mixture has melted. Stir in rice krispies. Drop by tablespoon onto wax paper. Makes 2 dozen.

QUICK VANILLA FUDGE

2 cups vanilla chocolate chips

1 cup sweetened condensed milk

2 cups chopped almonds, toasted

½ teaspoon vanilla extract

In slow cooker, combine chips and milk. Mix well. Cover. Cook on high 1 hour. Mix well. Cook on low until mixture is hot and smooth. Add almonds and vanilla. Mix well. Spread in greased baking pan. Cover, chill. Cut into squares. Makes 2 dozen.

SWEET TREAT FUDGE

3 cups semisweet chocolate chips

1 (14 ounce) can sweetened condensed milk

1 cup chopped nuts

1½ teaspoons vanilla

In slow cooker, combine chocolate chips and milk. Cover. Cook on low 2 hours. Add nuts and vanilla. Mix well. Spread mixture into greased 9 inch square pan. Chill until firm. Cut into squares. Makes 2 pounds.

CORAZON AQUINO *ran for president of the Philippines after her husband was killed by government agents. Both sides claimed victory in the 1986 election and Fernando Marcos refused to step down. Aquino organized strikes and boycotts, Marcos accepted asylum in the U.S., and she became the first woman president of the country. There were six coups attempts against her, and she did not run again.*

CHOCOLATE CLUSTERS

2 cups semisweet chocolate chips

1 (4 ounce) package sweet chocolate

2 pounds white chocolate, chopped

1½ cups peanuts

In slow cooker, combine all ingredients, except peanuts. Cook on high 1 hour. Mix well. Cook on low until chocolate has melted. Add peanuts. Mix well. Drop by teaspoonful on wax paper. Makes 3 dozen.

JAZZ UP CLUSTERS

1⅔ cups peanut butter chips

2 tablespoons shortening

1½ cups crushed thin pretzel sticks

1 cup honey graham cereal

½ cup sliced almonds

In slow cooker, combine peanut butter chips and shortening. Mix well. Cook on high 1½ hours or until mixture has melted. Add pretzel sticks, cereal and almonds. Drop mixture by heaping tablespoon on wax paper. Cool. Makes 15 clusters.

*In 1945 **BETTY MAE JUMPER** and her cousin became the first Florida Seminole to graduate from high school (a school in Cherokee, NC). She became a nurse and launched a tribal newsletter. In 1967 she was elected head of the Tribal Council, the first woman leader of the Seminoles. After she left office she became publisher of the Seminole Tribune newspaper.*

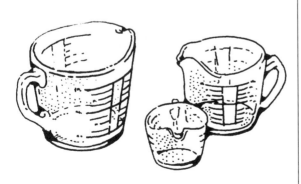

239

CRAVING FOR CLUSTERS

4 cups peanut butter

2 (16 ounce) packages semisweet chocolate chips

2 (12 ounce) packages salted peanuts

In slow cooker, combine peanut butter and chocolate chips. Cover. Cook on low 2 hours or until mixture has melted. Add peanuts. Mix well. Drop mixture by heaping teaspoon on wax paper. Cool. Makes 3½ dozen

CANDIED PRETZEL TREATS

2 (16 ounce) packages almond bark

4 tablespoons vegetable oil

4 dozen pretzels

1 cup confectioners' sugar

In slow cooker, combine almond bark and oil. Cook on high 1½ hours until melted. Mix well. Dip pretzel in mixture. Roll in sugar. Place on wax paper and chill. Makes 48 pretzels.

MYRA C. SELBY *was the first woman and the first African-American to serve as an associate justice on the Indiana Supreme Court, 1995–99. She helped make major decisions regarding insurance, state property taxes and tort law reform. She lectures widely and is a columnist for the Indianapolis Business Journal.*

NO FUSS CHOCOLATE DROPS

4 cups milk chocolate chips

2 teaspoons shortening

1 cup raisins

1 cup walnuts

In slow cooker, combine chocolate chips and shortening. Cover. Cook on high 1 hour. Reduce heat to low, cook until mixture has melted. Add raisins and walnuts. Mix well. Drop mixture by heaping tablespoon on wax paper. Chill. Makes 3½ dozen.

CHOCOLATE COVERED PEANUTS

2 pounds chocolate flavored almond bark

1 (12 ounce) package semi sweet chocolate chips

3½ cups dry roasted peanuts

In slow cooker, combine all ingredients, except peanuts. Cover. Cook on low, stirring every 15 minutes for 1½ hours. Add peanuts. Cook an additional 15 minutes. Drop by tablespoon onto wax paper. Cool.

CARRIE CHAPMAN CATT was a leader for women's suffrage not only in this country, but in Canada and Europe. As head of the National American Women Suffrage Association, she helped develop the winning plan that led to state-by-state enactments of suffrage and the final victory in 1920. She also founded the League of Women Voters.

MILK CHOCOLATE FONDUE

1 (16 ounce) can chocolate flavored syrup

1 (14 ounce) can sweetened condensed milk

1½ teaspoons vanilla extract

In slow cooker, combine chocolate and milk. Mix well. Cover. Cook on low 1½ hours. Add vanilla just before serving. Mix well. Serve with marshmallows, pound cake, angel food cake, fresh fruit chunks.

FUDGY PEANUT BUTTER FONDUE

⅓ cup unsweetened cocoa powder

½ cup sugar

½ cup sweetened condensed milk

3 tablespoons peanut butter

1 teaspoon vanilla

In slow cooker, combine cocoa powder, sugar, milk, and peanut butter. Mix well. Cover. Cook on low 1½ hours. Add vanilla just before serving. Mix well. Serve with fruit chunks or cake.

PEANUT BUTTER FONDUE

1⅓ cups peanut butter

1⅓ cups sweetened condensed milk

1 cup honey

1 teaspoon cinnamon

In slow cooker, combine all ingredients. Cover. Cook on low 1½ hours. Mix after 30 minutes. Serve with sliced fruit or French bread chunks.

MARY BARRET DYER (?–1660) *was banished from the Massachusetts Bay Colony, moved back to England and became a disciple of the founder of Quakerism. She returned to Boston, was arrested, imprisoned and expelled for teaching the Quaker faith. She kept returning to Boston until she was arrested and hanged. Her death helped bring about a move for religious tolerance in the colonies.*

MOCHA FONDUE

½ pound milk chocolate, broken in pieces

1 cup sweetened condensed milk

¼ cup water

3 teaspoons instant coffee

½ teaspoon vanilla

In slow cooker, combine chocolate, condensed milk, and water. Cover. Cook on low 1 hour. Stir after 30 minutes. Add coffee and vanilla. Mix well. Cover. Cook an additional 30 minutes. Serve with pound or angel food cake and fruit slices.

CANDY BAR FONDUE

Butter flavored cooking spray

16 (1 ounce) chocolate candy bars, broken into pieces

30 large marshmallows

⅓ cup sweetened condensed milk

½ pint whipping cream

In slow cooker, spray with cooking spray. Add candy bars, marshmallows, and milk. Cover. Cook on low 1 hour. Stir every 30 minutes. Add whipping cream slowly. Mix well. Cover. Cook an additional 1½ to 2 hours. Serve with pound or angel food cake and sliced fruit.

SYLVIA EARLE, PH.D., is an internationally known marine biologist, sometimes known as "Her Deepness" or "The Sturgeon General." She has led more than 50 expeditions totaling over 6,000 hours underwater. She holds numerous diving records, including the women's depth record for solo diving, 3,300 feet.

CARAMEL FONDUE

1 (12 ounce) can sweetened condensed milk

1 cup brown sugar

½ cup light corn syrup

½ cup butter

In slow cooker, combine all ingredients. Mix well. Cover. Cook on low 2 to 3 hours. Serve with fruit slices and cookies. Makes 3 cups of dip.

PEACHES AND CREAM FONDUE

2 (16 ounce) cans sliced peaches, drained

1¼ cups sweetened condensed milk

2 tablespoons confectioners' sugar

In blender, puree peaches. In slow cooker, combine all ingredients. Cover. Cook on low 1½ hours. Serve with pound or angel food cake.

CRYSTAL EASTMAN *was co-founder of the American Civil Liberties Union and wrote the first national labor safety law guidelines. She was one of four authors of the Equal Rights Amendment proposed in 1923. She was blacklisted for her left-wing political views and spent several years in England.*

Adaptations, Substitutions, Herbs & Spices

ADAPT MOST RECIPES TO A SLOW COOKER FOR HASSLE FREE COOKING

CROCK POT® AND SLOW COOKERS ARE THE SAME

YOU CAN PREPARE just about any type of meal in a Slow Cooker. There is nothing easier then putting ingredients into a Slow Cooker in the morning, and coming home to a hot cooked meal. Here are some tips to help adapt your recipes for successful cooking in your Slow Cooker. Several factors can affect your recipes, so REMEMBER THESE TIPS.

Cooking time in all recipes are approximations, affected by how much food is in the cooker, humidity, the temperature of the ingredients when you add them; so note that cooking times in the recipes are ranges only.

To make cleanup easier, spray the inside of the Slow Cooker with non-stick cooking spray before adding food.

Meats will not brown in a Slow Cooker. If a recipes calls for meat to be browned, brown it in a skillet. The recipe will be better, it will enhance the flavor and decrease fat.

A Slow Cooker is great for tougher cuts of meat.

It is always better to thaw meat before placing it in the Slow Cooker. It will cook faster.

Fill cooker between half and two-thirds full.

Add vegetables to cooker first, then add meat. Vegetables cook slower than meat.

Cut vegetables in smaller pieces to ensure proper cooking.

Do not add as much water as regular recipes indicate. Use about half the recommended amount, unless it calls for rice or pasta. Liquids don't boil away as in conventional cooking.

If recipe calls for raw rice, add ¼ cup extra liquid per ¼ cup of raw rice

If recipe calls for pasta or rice, cook until slightly tender.

If recipe calls for dry beans, it is best to cook beans before adding to recipe.

In the last hour of cooking it is better to add milk, sour cream or cream to the recipe. Dairy products tend to curdle over long cooking periods. Condensed cream of soup or evaporated milk can be substituted in some recipes.

Processed cheeses tend to work better in Slow Cookers than natural cheese.

Juices can be thickened by adding corn starch during the last hour of cooking. Turn heat to high.

It is best to add ground seasoning near the end of cooking.

COOKING GUIDE
FOR ADAPTING RECIPES

TIME GUIDE

If recipe says cook or bake	Slow Cooker on Low	Slow Cooker on High
15 to 30 minutes	4 to 6 hours	1½ to 2 hours
35 to 45 minutes	6 to 10 hours	3 to 4 hours
50 minutes to 3 hours	8 to 15 hours	4 to 6 hours

SLOW COOKER DON'TS

• DON'T remove the lid during cooking unless recipe calls for it. Every time you lift the lid you will slow the cooking time by 20 to 30 minutes.

• DON'T leave food in the Crock Pot®. Remove food within one hour.

• DON'T reheat food in a Crock Pot® because it takes too much time for food to reach a safe temperature.

• DON'T add water to clean the cooker until it has cooled.

• DON'T use metal utensils; use rubber, plastic or wood to avoid damaging interior of the Crock Pot®s.

SUBSTITUTIONS
OUT OF THIS INGREDIENT?
THEN SUBSTITUTE:

INGREDIENT	AMOUNT	SUBSTITUTE
Allspice	1 teaspoon	½ teaspoon cinnamon and ½ teaspoon ground cloves
Baking Powder	1 teaspoon	¼ teaspoon baking soda and 1 teaspoon cream of tartar
Broth-beef or chicken	1 cup	1 bouillon cube dissolved in 1 cup boiling water
Catsup	1 cup	1 cup tomato sauce, ½ cup sugar and 2 teaspoons vinegar
Chives, finely chopped	2 teaspoons	2 teaspoons finely chopped green onion tips
Chocolate chips-semi sweet	1 ounce	1 ounce sweet cooking chocolate
Cornstarch-for thickening	1 tablespoon	2 tablespoons all-purpose flour 4 to 6 teaspoons quick cooking tapioca
Cracker Crumbs	¾ cup	1 cup bread crumbs
Cream Cheese	1 cup	cottage cheese beaten until smooth
Dry Mustard	1 teaspoon	1 tablespoon prepared mustard
Flour, cake	1 cup sifted	1 cup minus 2 teaspoons all-purpose flour
Flour, self rising	1 cup	1 cup minus 2 teaspoons all-purpose flour plus 1½ teaspoons baking powder and ½ teaspoon salt
Herbs, fresh	1 tablespoon	1 teaspoon dried herbs
Milk, sour	1 cup	1 tablespoon lemon juice and 1 cup milk
Milk, buttermilk	1 cup	1 cup plain yogurt

INGREDIENT	AMOUNT	SUBSTITUTE
Milk, whole	1 cup	½ cup evaporated milk
Onion, fresh	1 small	1 tablespoon minced onion, dehydrated
Sugar, brown	½ cup	2 tablespoons molasses in ½ cup granulated sugar
Sugar, confectioner's	1 cup	1 cup granulated sugar plus 1 teaspoon cornstarch
Sugar, maple	½ cup	1 cup maple syrup
Tomatoes, fresh	2 cups	1 (16 ounce) can diced tomatoes
Tomato sauce	1 (15-ounce) can	1 (6-ounce) can tomato paste plus cup water
Wine	1 cup	13 tablespoons water, 3 tablespoons lemon juice and 1 tablespoon sugar
Worcestershire sauce	1 teaspoon	1 teaspoon bottled steak sauce
Yogurt	1 cup	1 cup sour cream

MEASUREMENTS FOR COOKING

3 teaspoons... 1 tablespoon

2 tablespoons.. 1 fluid ounce

4 tablespoons.. ¼ cup

5 tablespoons plus 1 teaspoon .... ⅓ cup

8 tablespoons.. ½ cup

16 tablespoons....................................... 1 cup

Dash.. less than ⅛ teaspoon

Pinch.. as much as can be taken between tip of fingers and thumb

HERBS AND SPICES
ARE USED FOR WHAT?

BASIL — Good with stews, roast beef, ground beef, lamb, fish, vegetables, and omelets.

BAY LEAVES — Has a pungent flavor. Good in seafood, stews, and vegetable dishes.

CARAWAY — Use in breads, soups, cakes, cheese, and sauerkraut.

CHIVES — Good in salads, fish, soups, and potatoes.

CILANTRO — Southwestern dishes, rice, beans, salads, fish, and chicken.

CURRY POWDER — A combination of spices that give a distinct flavor to meat, poultry, fish, and vegetables.

DILL — Both seeds and leaves may be used. Leaves can be used as a garnish or cooked with soup, fish, potatoes, and beans.

FENNEL — Has a hot, sweet flavor. Small quantities are used in pies and baked goods, and the leaves can be boiled with fish.

GINGER — It is a pungent root and is used in pickles, cakes, cookies, preserves, soups, and meat dishes.

MARJORAM — It adds flavor to stew, stuffing, lamb, fish, poultry, and omelets.

MINT — It is great in beverages, soup, peas, carrots, lamb, cheese, preserves and fruit desserts.

OREGANO — It can be used whole or ground, in pizza, tomato juice, fish, eggs, omelets, stew, gravy, poultry, and vegetables.

PAPRIKA — A bright red pepper that is used as a garnish for potatoes, salads, and eggs, and as a spice used in meat, vegetables, and soup.

PARSLEY — Can be used dried as seasoning or garnish. Use in fish, soup, meat, stuffing, and mixed greens.

ROSEMARY — It can be used to season fish, stuffing, beef, lamb, poultry, onions, eggs, bread, and potatoes. It is great in dressings.

SAFFRON — It is used in breads, soup, rice, and chicken.

SAGE — May be used in stuffing, fish, omelets, poultry, tomato juice, breads, and cheese spreads.

TARRAGON — Used in salads, sauces, fish, poultry, tomatoes, eggs, carrots, green beans, and dressing.

THYME — Leaves may be sprinkled on fish or poultry before baking or broiling.

IT MAKES HOW MUCH?

FOOD FOR INGREDIENTS	QUANTITY	YIELDS
Apple	1 medium	1 cup
Bread Crumbs	1 slice	¼ cup
Butter	1 stick	½ cup
Egg whites	8 to 10	1 cup
Egg yolks	10 to 12	1 cup
Lemon	1 medium	3 tablespoons lemon juice
Noodles, uncooked	1½ cups	2 to 3 cups cooked
Macaroni, uncooked	1¼ cups	2½ cups cooked
Spaghetti	8 ounces	4½ cups cooked
Nuts, chopped	¼ pound	1 cup
Nuts, walnuts, unshelled	1 pound	1½ cups
Onion, chopped	1 medium	½ cup
Rice, regular	1 cup	3 cups cooked
Rice, wild	1 cup	4 cups cooked
Sugar, brown	1 pound	2½ cups
Sugar, white	1 pound	2 cups

INDEX

A

A Little Chunky Applesauce, 234
A Robust Beef Brisket, 169
After the Game Tacos, 153
After Work Swiss Steak, 169
Alfredo Topped Baked Potatoes, 89
Almost Apple Crisp, 235
Almost Baked Ravioli, 122
Almost BBQ Chicken, 207
Almost Like Mom's Potato Soup, 50
Aloha Beanie Wiennie Casserole, 130
Alphabet Soup, 61
Amazing Asparagus & Chicken
  Casserole, 143
America's Pot Roast, 159
Another Pepper Chicken, 215
Anytime Roast, 165
Apple and Cranberry Fruit Dessert, 234
Apricot Chicken, 201
Apricot Glazed Chicken, 201
Artichoke Dip, 15

APPETIZERS (Also see: Dips and
Spreads)
  Barbecue Chicken Wings, 31
  Barbecued Meatballs, 35
  BBQ Cocktail Wieners, 30
  Beef Burger Bites, 34
  Budget Party Links, 30
  Cheddar Cheese Fondue, 36
  Gotta Have Hot Dog Roll Ups, 29
  Having a Party Cheese Ball, 27
  Jalapeno Cocktail Wieners, 28
  Just Wing It, 34
  Little Smokies Links, 30
  Mad About Mushrooms, 15
  Nachos, 27
  Nuts About Walnuts, 28
  Party Cocktail Wieners, 31
  Party Time Meatballs, 34
  Pretzel Twist Nibblers, 35
  Saucy Sweet Chicken Wings, 33
  Smoke'n Hot Wings, 32
  So Good Chicken Wings, 33
  Spicy Honey Wings, 32
  Sweet and Sour Cocktail Wieners, 29
  Swiss Cheese Fondue, 36

B

Backyard BBQ Chicken, 208
Bacon Potato Casserole, 139
Barbecue Chicken Breasts, 208
Barbecue Chicken Wings, 31
Barbecue Spareribs, 194
Barbecued Meatballs, 35
Barbeque Pork Ribs, 192
Barbeque Sandwiches, 156
Bayside Clam Chowder, 56
BBQ Cocktail Wieners, 30
BBQ Ham Slices, 198
BBQ Hamburgers, 155
BBQ Roast Beef, 166
Beanie Wienie Casserole, 130
Beans with Bacon Soup, 60
Beef & Mac, 112
Beef & Tater-Tots Casserole, 145
Beef Burger Bites, 43
Beef Chuck Roast, 162
Beef Green Chile Stew, 63
Beef Mixture on Rice, 150
Beef Potato Soup, 51
Beef Short Ribs, 167
Beef Sirloin Stew, 68
Beef Stew, 66

Beef Stroganoff, 126
Beefy Mushroom Stew, 67
Beefy Noodle Soup, 58
Bell Pepper Soup, 54
Berry-Licous Chicken, 202
Best Bow Tie Pasta, 113
Beyond Easy Beef Roast, 164
Bit Special Green Beans, 84
Black Bean Soup, 60
Black Eyed Pea Roast, 167
Boneless Pork Roast, 181
Bow Tie Pasta, 114
Brisket Marinade, 169
Broccoli Cheddar Cheese Soup, 40
Broccoli Cheese Dip, 24
Broccoli Cheese Soup, 39
Broccoli Cheese Soup, 41
Broccoli Dip, 24
Broccoli, 78
Broccoli, Cauliflower & Cheese, 77
Budget Party Links, 30
Butter Bean Soup, 46
Butterscotch Krispies, 238

BEANS
Aloha Beanie Wiennie Casserole, 130
Beanie Wiennie Casserole, 130
Beans With Bacon Soup, 60
Beans, Ham & Butter, 103
Bit Special Green Beans, 84
Black Bean Soup, 60
Butter Bean Soup, 46
Cajun Beans & Sausage, 104
Chuck Wagon BBQ Beans, 105
Don't Bake It Green Beans, 84
Just Beef & Beans, 85
Navy Beans & Ham Hack, 104
New Twist Bake Beans, 107
Not Just Beans 'N Wieners, 129
Pork & Beans Supper, 102
Quick Trick Bake Beans, 105
Refried Beans Dish, 102
Route 66 Baked Beans, 106
Salsa Beans, 107

Sausage & Beans Stew, 64
Shortcut Beans & Ham, 103
Shortcut Butter Beans, 102
Touchdown Baked Beans, 106

BEEF
A Robust Beef Brisket, 169
After Work Swiss Steak, 169
America's Pot Roast, 159
Anytime Roast, 165
Barbecued Meatballs, 35
Barbeque Sandwiches, 156
BBQ Hamburgers, 155
BBQ Roast Beef, 166
Beef & Mac, 112
Beef & Tater-Tots Casserole, 145
Beef Burger Bites, 34
Beef Chuck Roast, 162
Beef Green Chile Stew, 63
Beef Mixture on Rice, 150
Beef Potato Soup,51
Beef Short Ribs, 167
Beef Sirloin Stew, 68
Beef Stew, 66
Beef Stroganoff, 126
Beefy Mushroom Stew, 67
Beefy Noodle Soup, 58
Beyond Easy Beef Roast, 164
Black Eyed Pea Roast, 167
Brisket Marinade, 169
Cabbage With Beef, 134
Chill Out Beef Soup, 44
Chuck Roast, 160
Cook & Slice Brisket, 168
Corned Beef Pasta, 117
Corned Beef Ruebens, 180
Crazy Cajun Pot Roast, 166
Creamy Style Swiss Steak, 170
Delicious Chuck Roast, 163
Easy Fix'n Beef Soup, 43
Easy Supper, 143
Fixin Beef Burgers, 155
French Dip Sandwiches, 177
Game Time Joes, 145

Greek Pasta, 109
Ground Beef Soup, 45
Hearty Beef Stew, 68
Hearty Meat Loaf, 173
Home-Style Roast, 163
Irish Corned Beef Brisket, 168
Is It Goulash, 113
Italian Beef Roast, 161
Italian Style Beef Roast, 162
Italian Style Round Steak, 172
Just a Meatloaf, 175
Just Beef & Beans, 85
Lasagna, 108
Lazy Day Meatloaf, 174
Little Bite Beef Soup, 44
Mama Mia's Meatball Soup, 46
Meat Loaf, 176
Meatball Sandwiches, 178
Meatball Soup, 47
Meatballs and Gravy Sandwiches, 179
Meatloaf for Dinner, 175
Mexi Meatloaf, 173
Mix It & Go Roast, 160
Mix it Quick Meat Loaf, 172
Mix It Up Meatloaf, 176
No Fuss Veggie Beef Soup, 46
Oh So Delicious Roast, 161
Out All Day Beef Stroganoff, 127
Party Time Meatballs, 34
Peppers and Swiss Steak, 171
Pizza Sloppy Joes, 180
Pot Roast Dinner, 159
Pot Roast on the Go, 160
Round Steak and Mushroom Gravy, 171
Santa Fe Beef Fajitas, 178
Short Steps Stroganoff, 127
Shredded Beef Sandwiches, 177
Slow Cooker Swiss Steak, 170
Souped Up Beef Casserole, 128
Southwest Beef Roast, 164
Steak Casserole, 128
Sunday Supper Roast, 165

Tasty Beef Burgers, 179
Teriyaki Roast, 165
Texas Beef Stew, 67
Texas Meatloaf, 174
Veggie Beef Soup, 45

BEVERAGES
Caramel Apple Cider, 13
Chill Out Apple Juice, 14
Hot Cider Punch, 13
Hot Cran-Apple Cider, 14
Hot Irish Mocha, 12
Hot Juice Warm-Ups, 12
Hot Party Punch, 12
Mocha Cappuccino, 11
Mocha Coffee, 11
Sippin Apple Cider, 14
Spicy Hot Cider, 13
Wide Awake Coffee, 11

BREADS
Caramel Rolls for Dessert, 235
Easy to Make Dressing, 153
No Bake Dressing, 154
Raisin Bread Pudding, 236

C
C'mon Over Cheese Dip, 23
Cabbage & Corned Beef Casserole, 137
Cabbage & Ham, 81
Cabbage Patch Stew, 65
Cabbage With Beef, 134
Cabbage, 82
Cajun Beans & Sausage, 104
Candied Carrots, 86
Candied Pretzel Treats, 240
Candied Sweet Potatoes, 101
Candy Bar Fondue, 243
Caramel Apple Cider, 13
Caramel Apples, 232
Caramel Fondue, 244
Caramel Rolls for Dessert, 235

Caramels N' Apples, 232
Carrot Casserole, 147
Cauliflower & Broccoli, 77
Celery Around Pork Chops, 185
Cheddar & Broccoli, 78
Cheddar Cheese Fondue, 36
Cheddar Cheese Soup, 40
Cheddar Cheese Soup, 41
Cheddar Potatoes, 91
Cheese & Broccoli, 78
Cheese & Shrimp Dip, 17
Cheese Pasta Bake, 112
Cheesy Broccoli Soup, 40
Cheesy Crab Dip, 17
Cheesy Potato Soup, 52
Cheesy Steak Fries, 93
Cheesy Taters, 92
Cheesy Tuna Casserole, 145
Cherry Dump Dessert, 229
Chicken & Drop Dumplings, 142
Chicken & Rice Dish, 148
Chicken & Wild Rice Soup, 57
Chicken & Wild Rice, 152
Chicken and Broccoli Alfredo, 116
Chicken and Rice, 149
Chicken Burritos, 210
Chicken Cacciatore, 210
Chicken Cheese Spread, 26
Chicken Chili Made Special, 73
Chicken Chili, 70
Chicken Cordon Bleu, 214
Chicken Dump Soup, 59
Chicken in Mushroom Gravy, 205
Chicken Loaf, 217
Chicken N' Noodles, 114
Chicken Noodle Casserole, 115
Chicken Stew, 69
Chile Con Queso Dip, 19
Chili & Tamale Casserole, 133
Chili Con Carne, 73
Chili Dogs 'n One Pot, 74
Chili Soup, 49
Chili Spaghetti, 117

Chill Out Apple Juice, 14
Chill Out Beef Soup, 44
Chipped Beef Chicken, 212
Chipped Beef on Toast, 153
Chocolate Clusters, 239
Chocolate Covered Peanuts, 241
Chops Stick Ribs, 192
Chuck Roast, 160
Chuck Wagon BBQ Beans, 105
Chunky Chili, 74
City Slicker Bratwurst, 199
Classic Marinara Shrimp, 224
Classic Potatoes, 95
Complete BBQ Turkey Meal, 221
Con Queso Dip, 18
Cook & Slice Brisket, 168
Cook Don't Bake Brownies, 237
Corn & Green Chile Dish, 83
Corn Chowder, 55
Corned Beef Pasta, 117
Corned Beef Ruebens, 180
Country BBQ Ribs, 193
Cowboy Chili Casserole, 140
Crab Cheese Spread, 26
Cran-Apple Pork Chops, 185
Cranberry Lover's Chicken, 202
Cranberry Roast, 184
Craving for Clusters, 240
Crazy Cajun Pot Roast, 166
Creamed Corn, 83
Creamy Broccoli Soup, 39
Creamy Garlic Chicken, 219
Creamy Green Chile Rice, 151
Creamy Style Swiss Steak, 170
Creamy Tomato Soup, 48
Crock That Tuna, 226
Curry Tomato Soup, 48

CANDY
    Candied Pretzel Treats, 240
    Chocolate Clusters, 239
    Chocolate Covered Peanuts, 241
    Craving for Clusters, 240

Jazz up Clusters, 239
No Fuss Chocolate Drops, 241

CASSEROLES
Aloha Beanie Wiennie Casserole, 130
Amazing Asparagus Chicken
   Casserole, 143
Bacon Potato Casserole, 139
Beanie Wiennie Casserole, 130
Beef & Tater-Tots Casserole, 145
Cabbage & Corned Beef Casserole,
   137
Carrot Casserole, 147
Cheesy Tuna Casserole, 145
Chicken Noodle Casserole, 115
Chili & Tamale Casserole, 133
Cowboy Chili Casserole, 140
Enchilada Casserole, 131
Italian Sausage Potato Casserole, 139
Kids Love it Cheeseburger Casserole,
   138
Layered Casserole, 136
Layered Mexican Casserole, 132
Meatball & Hash Brown Casserole,
   136
Mexican Casserole, 133
On the Run Tuna Casserole, 1355
One Dish Chicken Casserole, 140
Potatoes & Sausage Casserole, 129
Potluck Tater Casserole, 135
Sausage and Hash Brown Casserole,
   138
Shoestring Casserole, 146
Souped Up Casserole, 128
Steak Casserole, 128
Stir Fry Chicken Casserole, 141
Taco Casserole, 132
Tuna & Spinach Casserole, 144
Tuna Casserole, 137
Veggi & Sausage Casserole, 148

CHICKEN/TURKEY
Almost BBQ Chicken, 207

Amazing Asparagus & Chicken
   Casserole, 143
Another Pepper Chicken, 215
Apricot Chicken, 201
Apricot Glazed Chicken, 201
Backyard BBQ Chicken, 208
Barbecue Chicken Breasts, 208
Barbecue Chicken Wings, 31
Berry-Licous Chicken, 202
Chicken & Drop Dumplings, 142
Chicken & Rice Dish, 148
Chicken & Rice, 149
Chicken & Wild Rice Soup, 57
Chicken & Wild Rice, 152
Chicken and Broccoli Alfredo, 116
Chicken Burritos, 210
Chicken Cacciatore, 210
Chicken Chili Made Special, 73
Chicken Chili, 70
Chicken Cordon Bleu, 214
Chicken Dump Soup, 59
Chicken in Mushroom Gravy, 205
Chicken Loaf, 217
Chicken N' Noodles, 114
Chicken Noodle Casserole, 115
Chicken Stew, 69
Chipped Beef Chicken, 212
Complete BBQ Turkey Meal, 221
Cranberry Lover's Chicken, 202
Creamy Garlic Chicken, 219
Easy to Make Turkey, 219
Family Pleasing Chicken, 219
Garlic Chicken, 213
Glaze Over Chicken Breast, 202
Green Chile Chicken Alfredo, 115
Honey Dijon Chicken, 200
Honey Mustard Chicken, 200
Hungry Man's Chicken, 216
Italian Chicken, 212
Just Wing It, 34
Keep it Simple Chicken, 211
Leftover Chicken and Vegetable Soup,
   61

Lemon Chicken, 203
Lemon Over Chicken, 203
Mediterranean Turkey, 222
Mixed Up Chicken, 211
More Than Chicken Soup, 42
Mushroom Chicken, 206
Nacho Chicken, 209
New Mexico Style Chicken, 209
Olive Chicken, 216
One Dish Chicken Casserole, 140
One for all Chicken Dinner, 141
One Pot Chicken Dinner, 146
Pepper Chicken, 214
Pineapple Chicken, 201
Pizza Chicken Pasta, 109
Play 'N Eat Chicken Dinner, 142
Roasted Chicken, 206
Roasted Turkey Breast, 222
Salsa Chicken, 209
Saucy Chicken Sandwiches, 217
Saucy Sweet Chicken Wings, 33
Seasoned Turkey, 221
Shopping Day Chicken, 207
Simply Chicken, 212
Smoke'n Hot Wings, 32
So Good Chicken Wings, 33
Spicy Honey Wings, 32
Spinach & Chicken Pasta, 111
Spunky BBQ Chicken, 208
Stir Fy Chicken Casserole, 141
Stuffing Top Chicken, 218
Sweet & Sour Chicken, 204
Sweet & Tasty Chicken, 204
Sweet Potato Chicken, 215
Swiss Slow Cooked Chicken, 213
Taste of the Orient Chicken, 205
Tasty Chicken Italiano, 218
Tasty Turkey, 223
Turkey & Vegetable Soup, 49
Turkey & Vegetable Soup, 49
Turkey and Stuffing, 220
Turkey and Vegetables, 223
Turkey Anytime, 220

Turkey Loaf, 223
Turkey Sloppy Joes, 155

CHILI
Chicken Chili Made Special, 73
    Chicken Chili, 70
    Chili Con Carne, 73
    Chili Dogs 'n One Pot, 74
    Chili Soup, 49
    Chili Spaghetti, 117
    Chunky Chili, 74
    Cowboy Chili Casserole, 140
    Everyday Chili, 71
    Hurry Up Chili, 70
    Out All Day Chili, 72
    Quick Draw Chili, 71
    Slow Cooked Chili, 72

CHOCOLATE
    Candied Pretzel Treats, 240
    Candy Bar Fondue, 243
    Chocolate Clusters, 239
    Chocolate Covered Peanuts, 241
    Cook Don't Bake Brownies, 237
    Craving for Clusters, 240
    Fudgy Peanut Butter Fondue, 242
    Milk Chocolate Fondue, 242
    Mocha Fondue, 243
    No Fuss Chocolate Drops, 241
    Pack-N-Go Cookies, 237
    Sweet Treat Fudge, 238

COOKIES, BROWNIES AND BARS
    Butterscotch Krispies, 238
    Cook Don't Bake Brownies, 237
    Pack-N-Go Cookies, 237

D
Delicious Chuck Roast, 163
Delicious Creamy Potatoes, 93
Don't Bake it Green Beans, 84
Don't Be a Crab Dip, 16

Don't Pass Up Topper, 125

DESSERTS
  A Little Chunky Applesauce, 234
  Almost Apple Crisp, 235
  Apple and Cranberry Fruit Dessert, 234
  Caramel Apples, 232
  Caramels N' Apples, 232
  Cherry Dump Dessert, 229
  Glazed Pineapple, 231
  Hawaii Pineapple Dessert, 231
  Just Like Peach Cobbler, 229
  Peach Tree Peaches, 230
  Peaches & Cream, 230
  Peaches and Cream Fondue, 224
  Raisin Bread Pudding, 236
  Slow Cooked Baked Apples, 233
  Stuffed Apples, 233

DIPS AND SPREADS
  Artichoke Dip, 15
  Broccoli Cheese Dip, 24
  Broccoli Dip, 24
  C'mon Over Cheese Dip, 23
  Cheese & Shrimp Dip, 17
  Cheesy Crab Dip, 17
  Chicken Cheese Spread, 26
  Chile Con Queso Dip, 19
  Con Queso Dip, 18
  Crab Cheese Spread, 26
  Don't Be a Crab Dip, 16
  Easy Artichoke Dip, 16
  Easy Party Cheese Dip, 23
  Game Time Cheese Dip, 20
  Ham & Cheese Dip, 22
  Ham & Veggie Dip, 22
  Having a Party Cheese Ball, 27
  Italian Pizza Dip, 21
  Nacho Party Snack Dip, 19
  Onion Dip, 22
  Party Time Shrimp Dip, 17
  Pepperoni Dip, 21
  Pizza Dip, 21

  Pumpkin Butter Spread, 25
  Reuben Spread, 25
  Salsa Mexi Dip, 19
  Seaside Clam Dip, 16
  Sizzlin Beef Dip, 20
  Taco Cheese Dip, 18
  Taco Dip, 18
  Tipsy Cheese Dip, 20

E
Easy Artichoke Dip, 16
Easy Barbeque Ribs, 194
Easy Fix'n Beef Soup, 43
Easy Party Cheese Dip, 23
Easy Supper, 143
Easy to Make Dressing, 153
Easy to Make Turkey, 219
Easy Vegetable Dish, 79
Enchilada Casserole, 131
Everyday Chili, 71
Extra Cheesy Has Browns, 94

F
Family Pleasing Chicken, 219
Fettuccine Noodles, 116
Fix & Go Stew, 65
Fixin Beef Burgers, 155
Flavor of Florida Fish, 226
Flavor Packed Pork Roast, 181
Fork Tender Short Ribs, 194
French Dip Sandwiches, 177
Fresh Cod Fillets, 225
Fudgy Peanut Butter Fondue, 242

FRUIT
  A Little Chunky Applesauce, 234
  Almost Apple Crisp, 235
  Apple and Cranberry Fruit Dessert, 234
  Caramel Apples, 232
  Caramels N' Apples, 232
  Cherry Dump Dessert, 229

Cran-Apple Pork Chops, 185
Glazed Pineapple, 231
Hawaii Pineapple Dessert, 231
Just Like Peach Cobbler, 229
Peach Tree Peaches, 230
Peaches & Cream, 230
Peaches and Cream Fondue, 224
Raisin Bread Pudding, 236
Slow Cooked Baked Apples, 233
Stuffed Apples, 233

FONDUE
Candy Bar Fondue, 243
Caramel Fondue, 244
Cheddar Cheese Fondue, 36
Fudgy Peanut Butter Fondue, 242
Milk Chocolate Fondue, 242
Mocha Fondue, 243
Peaches and Cream Fondue, 224
Peanut Butter Fondue, 242
Swiss Cheese Fondue, 36

G
Game Time Cheese Dip, 20
Game Time Joes, 154
Garlic Chicken, 213
Garlic Pork Roast, 182
Garlic Vegetables, 88
Gee Whiz Hominy, 87
Get a Grip Onion Soup, 42
Glaze Over Chicken Breast, 202
Glazed Cover Pork Loin, 190
Glazed Pineapple, 231
Good 'n Tasty Ham, 196
Gotta Have Hot Dog Roll Ups, 29
Greek Pasta, 109
Green Chile Chicken Alfredo, 115
Green Chile Stew, 63
Ground Beef Soup, 45

H
Ham & Cheese Dip, 22

Ham & Navy Beans, 103
Ham & Veggie Dip, 22
Ham with Cola, 196
Having a Party Cheese Ball, 27
Hawaii Pineapple Dessert, 231
Hearty Beef Stew, 68
Hearty Meat Loaf, 173
Home-Style Roast, 163
Honey Baked Ham, 197
Honey Dijon Chicken, 200
Honey Mustard Chicken, 200
Honey Mustard Ham, 197
Hot Cider Punch, 13
Hot Cran-Apple Cider, 14
Hot Dog Macaroni, 120
Hot Irish Mocha, 12
Hot Juice Warm-Ups, 12
Hot Party Punch, 12
Hot Tex-Mex Stew, 64
Hungry Man's Chicken, 216
Hurry Up Chili, 70

I
I'll Bring the Cauliflower, 87
Imitation Crab Pasta, 118
In A Hurry Pork Chops, 190
Irish Corned Beef Brisket, 168
Is It Goulash, 113
It's so Cheesy Potato Hash Browns, 94
Italian Beef Roast, 161
Italian Chicken, 212
Italian Pizza Dip, 21
Italian Potato Soup, 50
Italian Sausage Dinner, 199
Italian Sausage Potato Casserole, 139
Italian Style Beef Roast, 162
Italian Style Round Steak, 172
Italian Zucchini, 80

J,K
Jalapeno Cocktail Wieners, 28
Jambalaya, 152

Jazz up Clusters, 239
Just a Meatloaf, 175
Just Ahead Potatoes & Beef, 144
Just Beef & Beans, 85
Just Like Peach Cobbler, 229
Just Mac & Cheese, 121
Just Spam it Rice, 150
Just Wing It, 34
Keep it Simple Chicken, 211
Kids Love it Cheeseburger Casserole, 138
Kind of a Ham Pasta, 147
Kraut & Chops, 184

L

Lasagna, 108
Layered Casserole, 136
Layered Mexican Casserole, 132
Lazy Day Meatloaf, 174
Lazy Lasagna Soup, 55
Leftover Chicken and Vegetable Soup, 61
Leisure Day Lamb Chops, 200
Lemon Chicken, 203
Lemon Over Chicken, 203
Little Bite Beef Soup, 44
Little Smokies Links, 30
Louisiana Shrimp Gumbo, 59

M

Mac N' Cheese for Lunch, 119
Macaroni & Cheese, 120
Mad About Mushrooms, 15
Mama Mia's Meatball Soup, 46
Maple Glazed Squash, 86
Mashed Red Potatoes, 92
Meat Loaf, 176
Meat Lovers Pizza Pasta, 110
Meatball & Hash Brown Casserole, 136
Meatball Sandwiches, 178
Meatball Soup, 47
Meatballs and Gravy Sandwiches, 179
Meatloaf for Dinner, 174

Mediterranean Turkey, 222
Mexi Meatloaf, 173
Mexican Casserole, 133
Mexican Pasta Sauce, 123
Mexican Split Pea Soup, 57
Milk Chocolate Fondue, 242
Minestrone Soup, 53
Mix It & Go Roast, 160
Mix it Quick Meat Loaf, 172
Mix It Up Meatloaf, 176
Mixed Up Chicken, 211
Mocha Cappuccino, 11
Mocha Coffee, 11
Mocha Fondue, 243
More Than Chicken Soup, 42
Mouth Watering Ham, 196
Mushroom Chicken, 206
Mustard Glazed Carrots, 85

MEXICAN
After the Game Tacos, 153
Beef Green Chile Stew, 63
Chicken Burritos, 210
Chile Con Queso Dip, 19
Chili & Tamale Casserole, 133
Con Queso Dip, 18
Corn & Green Chile Dish, 83
Creamy Green Chile Rice, 151
Enchilada Casserole, 131
Game Time Cheese Dip, 20
Green Chile Stew, 63
Hot Tex-Mex Stew, 64
Layered Mexican Casserole, 132
Mexi Meatloaf, 173
Mexican Casserole, 133
Mexican Pasta Sauce, 123
Mexican Split Pea Soup, 57
Nacho Chicken, 209
Nacho Party Snack Dip, 19
New Mexico Stew, 62
New Mexico Style Chicken, 209
Rolled Up Enchiladas, 131
Salsa Chicken, 209

Salsa Mexi Dip, 19
Santa Fe Beef Fajitas, 178
Santa Fe Soup, 53
Sizzlin Beef Dip, 20
South West Taco Pie, 134
Southwest Beef Roast, 164
Taco Casserole, 132
Taco Cheese Dip, 18
Taco Dip, 18
Texas Beef Stew, 67
Texas Meatloaf, 174
Tipsy Cheese Dip, 20

N

Nacho Chicken, 209
Nacho Party Snack Dip, 19
Nacho Pasta, 111
Nachos, 27
Navy Beans & Ham Hock, 104
New Mexico Stew, 62
New Mexico Style Chicken, 209
New Twist Bake Beans, 107
No Bake Dressing, 154
No Fuss Chocolate Drops, 241
No Fuss Veggie Beef Soup, 46
Noodle Lovers Soup, 58
Not Just Beans 'N Wieners, 129
Now That's a Baked Potato, 89
Nuts About Pork, 191
Nuts About Walnuts, 28
Nutty Maple Chops, 186

O

Oh So Delicious Roast, 161
Olive Chicken, 216
On for all Chicken Dinner, 141
On the Go Onion Soup, 43
On the Road Clam Chowder, 56
On the Run Tuna Casserole, 135
One Dish Chicken Casserole, 140
One Pot Chicken Dinner, 146

Onion Dip, 22
Orange Glazed Ham, 195
Orange Glazed Pork Roast, 183
Orange Sweet Potatoes & Pork, 100
Oriental Chops, 187
Out All Day Beef Stroganoff, 127
Out All Day Chili, 72

P

Pack-N-Go Cookies, 237
Party Cocktail Wieners, 31
Party Time Meatballs, 34
Party Time Shrimp Dip, 17
Pasta & Smoked Sausage, 118
Peach Glazed Ham, 198
Peach Tree Peaches, 230
Peaches & Cream, 230
Peaches and Cream Fondue, 224
Peachy Pie Sweet Potatoes, 101
Peanut Butter Fondue, 242
Peas Au Gratin, 79
Pepper Chicken, 214
Pepperoni Dip, 21
Peppers and Swiss Steak, 171
Pineapple Chicken, 201
Pineapple Over Ham, 198
Pizza Chicken Pasta, 109
Pizza Dip, 21
Pizza Sauce for Pasta, 124
Pizza Sloppy Joes, 180
Pizza Tasting Pasta, 110
Pizza Tasting Pork Chops, 184
Play 'N Eat Chicken Dinner, 142
Pork & Beans Supper, 102
Pork & Veggie Supper, 130
Pork Baby Back Ribs, 193
Pork Chops & Sweet Potatoes, 186
Pork Chops, 188
Pork Loin Roast, 182
Pork Ribs & Kraut, 195
Pork Roast & Cherries, 182
Pork Roast, 183

Pork Stew, 69
Pork Tenderloins, 190
Pot Roast Dinner, 159
Pot Roast on the Go, 160
Potato and Carrot Soup, 52
Potato Surprise, 90
Potatoes & Gravy With Chops, 97
Potatoes & Sausage Casserole, 129
Potluck Tater Casserole, 135
Pretzel Twist Nibblers, 35
Pumpkin Butter Spread, 25

PASTA
   Almost Baked Ravioli, 122
   Alphabet Soup, 61
   Beef & Mac, 112
   Beefy Noodle Soup, 58
   Best Bow Tie Pasta, 113
   Bow Tie Pasta, 114
   Cheese Pasta Bake, 112
   Chicken and Broccoli Alfredo, 116
   Chicken N' Noodles, 114
   Chicken Noodle Casserole, 115
   Chili Spaghetti, 117
   Corned Beef Pasta, 117
   Fettuccine Noodles, 116
   Greek Pasta, 109
   Green Chile Chicken Alfredo, 115
   Hot Dog Macaroni, 120
   Imitation Crab Pasta, 118
   Is It Goulash, 113
   Just Mac & Cheese, 121
   Lasagna, 108
   Lazy Lasagna Soup, 55
   Mac N' Cheese for Lunch, 119
   Macaroni & Cheese, 120
   Meat Lovers Pizza Pasta, 110
   Nacho Pasta, 111
   Noodle Lovers Soup, 58
   Pasta & Smoked Sausage, 118
   Pizza Chicken Pasta, 109
   Pizza Tasting Pasta, 110
   Ranch Ravioli, 122

Rave About Ravioli, 123
Ravioli Lasagna, 121
Spinach & Chicken Pasta, 111
Terrific Tortellini, 108
Tortellini Soup, 54
What's Cookin Macaroni, 119

PORK
   Barbecue Spareribs, 194
   Barbeque Pork Ribs, 192
   BBQ Ham Slices, 198
   Boneless Pork Roast, 181
   Celery Around Pork Chops, 185
   Chops Stick Ribs, 192
   City Slicker Bratwurst, 199
   Country BBQ Ribs, 193
   Cran-Apple Pork Chops, 185
   Cranberry Roast, 184
   Easy Barbeque Ribs, 194
   Flavor Packed Pork Roast, 181
   Fork Tender Short Ribs, 194
   Garlic Pork Roast, 182
   Glazed Cover Pork Loin, 190
   Good 'n Tasty Ham, 196
   Ham with Cola, 196
   Honey Baked Ham, 197
   Honey Mustard Ham, 197
   In A Hurry Pork Chops, 190
   Italian Sausage Dinner, 199
   Kraut & Chops, 184
   Mouth Watering Ham, 196
   Nuts About Pork, 191
   Nutty Maple Chops, 186
   Orange Glazed Ham, 195
   Orange Glazed Pork Roast, 183
   Oriental Chops, 187
   Peach Glazed Ham, 198
   Pineapple Over Ham, 198
   Pizza Tasting Pork Chops, 184
   Pork & Veggie Supper, 130
   Pork Baby Back Ribs, 193
   Pork Chops & Sweet Potatoes, 186
   Pork Chops, 188

Pork Loin Roast, 182
Pork Ribs & Kraut, 195
Pork Roast & Cherries, 182
Pork Roast, 183
Pork Stew, 69
Pork Tenderloins, 190
Shortcut Pork Chops, 188
Shredded Pork for Tacos, 191
Spout About BBQ Pork, 191
Sweet & Sour Chops, 187
Sweet Orange Pork Chops, 187
Swiss Pork Chops, 189
Tangy Ribs, 195
Teriyaki Chops, 189
Texas Style Chops, 188

POTATOES
  Alfredo Topped Baked Potatoes, 89
  Almost Like Mom's Potato Soup, 50
  Bacon Potato Casserole, 139
  Beef Potato Soup, 51
  Candied Sweet Potatoes, 101
  Cheddar Potatoes, 91
  Cheesy Potato Soup, 52
  Cheesy Steak Fries, 93
  Cheesy Taters, 92
  Classic Potatoes, 95
  Delicious Creamy Potatoes, 93
  Extra Cheesy Hash Browns, 94
  It's so Cheesy Potato Hash Browns, 94
  Italian Potato Soup, 50
  Just Ahead Potatoes & Beef, 144
  Mashed Red Potatoes, 92
  Now That's a Baked Potato, 89
  Orange Sweet Potatoes & Pork, 100
  Peachy Pie Sweet Potatoes, 101
  Potato and Carrot Soup, 52
  Potato and Carrot Soup, 52
  Potatoes & Gravy With Chops, 97
  Potatoes & Sausage Casserole, 129
  Potatoes Surprise, 90
  Ranch Potatoes, 96
  Santa Fe Style Scalloped Potatoes &
    Ham, 98

Saturday Night Potato Skins, 90
Sausage & Potato Dinner, 91
Scalloped Potato Bake, 97
Scalloped Potatoes & Chops, 99
Scalloped Potatoes & Ham, 97
Scalloped Potatoes & Ham, 99
Souper Hash Browns, 95
Sour Cream Scalloped Potatoes &
  Ham, 98
Southern Style Potatoes, 96
Sweet Potato Chicken, 215
Sweet Potatoes & Ham, 100
Sweet Potatoes, 100
Thick Potato Soup, 51

Q
Quick Beef Topper, 126
Quick Draw Chili, 71
Quick Trick Bake Beans, 105
Quick Vanilla Fudge, 238

R
Raisin Bread Pudding, 236
Raisin Bread Pudding, 236
Ranch Potatoes, 96
Ranch Ravioli, 122
Rave About Ravioli, 123
Ravioli Lasagna, 121
Red Snapper, 225
Refried Beans Dish, 102
Reuben Spread, 25
Rice & Shrimp Dish, 149
Rice Pudding, 236
Roasted Chicken, 206
Roasted Turkey Breast, 221
Rolled Up Enchiladas, 131
Round Steak and Mushroom Gravy, 171
Route 66 Baked Beans, 106

RICE
  Beef Mixture on Rice, 150
  Chicken & Rice Dish, 148

Chicken & Rice, 149
Chicken & Wild Rice Soup, 57
Chicken & Wild Rice, 152
Creamy Green Chile Rice, 151
Jambalaya, 152
Just Spam it Rice, 150
Rice & Shrimp Dish, 149
Rice Pudding, 236
Wild Rice Dish, 151

S

Salsa Beans, 107
Salsa Beans, 107
Salsa Chicken, 209
Salsa Mexi Dip, 19
Santa Fe Beef Fajitas, 178
Santa Fe Soup, 53
Santa Fe Style Scalloped Potatoes & Ham, 98
Saturday Night Potato Skins, 90
Saucy Chicken Sandwiches, 217
Saucy Corn & Broccoli, 88
Saucy Stuffed Peppers, 80
Saucy Sweet Chicken Wings, 33
Sausage & Beans Stew, 64
Sausage & Potatoes Dinner, 91
Sausage and Hash Brown Casserole, 136
Sausage Soup, 62
Sausage Topper for Fettuccini, 125
Scalloped Potato Bake, 97
Scalloped Potatoes & Chops, 99
Scalloped Potatoes & Ham, 97
Scalloped Potatoes & Ham, 99
Seaside Clam Dip, 16
Seasoned Turkey, 221
Shoestring Casserole, 146
Shopping Day Chicken, 207
Short Steps Stroganoff, 127
Shortcut Beans & Ham, 103
Shortcut Butter Beans, 102
Shortcut Pork Chops, 188
Shredded Beef Sandwiches, 177
Shredded Pork for Tacos, 191

Side Dish Cabbage, 81
Simply Chicken, 212
Sippin Apple Cider, 14
Sizzlin Beef Dip, 20
Slow Cooked Baked Apples, 233
Slow Cooked Chili, 72
Slow Cooker Swiss Steak, 170
Smoke'n Hot Wings, 32
So Good Chicken Wings, 33
Souped Up Beef Casserole, 128
Souper Hash Browns, 95
Sour Cream Scalloped Potatoes & Ham, 98
Southern Style Cabbage, 82
Southern Style Potatoes, 96
Southwest Beef Roast, 164
Southwest Taco Pie, 134
Spaghetti Sauce, 124
Spicy Honey Wings, 32
Spicy Hot Cider, 13
Spinach & Chicken Pasta, 111
Spout About BBQ Pork, 191
Spunky BBQ Chicken, 208
Steak Casserole, 128
Stew On It, 66
Stewed Tomatoes, 88
Stir Fry Chicken Casserole, 141
Stuffed Apples, 233
Stuffing Top Chicken, 218
Sunday Supper Roast, 165
Sweet & Sour Chicken, 204
Sweet & Sour Chops, 187
Sweet & Tasty Chicken, 204
Sweet and Sour Cocktail Wieners, 29
Sweet and Sour Shrimp, 224
Sweet Orange Carrots, 86
Sweet Orange Pork Chops, 187
Sweet Potato Chicken, 215
Sweet Potatoes & Ham, 100
Sweet Potatoes, 100
Sweet Treat Fudge, 238
Swiss Cheese Fondue, 36
Swiss Pork Chops, 189
Swiss Slow Cooked Chicken, 213

SAUCES AND TOPPERS
Don't Pass Up Topper, 125
Mexican Pasta Sauce, 123
Pizza Sauce for Pasta, 124
Quick Beef Topper, 126
Sausage Topper for Fettuccini, 125
Spaghetti Sauce, 124

SEAFOOD
Bayside Clam Chowder, 56
Cheese & Shrimp Dip, 17
Cheesy Crab Dip, 17
Cheesy Tuna Casserole, 145
Classic Marinara Shrimp, 224
Crab Cheese Spread, 26
Crock That Tuna, 226
Don't Be a Crab Dip, 16
Flavor of Florida Fish, 226
Fresh Cod Fillets, 225
Imitation Crab Pasta, 118
Louisiana Shrimp Gumbo, 59
On the Road Clam Chowder, 56
On the Run Tuna Casserole, 135
Party Time Shrimp Dip, 17
Red Snapper, 225
Rice & Shrimp Dish, 149
Seaside Clam Dip, 16
Sweet and Sour Shrimp, 224
Tuna & Spinach Casserole, 144
Tuna Casserole, 137

SOUPS AND STEWS
Almost Like Mom's Potato Soup, 50
Alphabet Soup, 61
Bayside Clam Chowder, 56
Beans with Bacon Soup, 60
Beef Green Chile Stew, 63
Beef Potato Soup, 51
Beef Sirloin Stew, 68
Beef Stew, 66
Beefy Mushroom Stew, 67
Beefy Noodle Soup, 58
Bell Pepper Soup, 54
Black Bean Soup, 60

Broccoli Cheddar Cheese Soup, 40
Broccoli Cheese Soup, 39
Broccoli Cheese Soup, 41
Butter Bean Soup, 46
Cabbage Patch Stew, 65
Cheddar Cheese Soup, 40
Cheddar Cheese Soup, 41
Cheesy Broccoli Soup, 40
Cheesy Potato Soup, 52
Chicken & Wild Rice Soup, 57
Chicken Dump Soup, 59
Chicken Stew, 69
Chili Soup, 49
Chill Out Beef Soup, 44
Corn Chowder, 55
Creamy Broccoli Soup, 39
Creamy Tomato Soup, 48
Curry Tomato Soup, 48
Easy Fix'n Beef Soup, 43
Fix & Go Stew, 65
Get a Grip Onion Soup, 42
Green Chile Stew, 63
Ground Beef Soup, 45
Hearty Beef Stew, 68
Hot Tex-Mex Stew, 64
Italian Potato Soup, 50
Lazy Lasagna Soup, 55
Leftover Chicken and Vegetable Soup,
    61
Little Bite Beef Soup, 44
Louisiana Shrimp Gumbo, 59
Mama Mia's Meatball Soup, 46
Meatball Soup, 47
Mexican Split Pea Soup, 57
Minestrone Soup, 53
More Than Chicken Soup, 42
New Mexico Stew, 62
No Fuss Veggie Beef Soup, 46
Noodle Lovers Soup, 58
On the Go Onion Soup, 43
On the Road Clam Chowder, 56
Pork Stew, 69
Potato and Carrot Soup, 52
Santa Fe Soup, 53

Sausage & Beans Stew, 64
Sausage Soup, 62
Stew On It, 66
Terrific Tomato Soup, 47
Texas Beef Stew, 67
Thick Potato Soup, 51
Tortellini Soup, 54
Turkey & Vegetable Soup, 49
Vegetable Soup, 41
Veggie Beef Soup, 45

T
Taco Casserole, 132
Taco Cheese Dip, 18
Taco Dip, 18
Tangy Ribs, 195
Taste of the Orient Chicken, 205
Tasty Beef Burgers, 179
Tasty Chicken Italiano, 218
Tasty Corn on the Cob, 87
Tasty Turkey, 223
Teriyaki Pork, 189
Teriyaki Roast, 165
Terrific Tomato Soup, 47
Terrific Tortellini, 108
Texas Beef Stew, 67
Texas Meatloaf, 174
Texas Style Chops, 188
Thick Potato Soup, 51
Tipsy Cheese Dip, 20
Tortellini Soup, 54
Touchdown Baked Beans, 106
Tuna & Spinach Casserole, 144
Tuna Casserole, 137
Turkey & Vegetable Soup, 49
Turkey and Stuffing, 220
Turkey and Vegetables, 223
Turkey Anytime, 220
Turkey Loaf, 223
Turkey Sloppy Joes, 155

V
Vegetable Soup, 41
Veggi & Sausage Casserole, 148
Veggie Beef Soup, 45
Veggie Dish, 85

VEGETABLES *(Also See: Potatoes)*
Bell Pepper Soup, 54
Bit Special Green Beans, 84
Broccoli Cheddar Cheese Soup, 40
Broccoli Cheese Soup, 39
Broccoli Cheese Soup, 41
Broccoli, 78
Broccoli, Cauliflower & Cheese, 77
Cabbage & Ham, 81
Cabbage Patch Stew
Cabbage, 82
Candied Carrots, 86
Carrot Casserole, 147
Cauliflower & Broccoli, 77
Cheddar & Broccoli, 78
Cheese & Broccoli, 78
Cheesy Broccoli Soup, 40
Corn & Green Chile Dish, 83
Creamed Corn, 83
Creamy Broccoli Soup, 39
Creamy Tomato Soup, 48
Curry Tomato Soup, 48
Don't Bake it Green Beans, 84
Easy Vegetable Dish, 79
Garlic Vegetables, 88
Gee Whiz Hominy, 87
Get a Grip Onion Soup, 42
I'll Bring the Cauliflower, 87
Italian Zucchini, 80
Just Beef & Beans, 85
Maple Glazed Squash, 86
Mustard Glazed Carrots, 85
No Fuss Veggie Beef Soup, 46
On the Go Onion Soup, 43

Peas Au Gratin, 79
Saucy Corn & Broccoli, 88
Saucy Stuffed Peppers, 80
Side Dish Cabbage, 81
Southern Style Cabbage, 82
Stewed Tomatoes, 88
Sweet Orange Carrots, 86
Tasty Corn on the Cob, 87
Terrific Tomato Soup, 47
Turkey & Vegetable Soup, 49

Vegetable Soup, 41
Veggie Beef Soup, 45
Veggie Dish, 85

W
Wake up to Breakfast, 156
What's Cookin Macaroni, 119
Wide Awake Coffee, 11
Wild Rice Dish, 151

BUSY WOMAN'S COOKBOOK

By Sharon and Gene McFall

Published 2000, *Busy Woman's Cookbook* featured 3 and 4 ingredient recipes and had stories and informative bits about more than 250 women. For those who might be interested in them, they are listed here.

Abigail Adams
Annette Abbott Adams
Clara Adams
Jane Adams
Joy Adamson
Marion Anderson
Julie Andrews
Maya Angelou
Susan B. Anthony
Countess Geraldine Apponiji
Elizabeth Arden
Dorothy Arzner
Mary Kay Ash
Nan Jane Aspinwall
Jane Austin
Tracy Austin
Gladys Aylward
Sarah G. Bagley
Josephine Baker
Lucille Ball
Brigitte Bardot
Dr. James Barry
Clara Barton
Sylvia Beach
Helen Delich Bentley
Benazir Bhutto
Antionette Blackwell
Elizabeth Blackwell
Fanny Blankers-Koen
Nellie Bly
Lucretia Bori
Myra Bradwell
Margaret Bourke-White
Lee Ann Breedlove
Lucy Brewer
Charlotte Bronte

Margaret Ann Brewer
Emily Bronte
Gwendolyn Brooks
Taylor Caldwell
Mother Frances Cabrini
Helen Gurley Brown
Angela Burdett-Coutts
Rachael Carson
Martha Jane Canary
Annie Jump Cannon
Hattie Caraway
Barbara Cartland
Mary Cassatt
Catherine the Great
Edith Cavell
Coco Chanel
Wu Chao
Shirley Chisolm
Agatha Christie
Cleopatra
Ester Cleveland
Jacqueline Cochran
Little Mo Connolly
Kay Cottee
Harriet Converse
Joan Ganz Cooney
Jane Todd Crawford
Diane Crump
Marie Curie
Christine Davies
Emily Davison
Bette Davis
Doris Day
Maria De Camargo
Emily Dickinson
Mary Dodge
Elizabeth Dole

Rita Dove
Isadora Duncan
George Eliot
Katherine Dunham
Amelia Earhart
Mary Baker Eddy
Mary Fallin
Edna Ferber
Miriam Ma Ferguson
Geraldine Ferraro
Ella Fitzgerald
Margot Fonteyn
Betty Ford
Ann Franklin
Betty Friedan
Elizabeth Fritsch
Elizabeth Gurney Fry
Indira Gandhi
Ava Gardner
Janet Gaynor
Ruth Bader Ginzburg
Althea Gibson
Nadine Gordimer
Katherine Graham
Martha Graham
Sarah Moor Grinke
Angela Grinke
Janet Guthrie
Dame Joan Hamilton
Patricia Roberts Harris
Helen Hayes
Edith Head
Sonja Henie
Katherine Hepburn
Eva Hesse
Caroline Herschel
Billie Holliday

Grace Murray Hopper
Liz Holtzman
Vinnie Ream Hoxie
Doris Humphrey
Zora Neale Hurston
Marjorie Jackson
Dr. Arletta Jacobs
Joan of Arc
Mary Harris Jones
Amy Johnson
Barbara Jordan
Florence Griffith Joyner
Grace F. Kaercher
Frida Kahlo
Helen Keller
Grace Kelly
Elizabeth Kenny
Mary Kies
Billie Jean King
Jeanne Kirkpatrick
Roberta A. Knakus
Margaret Knight
Juanita Kreps
Lady Godiva
Ann Landers
Lillie Langtry
Lady Astor Langhorne
Estee Lauder
Jeannie Lawson
Gypsy Rose Lee
Margaret Leech
Vivian Leigh
Tillie Lewis
Jenny Lind
Belva Ann Lockwood
Juliette Gordon Low
Eliza Lucas
Clare Booth Luce
Shannon Lucid
Autherine Lucy
Ann Sullivan Macy
Dolly Madison
Wilma Mankiller
Beryl Markham
Belle Martell
Christa McAuliffe
Barbara McClintock

Marjorie Swank Matthews
Aimee McPherson
Golda Mier
Ethel Merman
Edna St. Vincent Millay
Gabriel Mistral
Jerry Mock
Marilyn Monroe
Marie Montessori
Julie Morgan
Esther Morris
Grandma Moses
Martina Navratilova
Louise Nevelson
Cynthia Nichols
Florence Nightingale
Queen Noor
Emma Nutt
Diane Nyad
Sandra Day O'Connor
Rosie O'Donnell
Georgia O'Keefe
Annie Oakley
Rosa Parks
Jacqueline Kennedy
Anne S. Peck
Frances Perkins
Mary Brooks Picken
Mary Pickford
Pocahontas
Judit Polgar
Beatrix Potter
Sally J. Priesand
Princess Diana
Queen Victoria
Queen Elizabeth II
Jeanette Rankin
Mabel Reinecke
Janet Reno
Judith Resnic
Ellen Swallows Richards
Sally Ride
Mary Robinson
Eleanor Roosevelt
Elizabeth Ross
Nellie Taylor Ross
Sacajawea

Margaret Sanger
Sappho
Anna Sewell
Eva Shain
Susie Sharp
Murasaki Shikibu
Bessie Smith
Julie Smith
Maria Ann Smith
Elizabeth Cady Stanton
Ruth Stapleton
Statue of Liberty
Harriet Beecher Stowe
Barbara Streisand
Rachel Summers
Mary Sutton
Louise Ann Swain
Ida M. Tarbell
Helen Taussig
Elizabeth Taylor
Shirley Temple
Valentina Tereshkova
Margaret Thatcher
The Virgin Mary
Dorothy Thompson
Harriet Ross Tubman
Naomi Uemura
Valentina
Abigail Van Buren
Diana Vreeland
Sarah Waldrake
Barbara Walters
Madame C.J. Walker
Maggie Mitchell Walker
Mary Ball Washington
Maud Watson
Phyllis Wheatly
Frances Whitcher
Laura Ingalls Wilder
Edith Wilson
Emma Hart Willard
Ellen Louise Wilson
Oprah Winfrey
Virginia Woolf
Natalie Wood
Jeana Yeager
Mildred Zaharias

OTHER COOKBOOKS AVAILABLE FROM CREATIVE IDEAS PUBLISHING

To order, fill out enclosed order form.

BUSY WOMAN'S COOKBOOK A national bestseller by Sharon and Gene McFall. Over 350,000 copies sold. It has over 500 mouth-watering 3 and 4 ingredient recipes and more than 200 short stories and facts about famous and influential women. $16.95

COOKIN' WITH WILL ROGERS by Sharon and Gene McFall. Has over 560 delicious country cookin' recipes with over 100 Will Rogers quotes, 60 pictures and 50 stories of one of America's most beloved humorists. "Only a fool argues with a skunk, a mule or a cook." Will Rogers. $19.95.

HOME MADE BLESSINGS by Diane Reasoner. Over 400 excellent tasting recipes, straight forward instructions and ingredients that are found in any pantry. Inspirational sayings on every page that will brighten your day. $19.95.

MILD TO WILD MEXICAN COOKBOOK by Linda Burgett. Over 400 tantalizing recipes from south of the border. Every recipe tells you if it is hot, medium or mild-so you have no big surprises. Also has fun facts on ingredients. One word for this book—Wonderful. $18.95.

GET ME OUT OF THE KITCHEN by Sharon and Gene McFall. 500 easy to prepare recipes. Special low-fat and low-cal recipes as well as helpful cooking hints. A wonderful cookbook. $18.95.

JUST AROUND THE CURVE by Sharon and Gene McFall. Designed for RVers and Campers, but is great for the home. Over 350 great quick and easy recipes. Recipes from all 50 states. Also contains some low-fat, low-cal and diabetic recipes. Intriguing American points of interest and travel tips and tidbits. A must for the traveler or at home. $16.95.

IF I GOTTA COOK MAKE IT QUICK by Shelley Plettl. Over 500 Hassle Free recipes using just a few ingredients. Includes: Easy to Prepare Slow Cooker Recipes; Helpful Hints and Fun Facts; How to Adapt Your Favorite Recipes to the Slow Cooker; How to Substitute One Ingredient for Another; Uses of Herbs and Spices; Basic Rules for Table Manners. $18.95

Please send _____ copies of _____

@ _____ (U.S.) each $_____

Postage and handling @ $3.50 each $_____

TOTAL $_____

Check or Credit Card (Canada-credit card only)

Charge to my ☐ Master Card or Visa Card

account # _____

expiration date _____

signature _____

> **MAIL TO:**
> **Creative Ideas Publishing**
> **7916 N.W. 23rd St.**
> **P.M.B. 115**
> **Bethany, OK 73008-5135**
> **1-800-673-0768**
> **www.busywomanscookbook.com**

Name _____

Address _____

City _____ State _____ Zip _____

Phone (day) _____ (night) _____

ORDER BY EMAIL: sharoncookin@aol.com

- -

Please send _____ copies of
Busy Woman's Slow Cooker Cookbook

@ $18.95 (U.S.) each $_____

Postage and handling @ $3.50 each $_____

TOTAL $_____

Check or Credit Card (Canada-credit card only)

Charge to my ☐ Master Card or Visa Card

account # _____

expiration date _____

signature _____

> **MAIL TO:**
> **Creative Ideas Publishing**
> **7916 N.W. 23rd St.**
> **P.M.B. 115**
> **Bethany, OK 73008-5135**
> **1-800-673-0768**
> **www.busywomanscookbook.com**

Name _____

Address _____

City _____ State _____ Zip _____

Phone (day) _____ (night) _____

ORDER BY EMAIL: sharoncookin@aol.com

SHARE YOUR
FAVORITE RECIPE

Do you have a favorite quick and easy recipe? Do family and friends ask you for it? Would you like to see it in a national cookbook?

If so, please send your favorite quick and easy recipe to us. If we use it in a future cookbook, you will be given credit in the book for the recipe, and will receive a free copy of the book.

Submit to: Creative Ideas Publishing
              PMB 115
              7916 N.W. 23rd Street
              Bethany, OK 73008-5135
              1-800-673-0768

NOTES

NOTES

NOTES

NOTES

NOTES

NOTES

NOTES

NOTES

NOTES

NOTES

NOTES

NOTES

NOTES

NOTES

NOTES

NOTES